THE
SILENT HOUSE

FERGUS HUME

1st WORLD LIBRARY Literary Society

The Silent House

Fergus Hume

© 1st World Library, 2006
PO Box 2211
Fairfield, IA 52556
www.1stworldlibrary.com
First Edition

LCCN: 2006935229

Softcover ISBN: 1-4218-2482-5
Hardcover ISBN: 1-4218-2382-9
eBook ISBN: 1-4218-2582-1

Purchase *"The Silent House"*
as a traditional bound book at:
www.1stWorldLibrary.com/purchase.asp?ISBN=1-4218-2482-5

1st World Library is a literary, educational organization
dedicated to:

- Creating a free internet library of downloadable ebooks

- Hosting writing competitions and offering book
  publishing scholarships.

Interested in more 1st World Library books?
contact: literacy@1stworldlibrary.com

Check us out at: www.1stworldlibrary.com

1ˢᵗ World Library Literary Society

Giving Back to the World

"If you want to work on the core problem, it's early school literacy."

- James Barksdale, former CEO of Netscape

"No skill is more crucial to the future of a child, or to a democratic and prosperous society, than literacy."

- Los Angeles Times

Literacy... means far more than learning how to read and write... The aim is to transmit... knowledge and promote social participation."

- UNESCO

"Literacy is not a luxury, it is a right and a responsibility. If our world is to meet the challenges of the twenty-first century we must harness the energy and creativity of all our citizens."

- President Bill Clinton

"Parents should be encouraged to read to their children, and teachers should be equipped with all available techniques for teaching literacy, so the varying needs and capacities of individual kids can be taken into account."

- Hugh Mackay

CONTENTS

CHAPTER I

THE TENANT OF THE SILENT HOUSE

Lucian Denzil was a briefless barrister, who so far departed from the traditions of his brethren of the long robe as not to dwell within the purlieus of the Temple. For certain private reasons, not unconnected with economy, he occupied rooms in Geneva Square, Pimlico; and, for the purposes of his profession, repaired daily, from ten to four, to Serjeant's Inn, where he shared an office with a friend equally briefless and poor.

This state of things sounds hardly enviable, but Lucian, being young and independent to the extent of L300 a year, was not dissatisfied with his position. As his age was only twenty-five, there was ample time, he thought, to succeed in his profession; and, pending that desirable consummation, he cultivated the muses on a little oatmeal, after the fashion of his kind. There have been lives less happily circumstanced.

Geneva Square was a kind of backwater of the great river of town life which swept past its entrance with speed and clamour without disturbing the peace within. One long, narrow street led from a roaring thoroughfare into a silent quadrangle of tall grey houses, occupied by lodging-house keepers, city clerks and two or three artists, who represented the Bohemian element of the place. In the centre there was an oasis of green lawn, surrounded by rusty iron railings the height of a man, dotted with elms of considerable age, and streaked with narrow paths of yellow gravel.

The surrounding houses represented an eminently respectable appearance, with their immaculately clean steps, white-curtained windows, and neat boxes of flowers. The windows glittered like diamonds, the door-knobs and plates shone with a yellow lustre, and there were no sticks, or straws, or waste paper lying about to mar the tidy look of the square.

With one exception, Geneva Square was a pattern of all that was desirable in the way of cleanliness and order. One might hope to find such a haven in some somnolent cathedral town, but scarcely in the grimy, smoky, restless metropolis of London.

The exception to the notable spotlessness of the neighborhood was No. 13, a house in the centre of the side opposite to the entrance. Its windows were dusty, and without blinds or curtains, there were no flower-boxes on the ledges, the steps lacked whitewash, and the iron railings looked rusty for want of paint. Stray straws and scraps of paper found their way down the area, where the cracked pavement was damp with green slime. Such beggars as occasionally wandered into the square, to the scandal of its inhabitants, camped on the door-step; and the very door itself presented a battered, dissolute appearance.

Yet, for all its ill looks and disreputable suggestions, those who dwelt in Geneva Square would not have seen it furbished up and occupied for any money. They spoke about it in whispers, with ostentatious tremblings, and daunted looks, for No. 13 was supposed to be haunted, and had been empty for over twenty years. By reason of its legend, its loneliness and grim appearance, it was known as the Silent House, and formed quite a feature of the place. Murder had been done long ago in one of its empty, dusty rooms, and it was since then that the victim walked. Lights, said the ghost-seers, had been seen flitting from window to window, groans were sometimes heard, and the apparition of a little old woman in brocaded silk and high-heeled shoes appeared on occasions. Hence the Silent House bore an uncanny reputation.

How much truth there was in these stories it is impossible to say; but sure enough, in spite of a low rental, no tenant would take No. 13 and face its ghostly terrors. House and apparition and legend had become quite a tradition, when the whole fantasy was ended in the summer of '95 by the unexpected occupation of the mansion. Mr. Mark Berwin, a gentleman of mature age, who came from nobody knew where, rented No. 13, and established himself therein to lead a strange and lonely life.

At first, the gossips, strong in ghostly tradition, declared that the new tenant would not remain a week in the house; but as the week extended into six months, and Mr. Berwin showed no signs of leaving, they left off speaking of the ghost and took to discussing the man himself. In a short space of time quite a collection of stories were told about the newcomer and his strange ways.

Lucian heard many of these tales from his landlady. How Mr. Berwin lived all alone in the Silent House without servant or companion; how he spoke to none, and admitted no one into the mansion; how he appeared to have plenty of money, and was frequently seen coming home more or less intoxicated; and how Mrs. Kebby, the deaf charwoman who cleaned out Mr. Berwin's rooms, declined to sleep in the house because she considered that there was something wrong about her employer.

To such gossip Denzil paid little attention, until his skein of life became unexpectedly entangled with that of the strange gentleman. The manner of their meeting was unforeseen and peculiar.

One foggy November night, Lucian, returning from the theatre, shortly after eleven o'clock, dismissed his hansom at the entrance to the square and walked thereinto through the thick mist, trusting to find his way home by reason of two years' familiarity with the precincts. As it was impossible to see even the glare of the near gas lamp in the murky air, Lucian felt his way cautiously along the railings. The square was filled with fog, dense to the eye and cold to the feel, so that Lucian shivered with the chill, in spite of the fur coat over his evening clothes.

As he edged gingerly along, and thought longingly of the fire and supper awaiting him in his comfortable rooms, he was startled by hearing a deep, rich voice boom out almost at his feet. To make the phenomenon still more remarkable, the voice shaped itself into certain well-known words of Shakespeare:

"Oh!" boomed this *vox et praeterea nihil* in rather husky tones, "Oh! that a man should put an enemy in his mouth to steal away his brains!" And then through the mist and darkness came the unmistakable sound of sobs.

"God bless me!" cried Lucian, leaping back, with shaken nerves. "Who is this? Who are you?"

"A lost soul!" wailed the deep voice, "which God will not bless!" And then came the sobbing again.

It made Denzil's blood run cold to hear this unseen creature weeping in the gloom. Moving cautiously in the direction of the sound, he stumbled against a man with his folded arms resting on the railings, and his face bent down on his arms. He made no attempt to turn when Lucian touched him, but with downcast head continued to weep and moan in a very frenzy of self-pity.

"Here!" said the young barrister, shaking the stranger by the shoulder, "what is the matter with you?"

"Drink!" stuttered the man, suddenly turning with a dramatic gesture. "I am an object lesson to teetotalers; a warning to topers; a modern helot made shameful to disgust youth with vice."

"You had better go home, sir," said Lucian sharply.

"I can't find home. It is somewhere hereabout, but where, I don't know."

"You are in Geneva Square," said Denzil, trying to sharpen the dulled wits of the man.

"I wish I was in No. 13 of it," sighed the stranger. "Where the deuce is No. 13? Not in this Cloudcuckooland, anyhow."

"Oh!" cried Lucian, taking the man's arm. "Come with me. I'll lead you home, Mr. Berwin."

Scarcely had the name passed his lips than the stranger drew back suddenly, with a hasty exclamation. Some suspicion seemed to engender a mixture of terror and defiance which placed him on his guard against undue intimacy, even when some undefined fear was knocking at his heart. "Who are you?" he demanded in a steadier tone. "How do you know my name?"

"My name is Denzil, Mr. Berwin, and I live in one of the houses of this square. As you mention No. 13, I know you can be none other than Mr. Mark Berwin, the tenant of the Silent House."

"The dweller in the haunted house," sneered Berwin, evidently relieved, "who stays there with ghosts, and worse than ghosts."

"Worse than ghosts?"

"The phantoms of my own sins, young man. I have sowed folly, and now I am reaping the crop. I am -" Here his further speech was interrupted by a fit of coughing, which shook his lean figure severely. At its conclusion he was so exhausted that he was forced to support himself against the railings. "A portion of the crop," he murmured.

Lucian was sorry for the man, who seemed scarcely capable of looking after himself, and he thought it unwise to leave him in such a plight. At the same time, he was impatient of lingering in the heart of the clammy fog at such a late hour; so, as his companion seemed indisposed to move, he caught him again by the arm without ceremony. The abrupt action seemed to waken again the fears of Berwin.

"Where would you take me?" he asked, resisting the gentle force used by Lucian.

"To your own house. You will be ill if you stay here."

"You are not one of them?" asked the man suddenly.

"One of whom?"

"One of those who wish to harm me?"

Denzil began to think he had to do with a madman, and to gain his ends he spoke to him in a soothing manner, as he would to a child: "I wish to do you good, Mr. Berwin," said he gently. "Come to your home."

"Home! home! Ah, God, I have no home!"

Nevertheless, he gathered himself together, and with his arm in that of his guide, stumbled along in the thick, chill mist. Lucian knew the position of No. 13 well, as it almost faced the lodgings occupied by himself, and by skirting the railings with due caution, he managed to half lead, half drag his companion to the house. When they stood before the door, and Berwin had assured himself that he was actually home by the use of his latch-key, Denzil wished him a curt good-night. "And I should advise you to go to bed at once," he concluded, turning to descend the steps.

"Don't go! Don't go!" cried Berwin, seizing the young man by the arm. "I am afraid to go in by myself - all is so dark and cold! Wait until I get a light!"

As the creature's nerves seemed to be unhinged by over-indulgence in alcohol, and he stood gasping and shivering on the threshold like some beaten animal, Lucian took compassion on him.

"I'll see you indoors," said he, and striking a match, stepped into the darkness after the man. The hall of No. 13 seemed to be almost as cold as the world without, and the trifling glimmer of the lucifer served rather to reveal than dispel the surrounding darkness. The light, as it were, hollowed a gulf out of the tremendous gloom and made the house tenfold more ghostly than before. The footsteps of Denzil and Berwin sounding on the bare boards - for the hall was uncarpeted - waked hollow echoes, and when they paused the silence which ensued seemed almost menacing. The grim reputation of the mansion, its gloom and silence, appealed powerfully to the latent superstition of Lucian. How much more nearly, then, would it touch the shaken and excited nerves of the tragic drunkard who dwelt continually amid its terrors!

Berwin opened a door on the right-hand side of the hall and turned up the light of a handsome oil-lamp which had been screwed down pending his arrival. This lamp was placed on a small square table covered with a white cloth and a dainty cold supper. The young barrister noted that the napery, cutlery, and crystal were all of the finest; that the viands were choice; that champagne and claret were the beverages. Evidently Berwin was a luxurious gentleman and indulgent to his appetites.

Lucian tried to gain a long look at him in the mellow light, but Berwin kept his face turned away, and seemed as anxious now for his visitor to go as he had been for him to enter. Denzil, quick in comprehension, took the hint at once.

"I'll go now, as you have the light burning," said he. "Good-night."

"Good-night," replied Berwin shortly, and added to his discourtesy by letting Lucian find his way out alone.

And so ended the barrister's first meeting with the strange tenant of the Silent House.

CHAPTER II

SHADOWS ON THE BLIND

The landlady of Denzil was a rather uncommon specimen of the class. She inclined to plumpness, was lively in the extreme, wore very fashionable garments of the brightest colours, and - although somewhat elderly - still cherished a hope that some young man would elevate her to the rank of a matron.

At present, Miss Julia Greeb was an unwedded damsel of forty summers, who, with the aid of art, was making desperate but ineffectual efforts to detain the youth which was slipping from her. She pinched her waist, dyed her hair, powdered her face, and affected juvenile dress of the white frock and blue sash kind. In the distance she looked a girlish twenty; close at hand various artifices aided her to pass for thirty; and it was only in the solitude of her own room that her real age was apparent. Never did woman wage a more resolute fight with Time than did Miss Greeb.

But this was the worst and most frivolous side of her character, for she was really a good-hearted, cheery little woman, with a brisk manner, and a flow of talk unequalled in Geneva Square. She had been born in the house she occupied, after the death of her father, and had grown up to assist her mother in ministering to the exactions of a continuous procession of lodgers. These came and went, married and died; but not one of the desirable young men had borne Miss Greeb to the altar, so that when her mother died the fair Julia almost despaired of attaining to the dignity of wifehood. Nevertheless, she continued to keep boarders, and to make attempts to captivate the hearts of such bachelors as she judged weak in character.

Hitherto all her efforts had been more or less of a mercantile character, with an eye to money; but when Lucian Denzil appeared on the scene, the poor little woman really fell in love with his handsome face. But, in strange contrast to her other efforts, Miss Greeb never for a moment deemed that Lucian would marry her. He was her god, her ideal of manhood, and to him she offered worship, and burnt incense after the manner of her kind.

Denzil occupied a bedroom and sitting-room, both pleasant, airy apartments, looking out on to the square. Miss Greeb attended to his needs herself, and brought up his breakfast with her own fair hands, happy for the day if her admired lodger conversed with her for a few moments before reading the morning paper. Then Miss Greeb would retire to her own sitting-room and indulge in day dreams which she well knew would never be realised. The romances she wove herself were even more marvellous than those she read in her favourite penny novelettes; but, unlike the printed tales, her romance never culminated in marriage. Poor brainless, silly, pitiful Miss Greeb; she would have made a good wife and a fond mother, but by some irony of fate she was destined to be neither; and the comedy of her husband-hunting youth was now changing into the lonely tragedy of disappointed spinsterhood. She was one of the world's unknown martyrs, and her fate merits tears rather than laughter.

On the morning after his meeting with Berwin, the young barrister sat at breakfast, with Miss Greeb in anxious attendance. Having poured out his tea, and handed him his paper, and ascertained that his breakfast was to his liking, Miss Greeb lingered about the room, putting this straight and that crooked, in the hope that Lucian would converse with her. In this she was gratified, as Denzil wished to learn details about the strange man he had assisted on the previous night, and he knew that no one could afford him more precise information than his brisk landlady, to whom was known all the gossip of the neighbourhood. His first word made Miss Greeb flutter back to the table like a dove to its nest.

"Do you know anything about No. 13?" asked Lucian, stirring his tea.

"Do I know anything about No. 13?" repeated Miss Greeb in shrill amazement. "Of course I do, Mr. Denzil. There ain't a thing I don't know about that house. Ghosts and vampires and crawling spectres live in it - that they do."

"Do you call Mr. Berwin a ghost?"

"No; nor nothing half so respectable. He is a mystery, sir, that's what Mr. Berwin is, and I don't care if he hears me commit myself so far."

"In what way is he a mystery?" demanded Denzil, approaching the matter with more particularity.

"Why," said Miss Greeb, evidently puzzled how to answer this leading question, "no one can find out anything about him. He's full of secrets and underhand goings on. It ain't respectable not to be fair and above board - that it ain't."

"I see no reason why a quiet-living old gentleman should tell his private affairs to the whole square," remarked Lucian drily.

"Those who have nothing bad to conceal needn't be afraid of speaking out," retorted Miss Greeb tartly. "And the way in which Mr. Berwin lives is enough to make one think him a coiner, or a thief, or even a murderer - that it is!"

"But what grounds have you to believe him any one of the three?"

This question also puzzled the landlady, as she had no

reasonable grounds for her wild statements. Nevertheless, she made a determined attempt to substantiate them by hearsay evidence. "Mr. Berwin," said she in significant tones, "lives all alone in that haunted house."

"Why not? Every man has the right to be a misanthrope if he chooses."

"He has no right to behave so, in a respectable square," replied Miss Greeb, shaking her head. "There's only two rooms of that large house furnished, and all the rest is given up to dust and ghosts. Mr. Berwin won't have a servant to live under his roof, and Mrs. Kebby, who does his charing, says he drinks awful. Then he has his meals sent in from the Nelson Hotel round the corner, and eats them all alone. He don't receive no letters, he don't read no newspapers, and stays in all day, only coming out at night, like an owl. If he ain't a criminal, Mr. Denzil, why does he carry on so?"

"He may dislike his fellow-men, and desire to live a secluded life."

Miss Greeb still shook her head. "He may dislike his fellow-men," she said with emphasis, "but that don't keep him from seeing them - ah! that it don't."

"Is there anything wrong in that?" said Lucian, contemptuous of these cobweb objections.

"Perhaps not, Mr. Denzil; but where do those he sees come from?"

"How do you mean, Miss Greeb?"

"They don't go in by the front door, that's certain," continued the little woman darkly. "There's only one entrance to this square, sir, and Blinders, the policeman, is frequently on duty there. Two or three nights he's met Mr. Berwin coming in after dark and exchanged friendly greetings with him, and each time Mr. Berwin has been alone!"

"Well! well! What of that?" said Denzil impatiently.

"This much, Mr. Denzil, that Blinders has gone round the square, after seeing Mr. Berwin, and has seen shadows - two or three of them - on the sitting-room blind. Now, sir," cried Miss Greeb, clinching her argument, "if Mr. Berwin came into the square alone, how did his visitors get in?"

"Perhaps by the back," conjectured Lucian.

Again Miss Greeb shook her head. "I know the back of No. 13 as well as I know my own face," she declared. "There's a yard and a fence, but no entrance. To get in there you have to go in by the front door or down the aiery steps; and you can't do neither without coming past Blinders at the square's entrance, and that," finished Miss Greeb triumphantly, "these visitors don't do."

"They may have come into the square during the day, when Blinders was not on duty."

"No, sir," said Miss Greeb, ready for this objection. "I thought of that myself, and as my duty to the square I have inquired - that I have. On two occasions I've asked the day policeman, and he says no one passed."

"Then," said Lucian, rather puzzled, "Mr. Berwin cannot live alone in the house."

"Begging your pardon, I'm sure," cried the pertinacious woman, "but he does. Mrs. Kebby has been all over the house, and there isn't another soul in it. No, Mr. Denzil, take it what way you will, there's something that ain't right about Mr. Berwin - if that's his real name, which I don't believe it is."

"Why, Miss Greeb?"

"Just because I don't," replied the landlady, with feminine logic. "And if you think of having anything to do with this mystery, Mr. Denzil, I beg of you not to, else you may come to something as is too terrible to consider - that you may."

"Such as -"

"Oh, I don't know," cried Miss Greeb, tossing her head and gliding towards the door. "It ain't for me to say what I think. I am the last person in the world to meddle with what don't concern me - that I am." And thus ending the conversation, Miss Greeb vanished, with significant look and pursed-up lips.

The reason of this last speech and rapid retreat lay in the fact that Miss Greeb could bring no tangible charge against her opposite neighbour; and therefore hinted at his complicity in all kinds of horrors, which she was quite unable to define save in terms more or less vague.

Lucian dismissed such hints of criminality from his mind as the outcome of Miss Greeb's very lively imagination; yet, even though he reduced her communications to bare facts, he could not but acknowledge that there was something queer about Mr. Berwin and his mode of life. The man's self-pity and self-condemnation; his hints that certain people wished to do him harm; the curious episode of the shadows on the blind - these things engaged the curiosity of Denzil in no ordinary degree; and he could not but admit to himself that it would greatly ease his mind to arrive at some reasonable explanation of Berwin's eccentricities.

Nevertheless, he held that he had no right to pry into the secrets of the stranger, and honourably strove to dismiss the tenant of No. 13 and his tantalising environments from his mind. But such dismissal of unworthy curiosity was more difficult to effect than he expected.

For the next week Lucian resolutely banished the subject from his thoughts, and declined to discuss the matter further with

Miss Greeb. That little woman, all on fire with curiosity, made various inquiries of her gossips regarding the doings of Mr. Berwin, and in default of reporting the same to her lodger, occupied herself in discussing them with her neighbours. The consequence of this incessant gossip was that the eyes of the whole square fixed themselves on No. 13 in expectation of some catastrophe, although no one knew exactly what was going to happen.

This undefinable feeling of impending disaster communicating itself to Lucian, stimulated his curiosity to such a pitch that, with some feeling of shame for his weakness, he walked round the square on two several evenings in the hope of meeting Berwin. But on both occasions he was unsuccessful.

On the third evening he was more fortunate, for having worked at his law books until late at night, he went out for a brisk walk before retiring to rest. The night was cold, and there had been a slight fall of snow, so Lucian wrapped himself up well, lighted his pipe, and proceeded to take the air by tramping twice or thrice round the square. Overhead the sky was clear and frosty, with chill glittering stars and a wintry moon. A thin covering of snow lay on the pavement, and there was a white rime on the bare branches of the central trees.

On coming to the house of Berwin, the barrister saw that the sitting-room was lighted up and the curtains undrawn, so that the window presented a square of illuminated blind. Even as he looked, two shadows darkened the white surface - the shadows of a man and a woman. Evidently they had come between the lamp and the window, and so, quite unknowingly, revealed their actions to the watcher. Curious to see the end of this shadow pantomime, Lucian stood still and looked intently at the window.

The two figures seemed to be arguing, for their heads nodded violently and their arms waved constantly. They retreated out of the sphere of light, and again came into it, still continuing their furious gestures. Unexpectedly the male shadow seized the female by the throat and swung her like a feather to and fro. The struggling figures reeled out of the radiance and Lucian heard a faint cry.

Thinking that something was wrong, he rushed up the steps and rang the bell violently. Almost before the sound died away the light in the room was extinguished, and he could see nothing more. Again and again he rang, but without attracting attention; so Lucian finally left the house and went in search of Blinders, the policeman, to narrate his experience. At the entrance of Geneva Square he ran against a man whom he recognised in the clear moonlight.

To his surprise he beheld Mark Berwin.

CHAPTER III

AN UNSATISFACTORY EXPLANATION

"Mr. Berwin!" cried Lucian, recognising the man. "Is it you?"

"Who else should it be?" replied Berwin, bending forward to see who had jostled him. "Who else should it be, Mr. Denzil?"

"But I thought - I thought," said the barrister, unable to conceal his surprise, "that is, I fancied you were indoors."

"Your fancy was wrong, you see. I am not indoors."

"Then who is in your house?"

Berwin shrugged his shoulders. "No one, so far as I know."

"You are mistaken, sir. There was a light in your room, and I saw the shadows of a man and a woman struggling together thrown on the blind."

"People in my house!" said Berwin, laying a shaking hand on the arm of Lucian. "Impossible!"

"I tell you it is so!"

"Come, then, and we will look for them," said Berwin in a tremulous voice.

"But they have gone by this time!"

"Gone!"

"Yes," said Denzil rapidly. "I rang the bell, as I fancied there was some fatal quarrel going on within. At once the light was put out, and as I could attract no one to the door, I suppose the man and woman must have fled."

For a moment or so Berwin said nothing, but his grip on Lucian's arm relaxed, and he moved forward a few steps. "You must be mistaken, Mr. Denzil," said he in altered tones, "there can be no person in my house. I locked the door before I went out, and I have been absent at least two hours."

"Then I must be mad, or dreaming!" retorted Lucian, with heat.

"We can soon prove if you are either of the two, sir. Come with me and examine the house for yourself."

"Pardon me," said Denzil, drawing back, "it is none of my business. But I warn you, Mr. Berwin, that others are more curious than I am. Several times people have been known to be in your house while you were absent, and your mode of life, secretive and strange, does not commend itself to the house-holders in this neighbourhood. If you persist in giving rise to gossip and scandal, some busybody may bring the police on the scene."

"The police!" echoed the old man, now greatly alarmed, as would appear from his shaking voice. "No! no! That will never do! My house is my castle! The police dare not break into it! I am a peaceful and very unfortunate gentleman, who wishes to live quietly. All this talk of people being in my house is nonsense!"

"Yet you seemed afraid when I told you of the shadows," said Lucian pointedly.

"Afraid! I am afraid of nothing!"

"Not even of those who are after you?" hinted Denzil, recalling the conversation of the previous occasion.

Berwin gave a kind of eldritch shriek and stepped back a pace, as though to place himself on his guard. "What - what do you know about such - such things?" he panted.

"Only so much as you hinted at when I last saw you."

"Yes, yes! I was not myself on that night. The wine was in and the wit was out."

"The truth also, it would seem," said Lucian drily, "judging by your agitation then and now."

"I am an unfortunate gentleman," whimpered Berwin tremulously.

"If you will excuse me, sir, I shall leave you," said Lucian ceremoniously. "It seems to be my fate to hold midnight conversations with you in the cold, but I think this one had better be cut short."

"One moment," Mr. Berwin exclaimed. "You have been good enough to place me on my guard as to the talk my quiet course of life is causing. Pray add to your kindness by coming with me to my house and exploring it from attic to basement. You will then see that there are no grounds for scandal, and that the shadows you fancy you saw on the blind are not those of real people."

"They can't be those of ghosts, at all events," replied Lucian, "as I never heard, to my knowledge, that spirits could cast shadows."

"Well, come and see for yourself that the house is empty."

Warmly as this invitation was given, Lucian had some scruples about accepting it. To explore an almost unfurnished mansion with a complete stranger - and one with an ill reputation - at the midnight hour, is not an enterprise to be coveted by any man, however bold he may be. Still, Lucian had ample courage, and more curiosity, for the adventure, as the chance of it stirred up that desire for romance which belongs peculiarly to youth. Also he was anxious to satisfy himself concerning the blind shadows, and curious to learn why Berwin inhabited so dismal and mysterious a mansion. Add to these reasons a keen pleasure in profiting by the occurrence of the unexpected, and you will guess that Denzil ended by accepting the strange invitation of Berwin.

Being now fully committed to the adventure, he went forward with cool courage and an observant eye, to spy out, if possible, the secret upon which hinged these mysteries.

As on the former occasion, Berwin inducted his guest into the sitting-room, and here, as previously, a dainty supper was spread. Berwin turned up the lamp light and waved his hand round the luxuriously furnished room, pointing particularly to the space between table and window.

"The figures whose shadows you saw," said he, "must have struggled together in this space, so as to be between the lamp and the blind for the performance of their pantomime. But I would have you observe, Mr. Denzil, that there is no disturbance of the furniture to show that such a struggle as you describe took place; also that the curtains are drawn across the window, and no light could have been thrown on the blind."

"The curtains were, no doubt, drawn after I rang the bell," said Lucian, glancing towards the heavy folds of crimson velvet which veiled the window.

"The curtains," retorted Berwin, stripping off his coat, "were drawn by me before I went out."

Lucian said nothing, but shook his head doubtfully. Evidently Berwin was trying, for his own ends, to talk him into a belief that his eyes had deceived him; but Denzil was too clear-headed a young man to be so gulled. Berwin's explanations and excuses only confirmed the idea that there was something in the man's life which cut him off from humanity, and which would not bear the light of day. Hitherto, Lucian had heard rather than seen Berwin; but now, in the clear light of the lamp, he had an excellent opportunity of observing both the man and his quarters.

Berwin was of medium height, and lean, with a clean-shaven face, hollow cheeks, and black, sunken eyes. His hair was grey and thin, his looks wild and wandering, and the hectic colouring of his face and narrow chest showed that he was far gone in consumption. Even as Lucian looked at him he was shaken by a hollow cough, and when he withdrew his handkerchief from his lips the white linen was spotted with blood.

He was in evening dress, and looked eminently refined, although worn and haggard in appearance. Denzil noted two peculiar marks about him; the first, a serpentine cicatrice extending on the right cheek from lip almost to ear; the second, the loss of the little finger of the left hand, which was cut off at the first joint. As he examined the man a second and more violent fit of coughing shook him.

"You seem to be very ill," said Lucian, pitying the feebleness of the poor creature.

"Dying of consumption - one lung gone!" gasped Berwin. "It will soon be over - the sooner the better."

"With your health, Mr. Berwin, it is sheer madness to dwell in this rigorous English climate."

"No doubt," replied the man, pouring himself out a tumbler of claret, "but I can't leave England - I can't leave this house, even; but on the whole," he added, with a satisfied glance around, "I am not badly lodged."

Lucian agreed with this speech. The room was furnished in the most luxurious manner. The prevailing hue was a deep, warm red - carpet, walls, hangings, and furniture were all of this cheerful tint. The chairs were deep, and softly cushioned; on the walls were several oil paintings by celebrated modern artists; there were dwarf bookcases filled with well-chosen books, and on a small bamboo table near the fire lay magazines and papers.

The mantelpiece, reaching nearly to the ceiling, was of oak, framing mirrors of bevelled glass; and on the numerous shelves, cups, saucers, and vases of old and valuable china were placed. There was also a gilt clock, a handsome sideboard, and a neat smoking-table, on which stood a cut-glass spirit-stand and a box of cigars. The whole apartment was furnished with taste and refinement, and Lucian saw that the man who owned such luxurious quarters must be possessed of money, as well as the capability of using it in the most civilised way.

"You have certainly all that the heart of man can desire in the way of material comforts," said he, looking at the supper table, which, with its silver and crystal and spotless covering, glittered like a jewel under the brilliant lamplight. "My only wonder is that you should furnish one room so finely and leave the others bare."

"My bedroom and bathroom are yonder," replied Berwin, pointing towards large folding doors draped with velvet curtains, and placed opposite to the window. "They are as well furnished as this. But how do you know the rest of this house is bare?"

"I can hardly help knowing it, Mr. Berwin. Your contrast of poverty and riches is an open secret in this neighbourhood."

"No one has been in my house save yourself, Mr. Denzil."

"Oh, I have said nothing. You turned me out so quickly the other night that I had no time for observation. Besides, I am not in the habit of remarking on matters which do not concern me."

"I beg your pardon," said Berwin weakly. "I had no intention of offending you. I suppose Mrs. Kebby has been talking?"

"I should think it probable."

"The skirling Jezebel!" cried Berwin. "I'll pack her off right away!"

"Are you a Scotchman?" asked Denzil suddenly.

"Why do you ask?" demanded Berwin, without replying.

"You used an essentially Scotch word - 'skirling.'"

"And I used an essentially American phrase - 'right away,'" retorted the man. "I may be a Scot, I may be a Yankee, but I would remind you that my nationality is my own secret."

"I have no wish to pry into your secrets," said Denzil, rising from the chair in which he had seated himself, "and in my turn I would remind you that I am here at your invitation."

"Don't take offense at a hasty word," said Berwin nervously. "I am glad of your company, although I seem rather brusque. You must go over the house with me."

"I see no necessity to do so."

"It will set your mind at rest regarding the shadows on the blind."

"I can trust my eyes," said Lucian, drily, "and I am certain that before I met you a man and a woman were in this room."

"Well," said Berwin, lighting a small lamp, "come with me and I'll prove that you are mistaken."

Fergus Hume

CHAPTER IV

MRS. KEBBY'S DISCOVERY

The pertinacity which Berwin displayed in insisting that Lucian should explore the Silent House was truly remarkable. He appeared to be bent upon banishing the idea which Denzil entertained that strangers were hiding in the mansion.

From attic to basement, from front to back premises, he led the way, and made Lucian examine every corner of the empty rooms. He showed him even the unused kitchen, and bade him remark that the door leading into the yard was locked and bolted, and, from the rusty condition of the ironwork, could not have been opened for years. Also, he made him look out of the window into the yard itself, with its tall black fence dividing it from the other properties.

This exploration finished, and Lucian being convinced that himself and his host were the only two living beings in the house, Berwin conducted his half-frozen guest back to the warm sitting-room and poured out a glass of wine.

"Here, Mr. Denzil," said he in good-natured tones, "drink this and draw near the fire; you must be chilled to the bone after our Arctic expedition."

Lucian willingly accepted both these attentions, and sipped his wine - it was particularly fine claret - before the fire, while Berwin coughed and shivered, and muttered to himself about the cold of the season. When Lucian stood up to take his departure, he addressed him directly:

"Well, sir," said he, with a sardonic smile, "are you convinced that the struggling shadows on yonder blind were children of your heated fancy?"

"No," said Denzil stoutly, "I am not!"

"Yet you have seen that there is no one in the house!"

"Mr. Berwin," said Lucian, after a moment's thought, "you propose a riddle which I cannot answer, and which I do not wish to answer. I cannot explain what I saw to-night, but as surely as you were out of this house, some people were in it. How this affects you, or what reason you have for denying it, I do not ask. Keep your own secrets, and go your own way. I wish you good-night, sir," and Lucian moved towards the door.

Berwin, who was holding a full tumbler of rich, strong port, drank the whole of it in one gulp. The strong liquor reddened his pallid face and brightened his sunken eyes; it even strengthened his already sonorous voice.

"At least you can inform my good neighbours that I am a peaceful man, desirous of being left to lead my own life," he said urgently.

"No, sir! I will have nothing to do with your business. You are a stranger to me, and our acquaintance is too slight to warrant my discussing your affairs. Besides," added Lucian, with a shrug, "they do not interest me."

"Yet they may interest the three kingdoms one day," said Berwin softly.

"Oh, if they deal with danger to society," said Denzil, thinking his strange neighbour spoke of anarchistic schemes, "I would -"

"They deal with danger to myself," interrupted Berwin. "I am a hunted man, and I hide here from those who wish me ill. I am dying, as you see," he cried, striking his hollow chest, "but I may not die quickly enough for those who desire my death."

"Who are they?" cried Lucian, rather startled by this outburst.

"People with whom you have no concern," replied the man sullenly.

"That is true enough, Mr. Berwin, so I'll say good-night!"

"Berwin! Berwin! Ha! ha! A very good name, Berwin, but not for me. Oh, was there ever so unhappy a creature as I? False name, false friend, in disgrace, in hiding! Curse everybody! Go! go! Mr. Denzil, and leave me to die here like a rat in its hole!"

"You are ill!" said Lucian, amazed by the man's fury. "Shall I send a doctor to see you?"

"Send no one," cried Berwin, commanding himself by a visible effort. "Only go away and leave me to myself. 'Thou can'st not minister to a mind diseased.' Go! go!"

"Good-night, then," said Denzil, seeing that nothing could be done. "I hope you will be better in the morning."

Berwin shook his head, and with a silent tongue, which contrasted strangely with his late outcry, ushered Denzil out of the house.

As the heavy door closed behind him Lucian descended the steps and looked thoughtfully at the grim mansion, which was tenanted by so mysterious a person. He could make nothing of Berwin - as he chose to call himself - he could see no meaning in his wild words and mad behaviour; but as he walked briskly back to his lodgings he came to the conclusion that the man was nothing worse than a tragic drunkard, haunted by terrors engendered by over-indulgence in stimulants. The episode of the shadows on the blind he did not attempt to explain, for the simple reason that he was unable to find any plausible explanation to account therefor.

"And why should I trouble my head to do so?" mused Lucian as he went to bed. "The man and his mysteries are nothing to me. Bah! I have been infected by the vulgar curiosity of the Square. Henceforth I'll neither see nor think of this drunken lunatic," and with such resolve he dismissed all thoughts of his strange acquaintance from his mind, which, under the circumstances, was perhaps the wisest thing he could do.

But later on certain events took place which forced him to alter his determination. Fate, with her own ends to bring about is not to be denied by her puppets; and of these Lucian was one, designed for an important part in the drama which was to be played.

Mrs. Margery Kebby, who attended to the domestic economy of Berwin's house, was a deaf old crone with a constant thirst, only to be assuaged by strong drink; and a filching hand which was usually in every pocket save her own. She had neither kith nor kin, nor friends, nor even acquaintances; but, being something of a miser, scraped and screwed to amass money she had no need for, and dwelt in a wretched little apartment in a back slum, whence she daily issued to work little and pilfer much.

Usually at nine o'clock she brought in her employer's breakfast from the Nelson Hotel, which was outside the Square, and while he was enjoying it in bed, after his fashion, she cleaned out and made tidy the sitting-room. Berwin then dressed and went out for a walk, despite Miss Greeb's contention that he took the air only at night, like an owl, and during his absence Mrs. Kebby attended to the bedroom. She then went about her own business, which was connected with the cleaning of various other apartments, and only returned at midday and at night to lay the table for Berwin's luncheon and dinner, or rather dinner and supper, which were also sent in from the hotel.

For these services Berwin paid her well, and only enjoined her to keep a quiet tongue about his private affairs, which Mrs. Kebby usually did until excited by too copious drams of gin, when she talked freely and unwisely to all the servants in the Square. It was to her observation and invention that Berwin owed his bad reputation.

Well-known in every kitchen, Mrs. Kebby hobbled from one to the other, gossiping about the various affairs of her various employers; and when absolute knowledge failed she took to inventing details which did no small credit to her imagination. Also, she could tell fortunes by reading tea-leaves and shuffling cards, and was not above aiding the maid servants in their small love affairs.

In short, Mrs. Kebby was a dangerous old witch, who, a century back, would have been burnt at the stake; and the worst possible person for Berwin to have in his house. Had he known of her lying and prating she would not have remained an hour under his roof; but Mrs. Kebby was cunning enough to steer clear of such a danger in the most dexterous manner. She had a firm idea that Berwin had, in her own emphatic phrase, "done something" for which he was wanted by the police, and was always on the look out to learn the secret of his isolated life, in order to betray him, or blackmail him, or get him in some way under her thumb. As yet she had been unsuccessful.

Deeming her a weak, quiet old creature, Berwin, in spite of his suspicious nature, entrusted Mrs. Kebby with the key of the front door, so that she could enter for her morning's work without disturbing him. The sitting-room door itself was not always locked, but Berwin usually bolted the portal of his bedroom, and had invariably to rise and admit Mrs. Kebby with his breakfast.

The same routine was observed each morning, and everything

went smoothly. Mrs. Kebby had heard of the blind shadows from several people, and had poked and pryed about all over the house in the hope of arriving at some knowledge of the substantial flesh and blood figures which cast them. But in this quest, which was intended to put money into her own pocket, she failed entirely; and during the whole six months of Berwin's tenancy she never saw a living soul in No. 13 save her employer; nor could she ever find any evidence to show that Berwin had received visitors during her absence. The man was as great a mystery to Mrs. Kebby as he was to the square, in spite of her superior opportunities of learning the truth.

On Christmas Eve the old woman brought in a cold supper for Berwin, as usual, making several journeys to and fro between hotel and house for that purpose. She laid the table, made up the fire, and before taking her leave asked Mr. Berwin if he wanted anything else.

"No, I think not," replied the man, who looked wretchedly ill. "You can bring my breakfast to-morrow."

"At nine, sir?"

"At the usual time," answered Berwin impatiently. "Go away!"

Mrs. Kebby gave a final glance round to see that all was in order, and shuffled out of the room as fast as her rheumatism would let her. As she left the house eight o'clock chimed from the steeple of a near church, and Mrs. Kebby, clinking her newly-received wages in her pocket, hurried out of the square to do her Christmas marketing. As she went down the street which led to it, Blinders, a burly, ruddy-faced policeman, who knew her well, stopped to make an observation.

"Is that good gentleman of yours home, Mrs. Kebby?" he asked, in the loud tones used to deaf people.

"Oh, he's home," grumbled Mrs. Kebby ungraciously, "sittin' afore the fire like Solomon in all his glory. What d'ye want to know for?"

"I saw him an hour ago," explained Blinders, "and I thought he looked ill."

"So he do, like a corpse. What of that? We've all got to come to it some day. 'Ow d'ye know but what he won't be dead afore morning? Well, I don't care. He's paid me up till to-night. I'm going to enj'y myself, I am."

"Don't you get drunk, Mrs. Kebby, or I'll lock you up."

"Garn!" grunted the old beldame. "Wot's Christmas Eve for, if it ain't for folk to enj'y theirselves? Y'are on duty early."

"I'm taking the place of a sick comrade, and I'll be on duty all night. That's my Christmas."

"Well! well! Let every one enj'y hisself as he likes," muttered Mrs. Kebby, and shuffled off to the nearest public house.

Here she began to celebrate the season, and afterwards went shopping; then she celebrated the season again, and later carried home her purchases to the miserable garret she occupied. In this den Mrs. Kebby, with the aid of gin and water, celebrated the season until she drank herself to sleep.

Next morning she woke in anything but an amiable mood, and had to fortify herself with an early drink before she was fit to go about her business.

It was almost nine when she reached the Nelson Hotel, and found the covered tray with Mr. Berwin's breakfast waiting for her; so she hurried with it to Geneva Square as speedily as possible, fearful of a scolding. Having admitted herself into the house, Mrs. Kebby took up the tray with both hands, and pushed open the sitting-room door with her foot. Here, at the sight which met her eyes, she dropped the tray with a crash, and let off a shrill yell.

The room was in disorder, the table was overturned, and amid the wreckage of glass and china lay Mark Berwin, with outspread hands - stone dead - stabbed to the heart.

CHAPTER V

THE TALK OF THE TOWN

Nowadays, events, political, social, and criminal, crowd so closely on one another's heels that what was formerly a nine days' wonder is scarcely marvelled at the same number of minutes. Yet in certain cases episodes of a mysterious or unexpected nature engage the attention of a careless world for a somewhat longer period, and provoke an immense amount of discussion and surmise. In this category may be placed the crime committed in Geneva Square; for when the extraordinary circumstances of the case became known, much curiosity was manifested regarding the possible criminal and his motive for committing so apparently useless a crime.

To add to the wonderment of the public, it came out in the evidence of Lucian Denzil at the inquest that Berwin was not the real name of the victim; so here the authorities were confronted with a three-fold problem. They had first to discover the name of the dead man; second, to learn who it was had so foully murdered him; and third, to find out the reason why the unknown assassin should have slain an apparently harmless man.

But these hidden things were not easily brought to light; and the meagre evidence collected by the police failed to do away with any one of the three obstacles - at all events, until after the inquest. When the jury brought in a verdict that the deceased had been violently done to death by some person or persons unknown, the twelve good men and true stated the full extent of knowledge gained by Justice in her futile scramble after clues. Berwin - so called - was dead, his assassin had melted into thin air, and the Silent House had added a second legend to its already uncanny reputation. Formerly it had been simply haunted, now it was also blood-stained, and its last condition was worse than its first.

The dead man had been found stabbed to the heart by some long, thin, sharp-pointed instrument which the murderer had taken away with him - or perhaps her, as the sex of the assassin, for obvious reasons, could not be decided. Mrs. Kebby swore that she had left the deceased sitting over the fire at eight o'clock on Christmas Eve, and that he had then been fairly well, though far from enjoying the best of health. When she returned, shortly after nine, on Christmas morning, the man was dead and cold. Medical aid was called in at the same time as the police were summoned; and the evidence of the doctor who examined the body went to prove that Berwin had been dead at least ten hours; therefore, he must have been assassinated between the hours of eleven and twelve of the previous night.

Search was immediately made for the murderer, but no trace could be found of him, nor could it be ascertained how he had entered the house. The doors were all locked, the windows were all barred, and neither at the back nor in the front was there any outlet left open whereby the man - if it was a man who had done the deed - could have escaped.

Blinders, the policeman on duty at the entrance of the square, gave evidence that he had been on duty there all night, and that although many servants and owners of houses belonging to the square had passed in from their Christmas marketings, yet no stranger had entered. The policeman knew every one, even to the errand-boys of the neighbourhood, who brought parcels of Christmas goods, and in many cases had exchanged greetings with the passers-by; but he was prepared to swear, and, in fact, did swear at the inquest, that no stranger either came into or went out of Geneva Square.

Also he deposed that when the traffic died away after midnight he had walked round the square, and had looked at every window, including that of No. 13, and had tried every door, also including that of No. 13, only to find that all was safe. Blinders declared on oath that he had not on Christmas Eve the slightest suspicion of the horrid tragedy which had taken place in the Silent House during the time he was on duty.

When the police took possession of the body and mansion, search was made in bedroom and sitting-room for papers likely to throw light on the identity of the victim, but in vain. No letters or telegrams, or even writing of any kind, could be discovered; there was no name in the dead man's books, no mark on his clothes, no initials on his linen.

The landlord of the house declared that the deceased had hired the mansion six months before, but had given no references, and as the landlord was glad to let the haunted No. 13 on any terms, he had not insisted upon having them. The deceased, said the landlord, had paid a month's rent in advance in ready money, and at the end of every month he had discharged his liability in the same way. He gave neither cheque nor notes, but paid always in gold; and beyond the fact that he called himself Mark Berwin, the landlord knew nothing about him.

The firm who had furnished the rooms made almost the same report, quite as meagre and unsatisfactory. Mr. Berwin - so the deceased had given his name - had ordered the furniture, and had paid for it in gold. Altogether, in spite of every effort, the police were obliged to declare themselves beaten. They could not find out the name of the victim, and therefore were unable to learn his past life, or trace thereby if he had an enemy likely to harm him.

Beyond the report given by Lucian of his conversation with the man, which showed that Berwin certainly had some enemy whom he dreaded, there was nothing discovered to show reason for the committal of the crime.

Berwin - so called - was dead; he was buried under his assumed name, and there, so far as the obtainable evidence went, was an end to the strange tenant of the Silent House. Gordon Link, the detective charged with the conduct of the case, confessed as much to Denzil.

"I do not see the slightest chance of tracing Berwin's past," said he to the barrister. "We are as ignorant about him as we are of the name of the assassin."

"Are you sure there is no clue, Mr. Link?"

"Absolutely none; even the weapon with which the crime was committed cannot be found."

"You have searched the house?"

"Every inch of it, and with the result that I have found nothing. The surroundings of the case are most mysterious. If we do not identify the dead we cannot hope to trace the murderer. How the wretch got into the house is more than I can discover."

"It is strange," admitted Lucian thoughtfully, "yet in some secret way people were in the habit of entering the house, and Berwin knew as much; not only that, but he protected them from curiosity by denying that they even existed."

"I don't quite follow you, Mr. Denzil."

"I allude to the shadows on the blind, which I saw myself a week before the murder took place. They were those of a man and a woman, and must have been cast by bodies of flesh and blood. Therefore, two people must have been in Berwin's sitting-room on that night; yet when I met Berwin who was absent at the time - he denied that anyone could have entered his house without his knowledge. More, he actually insisted that I should satisfy myself as to the truth of this by examining the house."

"Which you did?"

"Yes, but found nothing; yet," said Lucian, with an air of conviction, "however the man and woman entered, they were in the house."

"Then the assassin must have come in by the same way; but where that way can be, or how it can be found, is more than I can say."

"Does the landlord know of any secret passages?"

"No; I asked him," replied the detective, "but he stated that houses nowadays were not built with secret passages. When Berwin denied that anyone was in the house, was he afraid, Mr. Denzil?"

"Yes, he seemed to be nervous."

"And he told you he had enemies?"

"He hinted that there were people who wished to see him dead. From the way he spoke and the language he used I am satisfied that he was hiding from the vengeance of some one."

"Vengeance!" repeated Link, raising his eyebrows. "Is not that word a trifle melodramatic?"

"Perhaps; but to my mind there is more melodrama in actual life than people fancy. However, Mr. Link," added Lucian, "I have come to certain conclusions. Firstly, that Berwin was in hiding; secondly, that he saw people secretly who entered in some way we cannot discover; and thirdly, that to solve the problem it will be necessary to look into the past life of the dead man."

"Your third conclusion brings us round to the point whence we started," retorted Link. "How am I to discover the man's past?"

"By learning who he is, and what is his real name."

"An easy task," said the detective sarcastically, "considering the meagre material upon which we have to work. And how is the business to be accomplished?"

"By advertisement."

"Advertisement!"

"Yes. I wonder the idea did not strike you before, seeing how often it is used in similar cases. Advertise a full description of the man who called himself Berwin, note his physical peculiarities and looks, and circulate such description by means of handbills and newspapers."

Link looked angry, and laughed rather contemptuously, as his professional pride was touched by the fact of being advised by an individual not of his calling.

"I am not so ignorant of my business as you think," he said sharply. "What you suggest has already been done. There are handbills describing the appearance of Berwin in every police office in the kingdom."

"In the newspapers, also?" asked Lucian, nettled by the detective's tone.

"No; it is not necessary."

"I don't agree with you. Many people in private life are not likely to see your handbills. I don't pretend to advise, Mr. Link," he added in soothing tones, "but would it not be wise to use the medium of the daily papers?"

"I'll think of it," said Link, too jealous of his dignity to give way at once.

"Oh, I quite rely on your discretion," said Denzil hastily. "You know your own business best. But if you succeed in identifying Berwin, will you let me know?"

Link looked keenly at the young man.

"Why do you wish to know about the matter?" he asked.

"Out of simple curiosity. The case is so mysterious that I should like to watch you unravel it."

"Well," said Link, rather gratified by this tribute to his power, "I shall indulge your fancy."

The result of this conversation was that Lucian observed in the newspapers next day an advertisement describing the looks and name, and physical peculiarities of the deceased, with special mention of the loss of the left hand's little finger, and the strange cicatrice on the right cheek. Satisfied that the only way to learn the truth had been adopted by the authorities, Lucian impatiently waited for the development of the scheme.

Within the week he received a visit from the detective.

"You were right and I was wrong, Mr. Denzil," admitted Link generously. "The newspapers were of more use than the handbills. Yesterday I received a letter from a lady who is coming to see me to-morrow at my office. So if you care to be present at the interview you have only to say so."

"I should like it above all things," said Lucian eagerly. "Who is the lady?"

"A Mrs. Vrain, who writes from Bath."

"Can she identify the dead man?"

"She thinks she can, but, of course, she cannot be certain until she sees the body. Going by the description, however," added Link, "she is inclined to believe that Berwin was her husband."

Fergus Hume

CHAPTER VI

MRS. VRAIN'S STORY

Denzil was much pleased with the courtesy of the detective Link in permitting him to gain, at first hand, further details of this mysterious case. With a natural curiosity, engendered by his short acquaintance with the unfortunate Berwin, he was most anxious to learn why the man had secluded himself from the world in Geneva Square; who were the enemies he hinted at as desirous of his death; and in what manner and for what reason he had met with so barbarous a fate at their hands. It seemed likely that Mrs. Vrain, who asserted herself to be the wife of the deceased, would be able to answer these questions in full; therefore, he was punctual in keeping the appointment at the office of Link.

He was rather astonished to find that Mrs. Vrain had arrived, and was deep in conversation with the detective, while a third person, who had evidently accompanied her, sat near at hand, silent, but attentive to what was being discussed. As the dead man had been close on sixty years of age, and Mrs. Vrain claimed to be his wife, Denzil had quite expected to meet with an elderly woman. Instead of doing so, however, he beheld a pretty young lady of not more than twenty-five, whose raiment of widow's weeds set off her beauty to the greatest advantage. She was a charming blonde, with golden hair and blue eyes, and a complexion of rose-leaf hue. In spite of her grief her demeanour was lively and engaging, and her smile particularly attractive, lighting up her whole face in the most fascinating manner. Her hands and feet were small, her stature was that of a fairy, and her figure was perfect in every way.

Altogether, Mrs. Vrain looked like a sylph or a dainty shepherdess of Dresden china, and should have been arrayed in gossamer robes, rather than in the deep mourning she affected. Indeed, Lucian considered that such weeds were rather premature, as Mrs. Vrain could not yet be certain that the murdered man was her husband; but she looked so charming and childlike a creature that he forgave her being too eager to consider herself a widow. Perhaps with such an elderly husband her eagerness was natural.

From this charming vision Lucian's eyes wandered to the attentive third person, a rosy-cheeked, plump little man, of between fifty and sixty. From his resemblance to Mrs. Vrain - for he had the same blue eyes and pink-and-white complexion - Lucian guessed that he was her father, and such, indeed, proved to be the case. Link, on Lucian's entrance, introduced him to the sylph in black, who in her turn presented him to the silvery-haired, benevolent old man, whom she called Mr. Jabez Clyne.

At the first sound of their voices Lucian detected so pronounced a twang, and so curious a way of collocating words, as to conclude that Mrs. Vrain and her amiable parent hailed from the States. The little lady seemed to pride herself on this, and indicated her republican origin in her speech more than was necessary - at least, Denzil thought so. But then, on occasions, he was disposed to be hyper-critical.

"Say, now," said Mrs. Vrain, casting an approving glance on Lucian's face, "I'm right down glad to see you. Mr. Link here was just saying you knew my husband, Mr. Vrain."

"I knew him as Mr. Berwin - Mark Berwin," replied Denzil, taking a seat.

"Just think of that now!" cried Mrs. Vrain, with a liveliness rather subdued in compliment to her apparel; "and his real name was Mark Vrain. Well, I guess he won't need no name now, poor man," and the widow touched her bright eyes carefully with a doll's pocket-handkerchief, which Lucian noted, somewhat cynically, was perfectly dry.

"Maybe he's an angel by this time, Lyddy," said Mr. Clyne, in a cheerful, chirping voice, "so it ain't no use wishing him back, as I can see. We've all got to negotiate kingdom-come some time or another."

"Not in the same way, I hope," said Lucian dryly. "But I beg your pardon, Link, I interrupt your conversation."

"By no means," replied the detective readily. "We had just begun when you entered, Mr. Denzil."

"And it wasn't much of a talk, anyhow," said Mrs. Vrain. "I was only replying to some stupid questions."

"Stupid, if you will, but necessary," observed Link, with gravity. "Let us continue. Are you certain that this dead man is - or rather was - your husband?"

"I'm as sure as sure can be, sir. Berwin Manor is the name of our place near Bath, and it looks as though my husband called himself after it when he changed his colours. And isn't his first name Mark?" pursued the pretty widow. "Well, my husband was called Mark, too, so there you are - Mark Berwin."

"Is this all your proof?" asked Link calmly.

"I guess not, though it's enough, I should say. My husband had a mark on his right cheek - got it fighting a duel with a German student when he was having a high time as one of the boys at Heidelberg. Then he lost part of his little finger - left-hand finger - in an accident out West. What other proof do you want, Mr. Link?"

"The proofs you have given seem sufficient, Mrs. Vrain, but may I ask when your husband left his home?"

"About a year ago, eh, poppa?"

"You are overdoing it, Lyddy," corrected the father. "Size it up as ten months, and you'll do."

"Ten months," said Lucian suddenly, "and Mr. Berwin -"

"Vrain!" struck in Lydia, the widow, "Mark Vrain."

"I beg your pardon! Well, Mark Vrain took the house in Geneva Square six months back. Where was he during the other four?"

"Ask me something easier, Mr. Denzil. I know no more than you do."

"Did you not know where he went on leaving Berwin Manor?"

"Sakes! how should I? Mark and I didn't pull together nohow, so he kicked over the traces and made tracks for the back of beyond."

"And you might square it, Lyddy, by saying as 'twasn't you who upset the apple cart."

"Well, I should smile to think so," said Mrs. Vrain vigorously. "I was as good as pie to that old man."

"You did not get on well together?" said Link sharply.

"Got on as well as a cat hitched along with a dog. My stars! there was no living with him. If he hadn't left me, I'd have left him - that's an almighty truth."

"So the gist of all this is that Mr. Vrain left you ten months ago, and did not leave his address?"

"That's so," said the widow calmly. "I've not seen nor heard of him for most a year, till pop there tumbled across your paragraph in the papers. Then I surmised from the name and the missing finger and the scarred cheek, that I'd dropped right on to Mark. I wouldn't take all this trouble for any one else; no, sir, not me!"

"My Lyddy does not care about being a grass-widow, gentlemen."

"I don't mind being a grass-widow or a real one, so long as I know how to ticket myself," said the candid Lydia; "but seems to me there's no question that Mark's sent in his checks."

"I certainly think that this man who called himself Berwin was your husband," said Denzil, for Mrs. Vrain's eyes rested on him, and she seemed to expect an answer.

"Well, then, that means I'm Mr. Vrain's widow?"

"I should say so."

"And entitled to all his pile?"

"That depends on the will," said Lucian dryly, for the light tone of the pretty woman jarred upon his ear.

"Oh, that's all right," replied Mrs. Vrain, putting a gold-topped smelling bottle to her nose. "I saw the will made, and know exactly how I come out. The old man's daughter by his first wife gets the manor and the rents, and I take the assurance money!"

"Was Mr. Berwin - I beg pardon, Vrain - was he married twice?"

"I should think so!" said Lydia. "He was a widower with a grown-up daughter when I took him to church. Well, can I get this assurance money?"

"I suppose so," said Link, "provided you can prove your husband's death."

"Sakes alive!" cried Mrs. Vrain briskly. "Wasn't he murdered?"

"The man called Berwin was murdered."

"Well, sir," said the rosy-cheeked Clyne, with more sharpness than might have been expected from his peaceful aspect, "and ain't Berwin Vrain?"

"It would seem so," replied Link coolly. "All your evidence goes to prove it, yet the assurance company may not be satisfied with the proof. I expect the grave will have to be opened, and the remains identified."

"Ugh!" said Mrs. Vrain with a shrug, "how disgusting! I mean," she added, colouring as she saw that Lucian was rather shocked by her flippancy, "that sorry as I am for the old man, he wasn't a good husband to me, and corpses a week old ain't pleasant things to look on."

"Lyddy," interposed Clyne, hastening to obliterate, if possible, the impression made on the two men by this foolish speech, "how you do go on. But you know your heart is better than your tongue."

"It was, to put up so long with Mr. Vrain," said Lydia resentfully; "but I'm honest, if I'm nothing else. I guess I'm sorry that Vrain got stuck like a pig; but it wasn't my fault, and I've done my best to show respect by wearing black. But it is no good going on in this way, poppa, for I've no call to excuse myself to strangers. What I want to know is how I'm going to get the dollars."

"You'll have to see the assurance company about that," said Link coldly; "my business with you, Mrs. Vrain, is about this murder."

"I know nothing about it," retorted the widow. "I haven't set eyes on Mark for most a year."

"Have you any idea who killed him?"

"I guess not! How should I?"

"You might know if he had enemies."

"He," said Mrs. Vrain, with supreme contempt, "why, he hadn't backbone enough for folks to get riz at him! He was half baked!"

"Crazy, that is," remarked Clyne; "always thought the world was against him, and folks wanted to get quit of him."

"He said he had enemies," hinted Lucian.

"You bet! He no doubt made out that all Europe was against him," said Clyne. "That was my son-in-law all over. Lyddy and he had a tiff, just like other married couples, and he clears out to lie low in an out-of-the-way shanty in Pimlico. I tell you, gentlemen, that Vrain had a chip out of his head. He fancied things, he did; but no one wanted to harm him that I know of."

"Yet he died a violent death," said Denzil gravely.

"That's a frozen fact, sir," cried Clyne, "and both Lyddy and I want to lynch the reptile as did it; but we neither of us know who laid him out."

"I'm sure I don't," said Mrs. Vrain in a weeping voice. "Every one that I knew was civil to him; he had no one who wanted to kill him when he left Berwin Manor. Why he went away, or how he died, I can't say."

"If you want to know how he died," explained Link, "I can tell you. He was stabbed."

"So the journals said; with a bowie!"

"No, not with a bowie," corrected Lucian, "but with some long, sharp instrument."

"A dagger?" suggested Clyne.

"I should be even more precise," said Denzil slowly. "I should say a stiletto - an Italian stiletto."

"A stiletto!" gasped Mrs. Vrain, whose delicate pink colour had faded to a chalky white. "Oh! - oh! I - I -" and she fainted forthwith.

CHAPTER VII

THE ASSURANCE MONEY

Mrs. Vrain's fainting fit was of no great duration, and she shortly recovered her senses, but not her sprightliness. Her excuse was that the long discussion of her husband's murder, and the too precise details related to her by Link before Denzil's arrival, had so wrought on her nerves as to occasion her temporary indisposition.

This reason, which was a trifle weak, since she seemed to bear her husband's loss with great stoicism, awakened suspicions in Lucian's mind as to her truthfulness. However, these were too vague and confused to be put into words, so the young man remained silent until Mrs. Vrain and her father departed. This they did almost immediately, after the widow had given her London and country addresses to the detective, in case he should require her in the conduct of the case.

This matter being attended to, she left the room, with a parting smile and especial bow to Lucian.

Link smiled in his turn as he observed this Parthian shaft, the shooting of which was certainly out of keeping with Mrs. Vrain's character of a mourning widow.

"You seem to have made an impression on the lady, Mr. Denzil," he said, with a slight cough to conceal his amusement.

"Nonsense!" replied Lucian, his fair face crimsoning with vexation. "She seems to me one of those shallow women who would sooner flirt with a tinker than pass unnoticed by the male sex. I don't like her," he concluded, with some abruptness.

"On what grounds?"

"Well, she spoke very hardly about her husband, and seemed rather more concerned about this assurance money than his death. She is a flippant doll, with a good deal of the adventuress about her. I don't think," said the barrister significantly, "that she is altogether so ignorant of this matter as she pretends to be."

The detective raised his eyebrows. "You don't propose to accuse her of the murder?" he asked sceptically.

"Oh, no!" answered Denzil hastily. "I don't say she is as guilty as all that; but she knows something, or suspects something."

"How do you make that out?"

"She fainted at the mention of stiletto; and I am convinced that Vrain - as I suppose we must call him now - was killed with one. And again, Link, this woman admitted that she had married her elderly husband in Florence. Now, Florence, as you know, is an Italian town; a stiletto is an Italian weapon. Putting these two things together, what do you make of Mrs. Vrain's fainting?"

"I make nothing of it, Mr. Denzil. You are too suspicious. The woman had no reason to rid herself of her husband as you hint."

"What about the assurance money?"

"There is a motive there, certainly - a motive of gain. Still, I think you are making a mountain out of a molehill, for I am satisfied that she knows no more who committed the crime than does the Pope himself."

"It is as well to look in every direction," said Lucian obstinately.

"Meaning that I should follow this clue you suggest, which has no existence save in your own fancy. Well, I'll keep my eye on Mrs. Vrain, you may be sure of that. It won't be difficult, as she will certainly stay in town until she identifies the body of her dead husband and gets the money. If she is guilty, I'll track her down; but I am certain she has nothing to do with the crime. If she had, it is not likely that she would enter the lion's den by coming to see me. No, no, Mr. Denzil; you have found a mare's nest."

Lucian shrugged his shoulders, and took up his hat to go.

"You may be right," said he reluctantly, "but I have my doubts of Mrs. Vrain, and shall continue to have them until she supplies a more feasible explanation of her fainting. In the meantime, I'll leave you to follow out the case in the manner you judge best. We shall see who is right in the long run," and Denzil, still holding to his opinion, took his departure, leaving Link confident that the young man did not know what he was talking about.

As the detective sat thinking over the late conversation, and wondering if he could shape any definite course out of it, Denzil put his head in at the door.

"I say, Link," he called out, "you'd better find out if Mrs. Vrain is really the wife of this dead man before you are guided by her story!" After which speech he hurriedly withdrew, leaving Link to digest it at his leisure.

At first, Link was indignant that Denzil should deem him so easily hoodwinked as the speech implied. Afterwards he began to laugh.

"Wife!" said he to himself. "Of course she is the man's wife! She knows too much about him to be otherwise; but even granting that Denzil is right - which I don't for a moment admit - there is no need for me to prove the truth of his assumption. If this pretty woman is not the true wife of Berwin, or Vrain, or whatever this dead man's name actually may be, the assurance company will get at the rights of the matter before paying over the money."

Subsequent events reflected credit on this philosophical speech and determination of Mr. Link. Had Mrs. Vrain been an imposter, her house of cards would have been knocked down, as soon as reared, by the searching inquiry instituted by the Sirius Assurance Company. It appeared that the life of the late Mark Vrain was on the books of the company for no less a sum than twenty thousand pounds; and under the will this was to be paid over to Lydia Vrain, *nee* Clyne. The widow, aided by her father - who was a shrewd business man, in spite of his innocent looks - and the family lawyer of the Vrains, went systematically to work to establish her own identity, the death of her husband, and her consequent right to the money.

The first thing to be done was to prove that the dead man was really Vrain. There was some little difficulty in obtaining an order from the authorities for the opening of the grave and the exhumation of the body; but finally the consent of those in power was obtained, and there was little difficulty in the identification of the remains. The lawyer, Mr. Clyne, Mrs. Vrain herself, and several people brought up from Bath by the assurance company, swore that the corpse - buried under the false name of Berwin - was that of Mark Vrain, for decomposition had not proceeded so far but what the features could be recognised. There was even no need to unwrap the body from its cerements, as the face itself, and the scar thereon, were quite sufficient for the friends of the deceased to swear to the corpse. Thereupon the assurance company, on the fullest of evidence, was compelled to admit that their client was dead, and expressed themselves ready to pay over the money to Mrs. Vrain as soon as the will should be proved.

Pending the legal process necessary to do this, the widow made a great parade of her grief and affection for the dead man. She had the body re-enclosed in a new and sumptuous coffin, and removed the same to Berwin Manor, near Bath, where, after a short lapse of time, it was duly placed in the family vault of the Vrains.

The widow, having thus disposed of her husband, bethought herself of her stepdaughter, who at that time was on a visit to some friends in Australia. A long letter, giving full details, was despatched by Mrs. Vrain, and the daughter was requested, both by the widow and the lawyer, to come back to England at once and take up her abode in Berwin Manor, which, with its surrounding acres, had been left to her under the will.

Matters connected with the death and its consequences having been disposed of thus far, Mrs. Vrain sat down, and, folding her hands, waited till such time as she would receive the assurance money, and begin a new life as a wealthy and fascinating widow. Every one said that the little woman had behaved very well, and that Vrain - weak-headed as he was supposed to be - had shown excellent judgment in dividing his property, real and personal, so equally between the two claimants. Miss Vrain, as became the child of the first wife, received the home and acres of her ancestors; while the second wife obtained the assurance money, which every one candidly admitted she quite deserved for having sacrificed her youth and beauty to an old man like Vrain. In those days, when all these details were being settled, the widow was the most popular personage in Bath.

Matters went smoothly with Mrs. Vrain in every respect. The will was duly proved, the twenty thousand pounds was duly paid over; so, finding herself rich, the widow came with her father to take up her abode in London. When settled there one of her first acts was to send a note to Lucian, telling him that she was in town. The good looks of the young man had made a considerable impression on Mrs. Vrain, and she appeared anxious to renew the acquaintance, although it had been so inauspiciously begun in the purlieus of the police courts.

On his part, Lucian lost no time in paying his respects, for after the searching inquiry conducted by the Sirius Assurance Company, out of which ordeal Mrs. Vrain had emerged unscathed, he began to think that he had been too hasty in condemning the little widow. So he called upon her almost immediately after receiving the invitation, and found her, after the lapse of three months, as pretty as ever, and clothed in less heavy mourning.

"It's real sweet of you to call, Mr. Denzil," said she vivaciously. "I haven't seen anything of you since we met in Mr. Link's office. And sakes! have I not had a heap of trouble since then?"

"Your trouble has done you no harm, Mrs. Vrain. So far as your looks go, three minutes, rather than three months, might have passed."

"Oh, that's all right. I guess it's not good enough to cry one's self sick for what can't be helped. But I want to ask you, Mr. Denzil, how that policeman is progressing with the case."

"He has found out nothing," replied Lucian, shaking his head, "and, so far as I can see, there's not much chance of learning the truth."

"I never thought there was," said Mrs. Vrain, with a shrug. "Seems to me you don't get round much in this old country. Well, it don't seem as I can do much more. I've told all I know, and I've offered a reward of L500 to discover the man who stuck Mark. If he ain't found for dollars he won't be found at all."

"Probably not, Mrs. Vrain. It is now over three months since the crime was committed, and every day makes the chance of discovery less."

"But for all that, Diana Vrain's going on the trail, Mr. Denzil."

"Diana Vrain! Who is she?"

"My stepdaughter - Mark's only child. She was in Australia - out in the wild west of that country - and only lately got the news of her father's death. I got a letter from her last week, and it seems as she's coming back here to find out who laid her poppa out."

"I am afraid she'll not succeed," said Denzil dubiously.

"She'll do her best to," replied Mrs. Vrain, with a shrug. "She's as obstinate as a battery mule; but it's no use talking, she will have her own way," and dismissing the subject of Miss Vrain, the pretty widow, with an air of relief, talked on more frivolous subjects until Lucian took his departure.

CHAPTER VIII

DIANA VRAIN

Although over three months had elapsed since the murder of Mark Vrain, and the crime had been relegated to oblivion both by press and people, curiosity concerning it was still active in Geneva Square. The gossips in that talkative quarter had exhausted their tongues and imaginations in surmising who had committed the deed, and how it had been accomplished.

It was now known that the deceased had been of a good county family, who had left his pretty young wife in a fit of groundless suspicion; that he had no enemies; and had withdrawn to the Silent House to save himself from the machinations of purely imaginary beings. The general opinion was that Vrain had been insane; but even this did not explain the reason of his tragic and unforeseen death.

Since the murder the Silent House had acquired a tenfold interest in the eyes of all. The crime, added to its reputation for being haunted, invested it with horror; and its common-place looks assumed to fanciful onlookers a grim and menacing aspect, in keeping with its blood-stained floor and ghostly rooms.

Disheartened by the late catastrophe, which had so greatly enhanced the already evil reputation of the house, the landlord did not attempt to relet it, as he knew very well that no tenant would be bold enough to take it, even at a nominal rent. Mrs.

Vrain had sold off the furniture of the two apartments which her unfortunate husband had inhabited, and now these were as bare and lonely as the rest of the rooms.

The landlord made no effort to furbish up or renovate the mansion, deeming that such expense would be useless; so No. 13, deserted by man, and cursed by God, remained vacant and avoided. People came from far and near to look at it, but no one entered its doors lest some evil fate should befall them. Yet, in strange contradiction to the horror it created in every breast, the houses on either side continued to be occupied.

Miss Greeb frequently took a peep across the way at the empty house, with its curtainless, dusty windows and smokeless chimneys. She had theorised often on the murder of Vrain, and being unable to come to any reasonable conclusion, finally decided that a ghost - the ghost which haunted the mansion - had committed the crime. In support of this fantastic opinion she related to Lucian at least a score of stories in which people foolishly sleeping in haunted rooms had been found dead in the morning.

"With black finger-marks on their throats," said Miss Greeb dramatically, "and looks of horror in their eyes, and everything locked up, just like it was in No. 13, to show that nothing but a ghost could have killed them."

"You forget, Miss Greeb," said Lucian flippantly, "poor Vrain was stabbed with a stiletto. Ghosts don't use material weapons."

"How do you know the dagger was a real one?" replied Miss Greeb, sinking her voice to a horrified whisper. "Was it ever seen? No! Was it ever found? No! The ghost took it away. Depend upon it, Mr. Denzil, it wasn't flesh and blood as made a spirit of that crazy Berwin."

"In that case, the ghostly criminal can't be hanged," said Denzil, with a laugh. "But it's all nonsense, Miss Greeb. I am astonished that a woman of your sense should believe in such rubbish."

"Wiser people than I have faith in ghosts," retorted the landlady obstinately. "Haven't you heard of the haunted house in a West End square, where a man and a dog were found dead in the morning, with a valet as gibbered awful ever afterwards?"

"Pooh! Pooh! That's a story of Bulwer Lytton's."

"It is not, Mr. Denzil - it's a fact. You can see the very house in the square for yourself, and No. 13 is just such another."

"Nonsense! Why, I'd sleep in No. 13 to-morrow night, just to prove that your ghostly fears are all moonshine."

Miss Greeb uttered a screech of alarm. "Mr. Denzil!" she cried, with great energy, "sooner than you should do that, I'd - I'd - well, I don't know what I'd do!"

"Accuse me of stealing your silver spoons and have me locked up," said Lucian, laughing. "Make yourself easy, Miss Greeb. I have no intention of tempting Providence. All the same, I don't believe for one minute that No. 13 is haunted."

"Lights were seen flitting from room to room."

"No doubt. Poor Vrain showed me over the house before he died. His candle explains the lights."

"They have been seen since his death," said Miss Greeb solemnly.

"Then, as a ghost, Vrain must be walking about with the old woman phantom who wears brocade and high-heeled shoes."

Miss Greeb, seeing that she had a sceptic to deal with, retreated with great dignity from the argument, but nevertheless to other people maintained her opinion, with many facts drawn from her imagination and from books on the supernatural compiled from the imagination - or, as the various writers called it - the experience of others. Some agreed with her, others laughed at her; but one and all acknowledged that, however it came about, whether by ghostly or mortal means, the murder of Vrain was a riddle never likely to be solved; and, with other events of a like nature and mystery, it was relegated to the list of undiscovered crimes.

After several interviews with Link, the barrister was also inclined to take this view of the matter. He found the detective quite discouraged in his efforts to find the assassin.

"I have been to Bath," said Link dismally. "I have examined, so far as I was able, into the past life of Vrain, but I can find nothing likely to throw light on the subject. He did not get on well with his wife, and left Bath ten months before the murder. I tried to trace where he went to, but could not. He vanished from Bath quite unexpectedly, and four months later turned up in Geneva Square, as we know, but who killed him, or why he was killed, I can't say. I'm afraid I'll have to give it up as a bad job, Mr. Denzil."

"What! and lose a reward of five hundred pounds!" said Lucian.

"If it was five thousand, I must lose it," returned the dejected Link. "This case beats me. I don't believe the murderer will ever be run down."

"Upon my word, I am inclined to agree with you," said Denzil, and barrister and detective departed, each convinced that the Vrain case was ended, and that in the face of the insuperable obstacles presented by it there was not the slightest chance of avenging the murder of the unfortunate man. The reading of the mystery was beyond mortal powers to accomplish.

*　*　*　*　*

About the middle of April, nearly four months after the tragedy, Lucian received a letter containing an invitation which caused him no little astonishment. The note was signed Diana Vrain, and, having intimated that the writer had returned only that week from Australia, requested that Mr. Denzil would be kind enough to call the next day at the Royal John Hotel in Kensington. Miss Vrain ended by stating that she had a particular desire to converse with Mr. Denzil, and hoped that he would not fail to keep the appointment.

Wondering greatly how the lady - who was no doubt the stepdaughter referred to by Mrs. Vrain - had obtained his address, and why she desired to see him so particularly, Lucian, out of sheer curiosity, obeyed the summons. Next day, at four o'clock - the appointed hour - he presented himself as requested, and, on giving his name, was shown immediately into the presence of his correspondent, who occupied a small private sitting-room.

When Miss Vrain rose to greet him, Lucian was amazed to see how beautiful and stately she was. With dark hair and eyes, oval face, and firm mouth, majestic figure and imperial gait, she moved towards him an apparent queen. A greater contrast to Mrs. Vrain than her stepdaughter can scarcely be imagined: the one was a frivolous, volatile fairy, the other a dignified and reserved woman. She also was arrayed in black garments, but these were made in the plainest manner, and showed none of the coquetry of woe such as had characterised Mrs. Vrain's elaborate costume. The look of sorrow on the face of Diana was in keeping with her mourning apparel, and she welcomed Lucian with a subdued courtesy which prepossessed him greatly in her favour.

Quick in his likes and dislikes, the young man was as drawn towards this beautiful, sad woman as formerly he had been repulsed by the feigned grief and ensnaring glances of silly Mrs. Vrain.

"I am much obliged to you for calling, Mr. Denzil," said Miss Vrain in a deep voice, rather melancholy in its tone. "No doubt you wondered how I obtained your address."

"It did strike me as peculiar, I confess," said Lucian, taking a chair to which she pointed, "but on considering the matter I fancied that Mrs. Vrain had -"

"Mrs. Vrain!" echoed Diana in a tone of contempt. "No! I have not seen Mrs. Vrain since I returned, a week ago, to London. I got your address from the detective who examined into the death of my most unhappy father."

"You have seen Link?"

"Yes, and I know all that Link could tell me. He mentioned your name frequently in his narrative, and gave me to understand that on two occasions you had spoken with my father; therefore, I asked him to give me your address, so that I might speak with you personally on the matter."

"I am quite at your service, Miss Vrain. I suppose you wish to learn all that I know of the tragedy?"

"I wish for more than that, Mr. Denzil," said Diana quietly. "I wish you to help me in hunting down the assassin of my father."

"What! Do you intend to reopen the case?"

"Certainly; but I did not know that the case - as you call it - had been closed. I have come home from Australia especially to devote myself to this matter. I should have been in London long ago, but that out in Australia I was with some friends in a part of the country where it is difficult to get letters. As soon as Mrs. Vrain's letter about the terrible end of my father came to hand I arranged my affairs and left at once for England. Since my arrival I have seen Mr. Saker, our family lawyer, and Mr. Link, the detective. They have told me all they know, and now

I wish to hear what you have to say."

"I am afraid I cannot help you, Miss Vrain," said Lucian dubiously.

"Ah! You refuse to help me?"

"Oh, no! no! I shall only be too glad to do what I can," protested Lucian, shocked that she should think him so hard-hearted, "but I know of nothing likely to solve the mystery. Both myself and Link have done our best to discover the truth, but without success."

"Well, Mr. Denzil," said Diana, after a pause, "they often say that a woman's wit can do more than a man's logic, so you and I must put our heads together and discover the guilty person. Have you no suspicion?"

"No. I have no suspicion," replied Lucian frankly. "Have you?"

"I have. I suspect - a lady."

"Mrs. Vrain?"

"Yes. How do you know I meant her?"

"Because at one time I suspected her myself."

"You suspected rightly," replied Diana. "I believe that Mrs. Vrain killed her husband."

CHAPTER IX

A MARRIAGE THAT WAS A FAILURE

Denzil did not reply at once to the accusation levelled by Diana at Mrs. Vrain, as he was too astonished at her vehemence to find his voice readily. When he did speak, it was to argue on the side of the pretty widow.

"I think you must be mistaken," he said at length.

"But, Mr. Denzil, you declared that you suspected her yourself!"

"At one time, but not now," replied Lucian decisively, "because at the time of the murder Mrs. Vrain was keeping Christmas in Berwin Manor."

"Like Nero fiddling when Rome was burning," retorted Diana sharply; "but you mistake my meaning. I do not say that Mrs. Vrain committed the crime personally, but she inspired and guided the assassin."

"And who is the assassin, in your opinion?"

"Count Hercule Ferruci."

"An Italian?"

"As you may guess from the name."

"Now, that is strange," cried Lucian, with some excitement, "for, from the nature of the wound, I believe that your father was stabbed by an Italian stiletto."

"Aha!" said Diana, with satisfaction. "That strengthens the accusation I bring against Ferruci."

"And, again," continued Denzil, hardly listening to what she was saying, "when I mentioned my suspicion about the stiletto in the hearing of Mrs. Vrain, she fainted."

"Which showed that her guilty conscience pricked her. Oh, I am sure of it, Mr. Denzil! My stepmother and the count are the criminals!"

"Our evidence, as yet, is only circumstantial," said Lucian cautiously. "We must not jump to conclusions. At present I am completely in the dark regarding this foreigner."

"I can enlighten you, but it is a long story."

"The longer the better," said Denzil, thinking he could hear Diana speak and watch her face for hours without weariness. "I wish for all details, then I shall be in a better position to judge."

"What you say is only reasonable, Mr. Denzil. I shall tell you my father's history from the time he went to Italy some three years ago. It was in Italy - to be precise, in Florence - that he met with Lydia Clyne and her father."

"One moment," said Denzil. "Before you begin, will you tell me what you think of the couple?"

"Think!" cried Diana disdainfully. "I think they are a couple of adventurers; but she is the worst of the two. The old man, Jabez Clyne, I think moderately well of; he is a weak fool under the thumb of his daughter. If you only knew what I have suffered at the hands of that golden-haired doll!"

"I should think you could hold your own, Miss Vrain."

"Not against treachery and lies!" retorted Diana fiercely. "It is not my habit to employ such weapons, but my stepmother used no others. It was she who drove me out of the house and made me exile myself to the Antipodes to escape her falseness. And it was she," added Miss Vrain solemnly, "who treated my father so ill as to drive him out of his own home. Lydia Vrain is not the doll you think her to be; she is a false, cruel, clever adventuress, and I hate her - I hate her with all my heart and soul!"

This feminine outburst of anger rather bewildered Denzil, who saw very plainly that Diana was by no means the lofty angel he had taken her to be in the first appreciation of her beauty. But her passion of the moment suited so well with her stately looks that she seemed rather a Margaret of Anjou defying York and his faction than an injured woman concerned with so slight a thing as the rebuke of one of her own sex for whom she had little love. Diana saw the surprise expressed on Lucian's face, and her own flushed a little with annoyance that she should have betrayed her feelings so openly. With a vexed laugh, she recovered her temper and composed demeanour.

"You see I am no saint, Mr. Denzil," she said, resuming her seat, for in her anger she had risen to her feet. "But even if I were one, I could not have restrained myself from speaking as I did. When you know my stepmother as well as I do - but I must talk calmly about her, or you will not understand my reasons for thinking her concerned in the terrible fate of my poor father."

"I am all attention, Miss Vrain."

"I'll tell you all I know, as concisely as possible," she replied, "and you can judge for yourself if I am right or wrong. Three years ago my father's health was very bad. Since the death of my mother - now some ten years - he had devoted himself to hard study, and had lived more or less the life of a recluse in

Berwin Manor. He was writing a history of the Elizabethan dramatists, and became so engrossed with the work that he neglected his health, and consequently there was danger that he might suffer from brain fever. The doctors ordered him to leave his books and to travel, in order that his attention might be distracted by new scenes and new people. I was to go with him, to see that he did not resume his studies, so, in an evil hour for us both, we went to Italy."

"Your father was not mad?" said Lucian, thinking of the extraordinary behaviour of Vrain in the square.

"Oh, no!" cried Diana indignantly. "He was a trifle weak in the head from overwork but quite capable of looking after himself."

"Did he indulge in strong drink?"

Miss Vrain looked scandalised. "My father was singularly abstemious in eating and drinking," she said stiffly. "Why do you ask such a question?"

"I beg your pardon," replied Lucian, with all humility, "but it was reported in Geneva Square that Berwin - the name by which your father was known - drank too much; and when I met him he was certainly not - not quite himself," finished the barrister delicately.

"No doubt his troubles drove him to take more than was good for him," said Diana in a low voice. "Yet I wonder at it, for his health was none of the best. Sometimes, I admit, he took sleeping draughts and - and - drugs."

"He was consumptive," said Lucian, noticing Diana's hesitation to speak plainly.

"His chest was weak, and consumption may have developed itself, but when I left England, almost two years back, he was certainly not suffering from that disease. But I see how it is," said Diana, wringing her hands. "During my short absence, and under the tyranny of his wife, his physical health and moral principles gave way. Drink and consumption! Ah! God! were not these ills enough but what the woman must add murder to cap them both?"

"We do not know yet if she is guilty," said Lucian quietly. "Will you go on with your story, Miss Vrain? Later on we can discuss these matters, when I am in possession of the facts. You say it was an evil hour when you went to Italy."

"It was indeed," said Diana sorrowfully, "for in Florence, at the Pension Donizetti, on the Lung Arno, we met with Lydia Clyne and her father. They had only lately arrived in Italy - from New York, I suppose - but already she was said to be engaged to a needy Italian nobleman named Hercule Ferruci."

"Then I suppose the Clynes were rich," said Lucian, "for I know those Italian nobles too well to suspect that this Count Ferruci would pay attention to any one but an heiress."

"She was supposed to be rich, Mr. Denzil. All Americans, for some reason, are supposed to be millionaires; but after she married my father I learned that Mr. Clyne had a very moderate fortune indeed, and his daughter nothing. It was for that reason that Lydia threw over the count, to whom she was almost engaged, and began to pay attention to my father. She heard talk of his estates in the gossip of the Pension, and believing him to be rich, she decided to marry him instead of throwing herself away in a romantic fit on Ferruci."

"Did she love this Italian?"

"Yes, I am sure she did; and, what is more, she loves him still!"

"What! Is Count Ferruci still acquainted with Mrs. Vrain?"

"He is, as you shall hear. Miss Clyne, as I said, determined to make a rich marriage by becoming the second Mrs. Vrain. I never liked her, knowing that she was false and frivolous; but though I did my best to stop the marriage, my father would not be controlled. You know that this woman is pretty and fascinating."

"She is certainly the first, but not the last," interposed Lucian.

"At all events," resumed Diana disconsolately, "she was sufficiently fascinating to snare my poor foolish old father. We remained four months in Florence, and before we left it Lydia Clyne became Mrs. Vrain. I could do nothing with my father, as he was possessed of the headstrong passion of an old man, and, moreover, Lydia had learned to know his weak points so well that she could twist him round her finger. But, angered as I was at my father's folly, I loved him too well to leave him at the time, therefore I returned to Berwin Manor with the pair.

"There, Mr. Denzil," continued Miss Vrain, her face growing dark, "Lydia made my life so wretched, and insulted me so openly, that I was forced, out of self-respect, to leave the house. I had some relatives in Australia, to whom I went out on a visit. Alas! I wish I had not done so; yet remain with my colonial cousins I did, until recalled to England by the terrible intelligence of my father's untimely end."

"So the marriage was a failure?"

"Yes; even before I left, Lydia openly neglected my father. I am bound to say that Mr. Clyne, who is much the better of the two, tried to make her conduct herself in a more becoming manner. But she defied him and every one else. After my departure I received letters from a friend of mine, who told me that Lydia had invited Count Ferruci over on a visit. My father, finding that he could do nothing, and seeing what a mistake he had made, returned to his books, and soon became ill again. Instead of looking after him, Lydia - as I heard - encouraged him to study hard, hoping, no doubt, that he would die, and that she would be free to marry Count Ferruci. Then my father left the house."

"Why? That is a very necessary detail."

Diana thought for a moment, then shook her head despondingly. "That I cannot explain," she said, with a sigh, "as I was in Australia at the time. But I expect that his brain grew weaker with study, and perhaps with the strong drink and drugs which this woman drove him to take. No doubt the poor man grew jealous of Ferruci; and, unable to assert himself, seeing how ill he was, left the house and retired to Geneva Square to meet his death, as we know."

"But all this is supposition," remonstrated Lucian. "We really do not know why Mr. Vrain left the house."

"What does Lydia say?"

"She gives no feasible explanation."

"Nor will she. Oh!" cried Diana, "is there no way of getting at the truth of this matter? I feel certain that Lydia and the Count are guilty!"

"You have no proofs," said Denzil, shaking his head.

"No proofs! Why, you said yourself that a stiletto -"

"That is a supposition on my part," interrupted Lucian quickly. "I cannot say for certain that the deed was committed with such a weapon. Besides, if it was, how can you connect the Italian with the deed?"

"Can we not find a proof?"

"I fear not."

"But if we search the house?"

"There is little use in doing that," rejoined Lucian. "However, if it will give you any satisfaction, Miss Vrain, I will take you over the house to-morrow morning."

"Do!" cried Diana, "and we may find proof of Lydia's guilt in a way she little dreams of. Good-bye, Mr. Denzil - till to-morrow."

CHAPTER X

THE PARTI-COLOURED RIBBON

The beauty and high spirit of Diana made so deep an impression on Lucian that he determined to aid her by every means in his power in searching for the assassin of her father. As yet Denzil had reached the age of twenty-five without having been attracted in any marked degree towards woman-kind; or, to put it more precisely, he had not yet been in love. But now it seemed that the hour which comes to all of Adam's sons had come to him; for on leaving Diana he thought of nothing else but her lovely face and charming smile, and, until he met her again, her image was never absent from his mind.

He took but a languid interest in his daily business or social pursuits, and, wrapped up in inwardly contemplating the beauties of Diana, he appeared to move amongst his fellow-men like one in a dream. And dreamer he was, for there was no substantial basis for his passion.

Many people - particularly those without imagination - scoff at the idea that love can be born in a moment, but such is often the case, for all their ill-advised jibes. A man may be brought into contact with the loveliest and most brilliant of women, yet remain heart-whole; yet unexpectedly a face - not always the most beautiful - will fire him with sudden fervour, even against his better judgment. Love is not an affair of reason, to be clipped and measured by logic and calculation; but a devouring, destroying passion, impatient of restraint, and utterly regardless of common sense. It is born of a look, of a smile, of a sigh, of a word; it springs up and fructifies more speedily than did Jonah's gourd, and none can say how it begins or how it will end. It is the ever old, ever new riddle of creation, and the more narrowly its mystery is looked into the more impossible does it become of solution. The lover of to-day, with centuries of examples at his back, is no wiser in knowledge than was his father Adam.

Although Lucian was thus stricken mad after the irrational methods of Cupid, he had sufficient sense not to examine too minutely into the reasons for this sudden passion. He was in love, and admitting as much to himself, there was an end of all argument. The long lane of his youthful and loveless life had turned in another direction at the signpost of a woman's face, and down the new vista the lover saw flowering meadows, silver streams, bowers of roses, and all the landscape of Arcadia. He was a piping swain and Diana a complaisant shepherdess; but they had not yet entered into the promised Arcadia, and might never do so unless Diana was as kindly as he wished her to be.

Lucian was in love with Diana, but as yet he could not flatter himself that she was in love with him, so he resolved to win her affection - if it was free to be bestowed - by doing her will, and her will was to revenge the death of her father. This was hardly a pleasant task to Lucian in his then peace-with-all-the-world frame of mind; but seeing no other way to gain a closer intimacy with the lady of his love, he took the bitter with the sweet, and set his shoulder to the wheel.

The next morning, therefore, Lucian called on the landlord of No. 13 and requested the keys of the house. But it appeared that these were not in the landlord's keeping at the moment.

"I gave them to Mrs. Kebby, the charwoman," said Mr. Peacock, a retired grocer, who owned the greater part of the square. "The house is in such a state that I thought I'd have it cleaned up a bit."

"With a view to a possible tenant, I suppose?"

"I don't know," replied Peacock, with a rueful shake of his bald head, "although I'm hoping against hope. But what with the murder and the ghost, there don't seem much chance of letting it. What might you be wanting in No. 13, Mr. Denzil?"

"I wish to examine every room, to find, if possible, a clue to this crime," explained Lucian, suppressing the fact that he was to have a companion.

"You'll find nothing, sir. I've looked into every room myself. However, you'll find Mrs. Kebby cleaning up, and she'll let you in if you ring the bell. You aren't thinking of taking the house yourself, I suppose?" added Peacock wishfully.

"No, thank you. My nerves are in good order just now; I don't want to upset them by inhabiting a house with so evil a reputation."

"Ah! that's what every one says," sighed the grocer. "I wish that Berwin, or Vrain, or whatever he called himself, had chosen some other place to be killed in."

"I'm afraid people who meet with unexpected deaths can't arrange these little matters beforehand," said Lucian drily, and walked away, leaving the unfortunate landlord still lamenting over his unlucky possession of a haunted and blood-stained mansion.

Before going to No. 13, Lucian walked down the street leading into Geneva Square, in order to meet Diana, who was due at eleven o'clock. Punctual as the barrister was, he found that Miss Vrain, in her impatience, was before him; for he arrived to see her dismiss her cab at the end of the street, and met her half way down.

His heart gave a bound as he saw her graceful figure, and he felt the hot blood rise to his cheeks as he advanced to meet her.

Diana, quite unconscious of having, like her namesake, the moon, caused this springtide of the heart, could not forbear a glance of surprise, but greeted her coadjutor without embarrassment and with all friendliness. Her thoughts were too taken up with her immediate task of exploring the scene of the crime to waste time in conjecturing the reason of the young man's blushes. Yet the instinct of her sex might have told her the truth, and probably it would have but that it was blunted, or rather not exercised, by reason of her preoccupation.

"Have you the key, Mr. Denzil?" said she eagerly.

"No; but I have seen the landlord, and he has given us permission to go over the house. A charwoman who is cleaning up the place will let us in."

"A charwoman," repeated Miss Vrain, stopping short, "and cleaning up the house! Is it, then, about to receive a new tenant?"

"Oh, no; but the landlord wishes it to be aired and swept; to keep it in some degree of order, I presume."

"What is the name of this woman?"

"Mrs. Kebby."

"The same mentioned in the newspaper reports as having waited on my unhappy father?"

"The same," replied Lucian, with some hesitation; "but I would advise you, Miss Vrain, not to question her too closely about your father."

"Why not? Ah! I see; you think her answers about his drinking habits will give me pain. No matter; I am prepared for all that. I don't blame him so much as those who drove him to intemperance. Is this the house?" she said, looking earnestly at the neglected building before which they were standing.

"Yes," replied Lucian, ringing the bell, "it was in this house that your father came to his untimely end. And here is Mrs. Kebby."

That amiable crone had opened the door while the young man was speaking, and now stood eyeing her visitors with a blear-eyed look of dark suspicion.

"What is't ye want?" she demanded, with a raven-like croak.

"Mr. Peacock has given this lady and myself permission to go over the house," responded Lucian, trying to pass.

"And how do I know if he did?" grumbled Mrs. Kebby, blocking the way.

"Because I tell you so."

"And because I am the daughter of Mr. Vrain," said Diana, stepping forward.

"Lord love ye, miss! are ye?" croaked Mrs. Kebby, stepping aside. "And ye've come to look at your pa's blood, I'll be bound."

Diana turned pale and shuddered, but controlling herself by an effort of will, she swept past the old woman and entered the sitting-room. "Is this the place?" she asked Lucian, who was holding the door open.

"That it is, miss," cried the charwoman, who had hobbled after them, "and yonder is the poor gentleman's blood; it soaked right through the carpet," added Mrs. Kebby, with ghoulish relish. "Lor! 'ow it must 'ave poured out!"

"Hold your tongue, woman!" said Lucian roughly, seeing that Diana looked as though about to faint. "Get on with your work!"

"I'm going; it's upstairs I'm sweeping," growled the crone, retreating. "You'll bring me to you if ye give a holler. I'll show ye round for a shilling."

"You shall have double if you leave us alone," said Lucian, pointing to the door.

Mrs. Kebby's blear eyes lighted up, and she leered amiably at the couple.

"I dessay it's worth two shillings," she said, chuckling hoarsely. "Oh, I'm not so old but what I don't know two turtle doves. He! he! To kiss over yer father's blood! Lawks! what a match 'twill be! He! he!"

Still laughing hoarsely, Mrs. Kebby, in the midst of her unholy joy, was pushed out of the door by Lucian, who immediately afterwards turned to see if Diana had overheard her ill-chosen and ominous words. But Miss Vrain, with a hard, white face, was leaning against the wall, and gave no sign of such knowledge. Her eyes were fixed on a dull-looking red stain of a dark hue, irregular in shape, and her hands the while were pressed closely against her bosom, as though she felt a cruel pain in her heart. With bloodless cheek and trembling lip the daughter looked upon the evidence of her father's death. Lucian was alarmed by her unnatural pallor.

"Miss Vrain!" he exclaimed, starting forward, "you are ill! Let me lead you out of this house."

"No!" said Diana, waving him back. "Not till we examine every inch of it; don't speak to me, please. I wish to use my eyes rather than my tongue."

Denzil, both as a lover and a friend, respected this emotion of the poor young lady, so natural under the circumstances; and in silence conducted her from room to room. All were empty and still dusty, for Mrs. Kebby's broom swept sufficiently light, and the footfalls of the pair echoed hollowly in the vast spaces.

Diana looked into every corner, examined every fireplace, attempted every window, but in no place could she find any extraneous object likely to afford a clue to the crime. They went down into the basement and explored the kitchen, the servant's parlour, the scullery, and the pantry, but with the same unsatisfactory result. The kitchen door, which led out into the back yard, showed signs of having been lately opened; but when Diana drew Lucian's attention to this fact, as the murderer having possibly entered thereby, he assured her that it had only lately been opened by the detective, Link, when he was searching for clues.

"I saw this door," added Lucian, striking it with his cane, "a week before your father was killed. He showed it to me himself, to prove that no one could have entered the house during his absence; and I was satisfied then, from the rusty condition of the bolts, and the absence of the key in the lock, that the door had not been opened - at all events, during his tenancy."

"Then how could those who killed him have entered?"

"That is what I wish to learn, Miss Vrain. But why do you speak in the plural?"

"Because I believe that Lydia and Ferruci killed my father."

"But I have proved to you that Mrs. Vrain remained at Bath."

"I know it," replied Diana quickly, "but she sent Ferruci up to kill my father, and I speak in the plural because I think - in a moral sense - she is as guilty as the Italian."

"That may be, Miss Vrain, but as yet we have not proved their guilt."

Diana made no answer, but, followed by Lucian, ascended to

the upper part of the house, where they found Mrs. Kebby sweeping so vigorously that she had raised a kind of dust storm. As soon as she saw the couple she hobbled towards them to cajole them, if possible, into giving her money.

For a few moments Diana looked at her haughtily, not relishing the familiarity of the old dame, but unexpectedly she stepped forward with a look of excitement.

"Where did you get that ribbon?" she asked Mrs Kebby, pointing to a scrap of personal adornment on the neck of the rusty old creature.

"This?" croaked Mrs. Kebby. "I picked it up in the kitchen downstairs. It's a pretty red and yaller thing, but of no value, miss, so I don't s'pose you'll take it orf me."

Paying no attention to this whimpering, Diana twitched the ribbon out of the old woman's hands and examined it. It was a broad yellow ribbon of rich silk, spotted with red - very noticeably and evidently of foreign manufacture.

"It is the same!" cried Diana, greatly excited. "Mr. Denzil, I bought this ribbon myself in Florence!"

"Well," said Lucian, wondering at her excitement, "and what does that prove?"

"This: that a stiletto which my father bought in Florence, at the same time, has been used to kill him! I tied this ribbon myself round the handle of the stiletto!"

CHAPTER XI

FURTHER DISCOVERIES

The silence which followed Diana's announcement regarding the ribbon and stiletto - for Lucian kept silence out of sheer astonishment - was broken by the hoarse voice of Mrs. Kebby:

"If ye want the ribbon, miss, I'll not say no to a shilling. With what your good gentleman promised, that will be three as I'm ready to take," and Mrs. Kebby held out a dirty claw for the silver.

"You'll sell it, will you!" cried out Diana indignantly, pouncing down on the harridan. "How dare you keep what isn't yours? If you had shown the detective this," shaking the ribbon in Mrs. Kebby's face, "he might have caught the criminal!"

"Pardon me," interposed Lucian, finding his voice, "I hardly think so, Miss Vrain; for no one but yourself could have told that the ribbon adorned the stiletto. Where did you see the weapon last?"

"In the library at Berwin Manor. I hung it up on the wall myself, by this ribbon."

"Are you sure it is the same ribbon?"

"I am certain," replied Diana emphatically. "I cannot be mistaken; the colour and pattern are both peculiar. Where did you find it?" she added, turning to Mrs. Kebby.

"In the kitchen, I tell ye," growled the old woman sullenly. "I only found it this blessed morning. 'Twas in a dark corner, near the door as leads down to the woodshed. How was I to know 'twas any good?"

"Did you find anything else?" asked Lucian mildly.

"No, I didn't, sir."

"Not a stiletto?" demanded Diana, putting the ribbon in her pocket.

"I don't know what's a stiletter, miss; but I didn't find nothing; and I ain't a thief, though some people as sets themselves above others by taking ribbons as doesn't belong to 'em mayn't be much good."

"The ribbon is not yours," said Diana haughtily.

"Yes it are! Findings is keepings with me!" answered Mrs. Kebby.

"Don't anger her," whispered Denzil, touching Miss Vrain's arm. "We may find her useful."

Diana looked from him to the old woman, and opened her purse, at the sight of which Mrs. Kebby's sour face relaxed. When Miss Vrain gave her half a sovereign she quite beamed with joy. "The blessing of heaven on you, my dear," she said, with a curtsey. "Gold! good gold! Ah! this is a brave day's work for me - thirteen blessed shillings!"

"Ten, you mean, Mrs. Kebby!"

"Oh, no, sir," cried Mrs. Kebby obsequiously, "the lady gave me ten, bless her heart, but you've quite forgot your three."

"I said two."

"Ah! so you did, sir. I'm a poor schollard at 'rithmetic."

"You're clever enough to get money out of people," said Diana, who was disgusted at the avarice of the hag. "However, for the present you must be content with what I have given you. If, in cleaning this house, you find any other article, whatever it may be, you shall have another ten shillings, on consideration that you take it at once to Mr. Denzil."

Mrs. Kebby, who was tying up the piece of gold in the corner of her handkerchief, nodded her old head with much complacency. "I'll do it, miss; that is, if the gentleman will pay on delivery. I like cash."

"You shall have cash," said Lucian, laughing; and then, as Diana intimated her intention of leaving the house, he descended the stairs in her company.

Miss Vrain kept silence until they were outside in the sunshine, when she cast an upward glance at the warm blue sky, dappled with light clouds.

"I am glad to be out of that house," she said, with a shudder. "There is something in its dark and freezing atmosphere which chills my spirits."

"It is said to be haunted, you know," said Lucian carelessly; then, after a pause, he spoke on the subject which was uppermost in his mind. "Now that you have this piece of evidence, Miss Vrain, what do you intend to do?"

"Make sure that I have made no mistake, Mr. Denzil. I shall go down to Berwin Manor this afternoon. If the stiletto is still hanging on the library wall by its ribbon, I shall admit my mistake; if it is absent, why then I shall return to town and consult with you as to what is best to be done. You know I rely on you."

"I shall do whatever you wish, Miss Vrain," said Lucian fervently.

"It is very good of you," replied the lady gratefully, "For I have no right to take up your time in this manner."

"You have every right - that is, I mean - I mean," stammered Denzil, thinking from the surprised look of Miss Vrain that he had gone too far at so early a stage of their acquaintance. "I mean that as a briefless barrister I have ample time at my command, and I shall only be too happy to place it and myself at your service. And moreover," he added in a lighter tone, "I have some selfish interest in the matter, also, for it is not every one who finds so difficult a riddle as this to solve. I shall never rest easy in my mind until I unravel the whole of this tangled skein."

"How good you are!" cried Diana, impulsively extending her hand. "It is as impossible for me to thank you sufficiently now for your kindness as it will be to reward you hereafter, should we succeed."

"As to my reward," said Lucian, retaining her hand longer than was necessary, "we can decide what I merit when your father's death is avenged."

Diana coloured and turned away her eyes, withdrawing her hand in the meantime from the too warm clasp of the young man. A sense of his meaning was suddenly borne in upon her by look and clasp, and she felt a maidenly confusion at the momentary boldness of this undeclared lover. However, with feminine tact she laughed off the hint, and shortly afterwards took her leave, promising to communicate as speedily as possible with Lucian regarding the circumstances of her visit to Bath.

The barrister wished to escort her back to the Royal John Hotel in Kensington, but Miss Vrain, guessing his feelings, would not permit this; so Lucian, hat in hand, was left standing in Geneva Square, while his divinity drove off in a prosaic hansom. With her went the glory of the sunlight, the sweetness of the spring; and Denzil, more in love than ever, sighed hugely as he walked slowly back to his lodgings.

For doleful moods, hard work and other interests are the sole cure; therefore, that same afternoon Lucian returned to explore the Silent House on his own account. It had struck him as suggestive that the parti-coloured ribbon to which Diana attached such importance should have been found in so out-of-the-way a corner as the threshold of the door which conducted to what Mrs. Kebby, with characteristic misre-presentation, called the woodshed. In reality the place in question was a cellar, which extended under the soil of the back yard, and was lighted from the top by a skylight placed on a level with the ground.

On being admitted again by Mrs. Kebby, and sending that ancient female to her Augean task of cleansing the house, Lucian descended to the basement in order to examine kitchen and cellar more particularly. If, as Diana stated, the ribbon had been knotted loosely about the hilt of the stiletto, it must have fallen off unnoticed by the assassin when, weapon in hand, he was retreating from the scene of crime.

"He must have come down here from the sitting-room," mused Denzil, as he stood in the cool, damp kitchen. "And - as the ribbon was found by Mrs. Kebby near yonder door - it is most probable that he left the kitchen by that passage for the cellar. Now it remains for me to find out how he made his exit from the cellar; and also I must look for the stiletto, which he possibly dropped in his flight, as he did the ribbon."

While thus soliloquising, Denzil lighted a candle which he had taken the precaution to bring with him for the purpose of making his underground explorations. Having thus provided himself with means to dispel the darkness, he stepped into the door and descended the stone stairs which led to the cellars.

At the foot of the steps he found himself in a passage running from the front to the back of the house, and forthwith turned to the right in order to reach the particular cellar, which was dug out in the manner of a cave under the back yard.

This, as Lucian ascertained by walking round, was faced with stone and had bins on all four sides for the storage of wine. Overhead there was a glass skylight, of which the glass was so dusty and dirty that only a few rays of light could struggle into the murky depths below. But what particularly attracted the attention of Denzil was a short wooden ladder lying on the stone pavement, and which probably was used to reach the wine in the upper bins.

"And I should not be surprised if it had been used for another purpose," murmured Lucian, glancing upward at the square aperture of the skylight.

It struck him as possible that a stranger could enter thereby and descend by the ladder. To test the truth of this he reared the ladder in the middle of the cellar so that its top rung rested against the lower edge of the square overhead. Ascending carefully - for the ladder was by no means stout - he pushed the glass frame upward and found that it yielded easily to a moderate amount of strength. Climbing up, step after step, Lucian arose through the aperture like a genie out of the earth, and soon found that he could jump easily out of the cellar into the yard.

"Good!" he exclaimed, much gratified by this discovery. "I now see how the assassin entered. No wonder the kitchen door was bolted and barred, and that no one was seen to visit Vrain by the front door. Any one who knew the position of that skylight could obtain admission easily, at any hour, by descending the ladder and passing through cellar and kitchen to the upper part of the house. So much is clear, but I must next discover how those who entered got into this yard."

And, indeed, there seemed no outlet, for the yard was enclosed

on three sides by a fence of palings the height of a man, and rendered impervious to damp by a coating of tar; on the fourth side by the house itself. Only over the fence - which was no insuperable obstacle - could a stranger have gained access to the yard; and towards the fence opposite to the house Lucian walked. In it there was no gate, or opening of any kind, so it would appear that to come into the yard a stranger would need to climb over, a feat easily achieved by a moderately active man.

As Denzil examined this frail barrier his eye was caught by a fluttering object on the left - that is, the side in a line with the skylight. This he found was the scrap of a woman's veil of thin black gauze spotted with velvet. At once his thoughts reverted to the shadow of the woman on the blind, and the suspicions of Diana Vrain.

"Great heavens!" he thought, "can that doll of a Lydia be guilty, after all?"

CHAPTER XII

THE VEIL AND ITS OWNER

As may be surmised, Lucian was considerably startled by the discovery of this important evidence so confirmative of Diana's suspicions. Yet the knowledge which Link had gained relative to Mrs. Vrain's remaining at Berwin Manor to keep Christmas seemed to contradict the fact; and he could by no means reconcile her absence with the presence on the fence of the fragment of gauze; still less with the supposition that she must have climbed over a tolerably difficult obstacle to enter the yard, let alone the necessity - by no means easy to a woman - of descending into the disused cellar by means of a shaky and fragile ladder.

"After all," thought Lucian, when he was seated that same evening at his dinner, "I am no more certain that the veil is the property of Mrs. Vrain than I am that she was the woman whose shadow I saw on the blind. Whosoever it was that gained entrance by passing over fence and through cellar, must have come across the yard belonging to the house facing the other road. Therefore, the person must be known to the owner of that house, and I must discover who the owner is. Miss Greeb will know."

Lucian made this last remark with the greatest confidence, as he was satisfied, from a long acquaintance with his landlady, that there was very little concerning her own neighbourhood of which she was ignorant. The result verified his belief, for when Miss Greeb came in to clear the table - a duty she invariably undertook so as to have a chance of conversing with her admired lodger - she was able to afford him the fullest information on the subject. The position of the house in question; the name of its owner; the character of its tenants; she was thoroughly well posted up in every item, and willingly imparted her knowledge with much detail and comment.

"No. 9 Jersey Street," said she, unhesitatingly; "that is the number of the house at the back of the haunted mansion, Mr. Denzil. I know it as well as I know my ten fingers."

"To whom does it belong?" asked Lucian.

"Mr. Peacock; he owns most of the property round about here, having bought up the land when the place was first built on. He's seventy years of age, you know, Mr. Denzil," continued Miss Greeb conversationally, "and rich! - Lord! I don't know how rich he is! Building houses cheap and letting them dear; he has made more out of that than in sanding his sugar and chicorying his coffee. He -"

"What is the name of the tenant?" interrupted Lucian, cutting short this rapid sketch of Peacock's life.

"Mrs. Bensusan, one of the largest women hereabouts."

"I don't quite understand."

"Fat, Mr. Denzil. She turns the scale at eighteen stone, and has pretty well broke every weighing machine in the place."

"What reputation has she, Miss Greeb?"

"Oh, pretty good," said the little woman, shrugging her shoulders, "though they do say she overcharges and underfeeds her lodgers."

"She keeps a boarding-house, then?"

"Well, she lets rooms," explained Miss Greeb in a very definite manner, "and those who live in them supply their own food, and pay for service and kitchen fire."

"Who is with her now?"

"No one," replied the landlady promptly. "She's had her bill up these three months. Her last lodger left about Christmas."

"What is his name - or her name?"

"Oh, it was a 'he,'" said Miss Greeb, smiling.

"Mrs. Bensusan prefers gentlemen, who are out of doors all day, to ladies muddling and meddling all day about the house. I must say I do, too, Mr. Denzil," ended the lady, with a fascinating glance.

"What is his name, Miss Greeb?" repeated Lucian, quite impervious to the hint.

"Let me see," said Miss Greeb, discomfited at the result of her failure. "A queer name that had to do with payments. Bill as the short for William. No, it wasn't that, although it does suggest an account. Quarterday? No. But it had something to do with quarter-days. Rent!" finished Miss Greeb triumphantly. "Rent, with a 'W' before it."

"W-r-e-n-t!" spelled Lucian.

"Yes. Wrent! Mr. Wrent. A strange name, Mr. Denzil - a kind of charade, as I may say. He was with Mrs. Bensusan six months; came to her house about the time Mr. Berwin hired No. 13."

"Very strange!" assented Lucian, to stop further comment. "What kind of a man was this Mr. Wrent?"

"I don't know. I never heard much about him," replied Miss

Greeb regretfully. "May I ask why you want to know all this, Mr. Denzil?"

Lucian hesitated, as he rather dreaded the chattering tongue of his landlady, and did not wish his connection with the Vrain case to become public property in Geneva Square. Still, Miss Greeb was a valuable ally, if only for her wide acquaintance with the neighbourhood, its inhabitants, and their doings. Therefore, after a moment's reflection, he resolved to secure Miss Greeb as a coadjutor, and risk her excessive garrulity.

"Can you keep a secret, Miss Greeb?" he asked, with impressive solemnity.

Struck by his serious air, and at once on fire with curiosity to learn its reason, Miss Greeb loudly protested that she should sooner die than breathe a word of what her lodger was about to divulge. She hinted, with many a mysterious look and nod, that secrets endangering the domestic happiness of every family in the square were known to her, and appealed to the fact that such families still lived in harmony as a proof that she was to be trusted.

"Wild horses wouldn't drag out of me what I know!" cried Miss Greeb earnestly. "You can confide in me as you would in a" - she was about to say mother, but recollecting her juvenile looks, substituted the word "sister."

"Very good," said Lucian, explaining just as much as would serve his purpose. "Then I may tell you, Miss Greeb, that I suspect the assassin of Mr. Vrain entered through Mrs. Bensusan's house, and so got into the yard of No. 13."

"Lord!" cried Miss Greeb, taken by surprise. "You don't say, sir, that Mr. Wrent is a murdering villain, steeped in gore?"

"No! No!" replied Lucian, smiling at this highly-coloured description. "Do not jump to conclusions, Miss Greeb. So far as I am aware, this Mr. Wrent you speak of is innocent. Do you know Mrs. Bensusan and her house well?"

"I've visited both several times, Mr. Denzil."

"Well, then, tell me," continued the barrister, "is the house built with a full frontage like those in this square? I mean, to gain Mrs. Bensusan's back yard is it necessary to go through Mrs. Bensusan's house?"

"No," replied Miss Greeb, shutting her eyes to conjure up the image of her friend's premises. "You can go round the back through the side passage which leads in from Jersey Road."

"H'm!" said Lucian in a dissatisfied tone. "That complicates matters."

"How so, sir?" demanded the curious landlady.

"Never mind just now, Miss Greeb. Do you think you could draw me a plan of this passage of Mrs. Bensusan's house, and of No. 13, with the yards between?"

"I never could sketch," said Miss Greeb regretfully, "and I am no artist, Mr. Denzil, but I think I can do what you want."

"Here is a sheet of paper and a pencil. Will you sketch me the houses as clearly as you can?"

With much reflection and nibbling of the pencil, and casting of her eyes up to the ceiling to aid her memory, Miss Greeb in ten minutes produced the required sketch.

"There you are, Mr. Denzil," said Miss Greeb, placing this work of art before the barrister, "that's as good as I can draw."

"It is excellent, Miss Greeb," replied Lucian, examining the plan. "I see that anyone can get into Mrs. Bensusan's yard through the side passage."

"Oh, yes; but I don't think a person could without being seen by Mrs. Bensusan or Rhoda."

"Who is Rhoda?"

"The servant. She's as sharp as a needle, but an idle slut, for all that, Mr. Denzil. They say she's a gypsy of some kind."

"Is the gate of this passage locked at night?"

"Not that I know of."

"Then what is to prevent any one coming in under cover of darkness and climbing the fence? He would escape then being seen by the landlady and her servant."

"I daresay; but he'd be seen climbing over the fence from the back windows of the houses on each side of No. 13."

"Not if he chose a dark night for the climbing."

"Well, even if he did, how could he get into No. 13?" argued Miss Greeb. "You know I've read the report of the case, Mr. Denzil, and it couldn't be found out (as the kitchen door was locked, and no stranger entered the square) how the murdering assassin got in."

"I may discover even that," replied Lucian, not choosing to tell Miss Greeb that he had already discovered the entrance. "With time and inquiry and observation we can do much. Thank you, Miss Greeb," he continued, slipping the drawing of the plan into his breast coat pocket. "I am much obliged for your information. Of course you'll repeat our conversation to no one?"

"I swear to breathe no word," said Miss Greeb dramatically, and left the room greatly pleased with this secret understanding, which had quite the air of an innocent intrigue such as was detailed in journals designed for the use of the family circle.

For the next day or two Lucian mused over the information he had obtained, and made a fresh drawing of the plan for his own satisfaction; but he took no steps on this new evidence, as he was anxious to submit his discoveries to Miss Vrain before doing so. At the present time Diana was at Bath, taking possession of her ancestral acres, and consulting the family lawyer on various matters connected with the property.

Once she wrote to Lucian, advising him that she had heard several pieces of news likely to be useful in clearing up the mystery; but these she refused to communicate save at a personal interview. Denzil was thus kept in suspense, and unable to rest until he knew precisely the value of Miss Vrain's newly acquired information; therefore it was with a feeling of relief that he received a note from her asking him to call at three o'clock on Sunday at the Royal John Hotel.

Since her going and coming a week had elapsed.

Now that his divinity had returned, and he was about to see her again, the sun shone once more in the heavens for Lucian, and he arrayed himself for his visit with the utmost care. His heart beat violently and his colour rose as he was ushered into the little sitting-room, and he thought less of the case at the moment than of the joy in seeing Miss Vrain once more, in hearing her speak, and watching her lovely face.

On her part, Diana, recollecting their last meeting, or more particularly their parting, blushed in her turn, and gave her hand to the barrister with a new-born timidity. She also was inclined to like Lucian more than was reasonable for the peace of her heart; so these two people, each drawn to the other, should have come together as lovers even at this second meeting.

But, alas! for the prosaicness of this workaday world, they had to assume the attitudes of lawyer and client; and discourse of crime instead of love. The situation was a trifle ironical, and must have provoked the laughter of the gods.

"Well?" asked Miss Vrain, getting to business as soon as Lucian was seated, "and what have you found out?"

"A great deal likely to be of service to us. And you?"

"I!" replied Miss Vrain in a satisfied tone. "I have discovered that the stiletto with the ribbon is gone from the library."

"Who took it away?"

"No one knows. I can't find out, although I asked all the servants; but it has been missing from its place for some months."

"Do you think Mrs. Vrain took it?"

"I can't say," replied Diana, "but I have made one discovery about Mrs. Vrain which implicates her still more in the crime. She was not in Berwin Manor on Christmas Eve, but in town."

"Really!" said Lucian much amazed. "But Link was told that she spent Christmas in the Manor at Bath."

"So she did. Link asked generally, and was answered generally. Mrs. Vrain went up to town on Christmas Eve and returned on Christmas Day; but," said Diana, with emphasis, "she spent the night in town, and on that night the murder was committed."

Lucian produced his pocketbook and took therefrom the fragment of gauze, which he handed to Diana.

"I found this on the fence at the back of No. 13," he said. "It is a veil - a portion of a velvet-spotted veil."

"A velvet-spotted veil!" cried Diana, looking at it. "Then it belongs to Lydia Vrain. She usually wears velvet-spotted veils. Mr. Denzil, the evidence is complete - that woman is guilty!"

CHAPTER XIII

GOSSIP

Going by circumstantial evidence, Diana certainly had good grounds to accuse Mrs. Vrain of committing the crime, for there were four points at least which could be proved past all doubt as incriminating her strongly in the matter.

In the first place, the female shadow on the blind seen by Lucian, showed that a woman had been in the habit of entering the house by the secret way of the cellar, and during the absence of Vrain.

Secondly, the finding of the parti-coloured ribbon in the Silent House, which had been knotted round the handle of the stiletto by Diana, and the absence of the stiletto itself from its usual place on the wall of the Berwin Manor library, proved that the weapon had been removed therefrom to London, and, presumably, used to commit the deed, seeing that otherwise there was no necessity for its presence in the Geneva Square mansion.

Thirdly, Diana had discovered that Lydia had spent the night of the murder in town; and, lastly, she also declared that the fragment of gauze found by Lucian on the dividing fence was the property of Mrs. Vrain.

This quartette of charges was recapitulated by Diana in support of her accusation of her stepmother.

"I always suspected Lydia as indirectly guilty," she declared in concluding her speech for the prosecution, "but I was not certain until now that she had actually struck the blow herself."

"But did she?" said Denzil, by no means convinced.

"I do not know what further evidence you require to prove it," retorted Diana indignantly. "She was in town on Christmas Eve; she took the stiletto from the library, and -"

"You can't prove that," interrupted Lucian decidedly. Then, seeing the look of anger on Diana's face, he hastened to apologise. "Excuse me, Miss Vrain," he said nervously. "I am not the less your friend because I combat your arguments; but in this case it is necessary to look on both sides of the question. Is it possible to prove that Mrs. Vrain removed this dagger?"

"Nobody actually saw it in her possession," replied Diana, who was more amenable to reason than the majority of her sex, "but I can prove that the stiletto, with its ribbon, remained in the library after the departure of my father. If Lydia did not take it, who else had occasion to bring it up to London?"

"Let us say Count Ferruci," suggested Denzil.

Diana pointed to the fragment of the veil lying on the table. "On the evidence of that piece of gauze," she said, "it was Lydia who entered the house. Again, you saw her shadow on the window blind."

"I saw two shadows," corrected Lucian hastily, "those of a man and a woman."

"In plain English, Mr. Denzil, those of Mrs. Vrain and Count Ferruci."

"We cannot be certain of that."

"But circumstantial evidence -"

"Is not always conclusive, Miss Vrain."

"Upon my word, sir, you seem inclined to defend this woman!"

"Miss Vrain," said Lucian seriously, "if we don't give her the benefit of every doubt the jury will, should she be tried on this charge. I admit that the evidence against this woman is strong, but it is not certain; and I argue the case looking at it from her point of view - the only view which is likely to be taken by her counsel. If Mrs. Vrain killed her husband she must have had a strong motive to do so."

"Well," said Diana impatiently, "there is the assurance money."

"I don't know if that motive is quite strong enough to justify this woman in risking her neck," responded the barrister. "As Mrs. Vrain of Berwin Manor she had an ample income, for your father seems to have left all the rents to her, and spent but little on himself; also she had an assured position, and, on the whole, a happy life. Why should she risk losing these advantages to gain more money?"

"She wanted to marry Ferruci," said Diana, driven to another point of defence. "She was almost engaged to him before she married my foolish father; she invited him to Berwin Manor against the wish of her husband, and showed plainly that she loved him sufficiently to commit a crime for his sake. With my father dead, and she in possession of L20,000, she could hope to marry this Italian."

"Can you prove that she was so reckless?"

"Yes, I can," replied Miss Vrain defiantly. "The same person who told me that Lydia was not at Berwin Manor on Christmas Eve can tell you that her behaviour with Count Ferruci was the talk of Bath."

"Who is this person?" asked Lucian, looking up.

"A friend of mine - Miss Tyler. I brought her up with me, so that you should get her information at first hand. You can see her at once," and Diana rose to ring the bell.

"One moment," interposed Lucian, before she could touch the button. "Tell me if Miss Tyler knows your reason for bringing her up."

"I have not told her directly," said Diana, with some bluntness, "but as she is no fool, I fancy she suspects. Why do you ask?"

"Because I have something to tell you which I do not wish your friend to hear, unless," added Lucian significantly, "you desire to take her into our confidence."

"No," said Diana promptly. "I do not think it is wise to take her into our confidence. She is rather - well, to put it plainly, Mr. Denzil - rather a gossip."

"H'm! As such, do you consider her evidence reliable?"

"We can pick the grains of wheat out of the chaff. No doubt she exaggerates and garbles, after the fashion of a scandal-loving woman, but her evidence is valuable, especially as showing that Lydia was not at Bath on Christmas Eve. We will tell her nothing, so she can suspect as much as she likes; if we do speak freely she will spread the gossip, and if we don't, she will invent worse facts; so in either case it doesn't matter. What is it you have to tell me?"

Lucian could scarcely forbear smiling at Diana's candidly expressed estimate of her ally's character, but, fearful of giving offence to his companion, he speedily composed his features. With much explanation and an exhibition of Miss Greeb's plan, he gave an account of his discoveries, beginning with his visit to the cellar, and ending with the important conversation with his landlady. Diana listened attentively, and when he concluded gave it as her opinion that Lydia had entered the first yard by the side passage and had climbed over the fence into the second, "as is clearly proved by the veil," she concluded decisively.

"But why should she take all that trouble, and run the risk of being seen, when it is plain that your father expected her?"

"Expected her!" cried Diana, thunderstruck. "Impossible!"

"I don't know so much about that," replied Lucian drily, "although I admit that on the face of it my assertion appears improbable. But when I met your father the second time, he was so anxious to prove, by letting me examine the house, that no one had entered it during his absence, that I am certain he was well aware the shadows I saw were those of people he knew were in the room. Now, if the woman was Mrs. Vrain, she must have been in the habit of visiting your father by the back way."

"And Ferruci also?"

"I am not sure if the male shadow was Ferruci, no more than I am certain the other was Mrs. Vrain."

"But the veil?"

Lucian shrugged his shoulders in despair. "That seems to prove it was she," he said dubiously, "but I can't explain your father's conduct in receiving her in so secretive a way. The whole thing is beyond me."

"Well, what is to be done?" said Diana, after a pause, during which they looked blankly at one another.

"I must think. My head is too confused just now with this conflicting evidence to plan any line of action. As a relief, let us examine your friend and hear what she has to say."

Diana assented, and touched the bell. Shortly, Miss Tyler appeared, ushered in by a nervous waiter, to whom it would seem she had addressed a sharp admonition on his want of deference. Immediately on entering she pounced down on Miss Vrain like a hawk on a dove, pecked her on both cheeks, addressed her as "my dearest Di," and finally permitted herself, with downcast eyes and a modest demeanour, to be introduced to Lucian.

It might be inferred from the foregoing description that Miss Tyler was a young and ardent damsel in her teens; whereas she was considerably nearer forty than thirty, and possessed an uncomely aspect unpleasing to male eyes. Her own were of a cold grey, her lips were thin, her waist pinched in, and - as the natural consequence of tight lacing - her nose was red. Her scanty hair was drawn off her high forehead very tightly, and screwed into a cast-iron knob at the nape of her long neck; and she smiled occasionally in an acid manner, with many teeth. She wore a plainly-made green dress, with a toby frill; and a large silver cross dangled on her flat bosom. Altogether, she was about as venomous a specimen of an unappropriated blessing as can well be imagined.

"Bella," said Miss Vrain to this unattractive female, "for certain reasons, which I may tell you hereafter, Mr. Denzil wishes to know if Mrs. Vrain was at Berwin Manor on Christmas Eve."

"Of course she was not, dearest Di," said Bella, drooping her elderly head on one scraggy shoulder, with an acid smile. "Didn't I tell you so? I was asked by Lydia - alas! I wish I could say my dearest Lydia - to spend Christmas at Berwin Manor. She invited me for my singing and playing, you know: and as we all have to make ourselves agreeable, I came to see her. On the day before Christmas she received a letter by the early post which seemed to upset her a great deal, and told me she would have to run up to town on business. She did, and stayed all night, and came down next morning to keep Christmas. I thought it *very* strange."

"What was her business in town, Miss Tyler?" asked Lucian.

"Oh, she didn't tell *me*," said Bella, tossing her head, "at least not directly, but I gathered from what she said that something was wrong with poor dear Mr. Clyne - her father, you know, dearest Di."

"Was the letter from him?"

"Oh, I couldn't say that, Mr. Denzil, as I don't know, and I never speak by hearsay. So much mischief is done in the world by people repeating idle tales of which they are not sure."

"Was Count Ferruci at Berwin Manor at the time?"

"Oh, dear me, no, Di! I told you that he was up in London the whole of Christmas week. I only hope," added Miss Tyler, with a venomous smile, "that Lydia did not go up to meet him."

"Why should she?" demanded Lucian bluntly.

"Oh, I'm not blind!" cried Bella, shrilly laughing. "No, indeed. The Count - a most amiable man - was *very* attentive to me at one time; and Lydia - a married woman - I regret to say, did not like him being so. I am indeed sorry to repeat scandal, Mr. Denzil, but the way in which Mrs. Vrain behaved towards me and carried on with the Count was not creditable. I am a gentlewoman, Mr. Denzil, and a churchwoman, and as such cannot countenance such conduct as his."

"You infer, then, that Mrs. Vrain was in love with the Italian?"

"I shouldn't be at all surprised to hear it," cried Bella again. "But he did not care for her! Oh, dear, no! It is my belief, Mr. Denzil, that Mrs. Vrain knows more about the death of her husband than she chooses to admit. Oh, I've read *all* the papers; I know *all* about the death."

"Miss Tyler!" said Lucian, alarmed.

"Bella!" cried Miss Vrain. "I -"

"Oh, I'm not blind, dearest," interrupted Bella, speaking very fast. "I know you ask me these questions to find out if Lydia killed her husband. Well, she did!"

"How do you know, Miss Tyler?"

"Because I'm sure of it, Mr. Denzil. Wasn't Mr. Vrain stabbed with a dagger? Very well, then. There was a dagger hanging in the library of the Manor, and I saw it there four days before Christmas. When I looked for it on Christmas Day it was gone."

"Gone! Who took it?"

"Mrs. Vrain!"

"Are you sure?"

"Yes, I am!" snapped Miss Tyler. "I didn't see her take it, but it was there before she went, and it wasn't there on Christmas Day. If Lydia did not take it, who did?"

"Count Ferruci, perhaps."

"He wasn't there! No!" cried Bella, raising her head, "I'm sure Mrs. Vrain stole it and killed her husband, and I don't care who hears me say so!"

Diana and Lucian looked at one another in silence.

CHAPTER XIV

THE HOUSE IN JERSEY STREET

As her listeners made no comment on Miss Tyler's accusation of Mrs. Vrain, she paused only for a moment to recover her breath, and was off again in full cry with a budget of ancient gossip drawn from a very retentive memory.

"Of the way in which Lydia treated her poor dear husband I know little," cried the fair Bella. "Only this, that she drove him out of the house by her scandalous conduct. Yes, indeed; although you may not believe me, Di. You were away in Australia at the time, but I kept a watch on Lydia in your interest, dear, and our housemaid heard from your housemaid the most dreadful things. Why, Mr. Vrain remonstrated with Lydia, and ordered Count Ferruci out of the house, but Lydia would not let him go; and Mr. Vrain left the house himself."

"Where did he go to, Miss Tyler?"

"I don't know; nobody knows. But it is my opinion," said the spinster, with a significant look, "that he went to London to see about a divorce. But he was weak in the head, poor man, and I suppose let things go on. When next I heard of him he was a corpse in Geneva Square."

"But did my father tell his wife that he was in Geneva Square?"

"Dearest Di, I can't say; but I don't believe he had anything to do with her after he left the house."

"Then if she did not know his whereabouts, how could she kill him?" asked Denzil pertinently.

Brought to a point which she could not evade, Bella declined to answer this question, but tossed her head and bit her lip, with a fine colour. All her accusations of Mrs. Vrain had been made generally, and, as Lucian noted, were unsupported by fact. From a legal point of view this spiteful gossip of a jealous woman was worth nothing, but in a broad sense it was certainly useful in showing the discord which had existed between Vrain and his wife. Lucian saw that little good was to be gained from this prejudiced witness, so thanking Miss Tyler courteously for her information, he arose to go.

"Wait for a moment, Mr. Denzil," said Diana hurriedly. "I want to ask you something. Bella, would you mind -"

"Leaving the room? Oh, dear, no!" burst out Miss Tyler, annoyed at being excluded. "I've said all I have to say, and anything I can do, dearest Di, to assist you and Mr. Denzil in hanging that woman, I -"

"Miss Tyler," interrupted Lucian sternly, "you must not speak so wildly, for as yet there is nothing to prove that Mrs. Vrain is guilty."

"She is guilty enough for me, Mr. Denzil; but like all men, I suppose you take her side, because she is supposed to be pretty. Pretty!" reflected Bella scornfully, "I never could see it myself; a painted up minx, dragged up from the gutter. I wonder at your taste, Mr. Denzil, indeed I do. Pretty, the idea! What fools men are! I'm glad I never married one! Indeed no! He! he!"

And with a shrill laugh to point this sour-grape sentiment, and mark her disdain for Lucian, the fair Bella took herself and her lean form out of the room.

Diana and the barrister were too deeply interested in their business to take much notice of Bella's hysterical outburst, but looked at one another gravely as she departed.

"Well, Mr. Denzil," said the former, repeating her earlier question, "what is to be done now? Shall we see Mrs. Vrain?"

"Not yet," replied Lucian quickly. "We must secure proofs of Mrs. Vrain's being in that yard before we can get any confession out of her. If you will leave it in my hands, Miss Vrain, I shall call on Mrs. Bensusan."

"Who is Mrs. Bensusan?"

"She is the tenant of the house in Jersey Street. It is possible that she or her servant may know something about the illegal use made of the right of way."

"Yes, I think that is the next step to take. But what am I to do in the meantime?"

"Nothing. If I were you I would not even see Mrs. Vrain."

"I will not seek her voluntarily," replied Diana, "but as I have been to Berwin Manor she is certain to hear that I am in England, and may perhaps find out my address, and call. But if she does, you may be sure that I will be most judicious in my remarks."

"I leave all that to your discretion," said Denzil, rising. "Good-bye, Miss Vrain. As soon as I am in possession of any new evidence I shall call again."

"Good-bye, Mr. Denzil, and thank you for all your kindness."

Diana made this remark with so kindly a look, so becoming a blush, and so warm a pressure of the hand, that Lucian felt quite overcome, and not trusting himself to speak, walked swiftly out of the room.

In spite of the gravity of the task in which he was concerned, at that moment he thought more of Diana's looks and speech than of the detective business which he had taken up for love's sake. But on reaching his rooms in Geneva Square he made a mighty effort to waken from these day dreams, and with a stern determination addressed himself resolutely to the work in hand.

In this case the bitter came before the sweet. But by accomplishing the desire of Diana, and solving the mystery of her father's death, Lucian hoped to win not only her smiles but the more substantial reward of her heart and hand.

Before calling on Mrs. Bensusan the barrister debated within himself as to whether it would not be judicious to call in again the assistance of Link, and by telling him of the new evidence which had been found place him thereby in possession of new material to prosecute the case. But Link lately had taken so pessimistic a view of the matter that Lucian fancied he would scoff at his late discoveries, and discourage him in prosecuting what seemed to be a fruitless quest.

Denzil was anxious, as Diana's knight, to do as much of the work as possible in order to gain the reward of her smiles. It is true that he had no legal authority to make these inquiries, and it was possible that Mrs. Bensusan might refuse to answer questions concerning her own business, unsanctioned by law; but on recalling the description of Miss Greeb, Lucian fancied that Mrs. Bensusan, as a fat woman, might only be good-natured and timid.

He therefore dismissed all ideas of asking Link to intervene, and resolved to risk a personal interview with the tenant of the Jersey Street house. It would be time enough to invite Link's assistance, he thought, when Mrs. Bensusan - as yet an unknown quantity in the case - proved obstinate in replying to his questions.

Mrs. Bensusan proved to be quite as stout as Miss Greeb had

reported. A gigantically fat woman, she made up in breadth what she lacked in length. Yet she seemed to have some activity about her, too, for she opened the door personally to Lucian, who was quite amazed when he beheld her monstrous bulk blocking up the doorway. Her face was white and round like a pale moon; she had staring eyes of a china blue, resembling the vacant optics of a wax doll; and, on the whole, appeared to be a timid, lymphatic woman, likely to answer any questions put to her in a sufficiently peremptory tone. Lucian foresaw that he was not likely to have much trouble with this mountain of flesh.

"What might you be pleased to want, sir?" she asked Lucian, in the meekest of voices. "Is it about the lodgings?"

"Yes," answered the barrister boldly, for he guessed that Mrs. Bensusan would scuttle back into the house like a rabbit to its burrow, did he speak too plainly at the outset, "that is - I wish to inquire about a friend of mine."

"Did he lodge here, sir?"

"Yes. A Mr. Wrent."

"Deary me!" said the fat woman, with mild surprise. "Mr. Wrent left me shortly after Christmas. A kind gentleman, but timid; he -"

"Excuse me," interrupted Lucian, who wanted to get into the house, "but don't you think you could tell me about my friend in a more convenient situation?"

"Oh, yes, sir - certainly, sir," wheezed Mrs. Bensusan, rolling back up the narrow passage. "I beg your pardon, sir, for my forgetfulness, but my head ain't what it ought to be. I'm a lone widow, sir, and not over strong."

Denzil could have laughed at this description, as the lady's bulk gave the lie to her assertion. However, on diplomatic grounds he suppressed his mirth, and followed his ponderous guide into a sitting-room so small that she almost filled it herself.

As he left the passage he saw a brilliant red head pop down the staircase leading to the basement; but whether it was that of a man or a woman he could not say. Still, on recalling Miss Greeb's description of the Bensusan household, he concluded that the red head was the property of Rhoda, the sharp servant, and argued from her appearance in the background, and rapid disappearance, that she was in the habit of listening to conversations she was not meant to hear.

Mrs. Bensusan sat down on the sofa, as being most accommodating to her bulk, and cast a watery look around the small apartment, which was furnished in that extraordinary fashion which seems to be the peculiar characteristic of boarding houses. The walls and carpet were patterned with glowing bunches of red roses; the furniture was covered with stamped red velvet; the ornaments consisted of shells, wax fruit under glass shades, mats of Berlin wool, vases with dangling pendants of glass, and such like elegant survivals of the early Victorian epoch.

Hideous as the apartment was, it seemed to afford Mrs. Bensusan - also a survival - great pleasure; and she cast a complacent look around as Lucian seated himself on an uncomfortable chair covered with an antimacassar of crochet work.

"My rooms are most comfortable, an' much liked," said Mrs. Bensusan, sighing, "but I have not had many lodgers lately. Rhoda thinks it must be on account of that horrible murder."

"The murder of Vrain in No. 13?"

"Ah!" groaned the fat woman, looking tearfully over her double chin, "I see you have heard of it."

"Everybody has heard of it," replied Lucian, "and I was one of the first to hear, since I live in Miss Greeb's house, opposite No. 13."

"Indeed, sir!" grunted Mrs. Bensusan, stiffening a little at the sound of a rival lodging-house keeper's name. "Then you are Mr. Denzil, the gentleman who occupies Miss Greeb's first floor front."

"Yes. And I have come to ask you a few questions."

"About what, sir?" said Mrs. Bensusan, visibly alarmed.

"Concerning Mr. Wrent."

"You are a friend of his?"

"I said so, Mrs. Bensusan, but as a matter of fact I never set eyes on the gentleman in my life."

Mrs. Bensusan gasped like a fish out of water, and patted her fat breast with her fat hand, as though to give herself courage. "It is not like a gentleman to say that another gentleman's his friend when he ain't," she said, with an attempt at dignity.

"Very true," answered Lucian, with great composure, "but you know the saying, 'All is fair in love and war.' I will be plain with you, Mrs. Bensusan," he added, "I am here to seek possible evidence in connection with the murder of Mr. Vrain, in No. 13, on Christmas Eve."

Mrs. Bensusan gave a kind of hoarse screech, and stared at Lucian in a horrified manner.

"Murder!" she repeated. "Lord! what mur - that murder! Mr. Vrain! Mr. Vrain - that murder!" she repeated over and over again.

"Yes, the murder of Mr. Vrain in No. 13 Geneva Square on

Christmas Eve. Now do you understand?"

With another gasp Mrs. Bensusan threw up her fat hands and raised her eyes to the ceiling.

"As I am a Christian woman, sir," she cried, "I am as innocent as a babe unborn!"

"Of what?" asked Lucian sharply.

"Of the murder!" wept Mrs. Bensusan, now dissolved in tears. "Rhoda said -"

"I don't want to hear what Rhoda said," interrupted Lucian impatiently, "and I am not accusing you of the murder. But - your house is at the back of No. 13."

"Yes," replied Mrs. Bensusan, weeping like a Niobe.

"And a fence divides your yard from that of No. 13?"

"I won't contradict you, sir - it do."

"And there is a passage leading from Jersey Street into your yard?"

"There is, Mr. Denzil; it's useful for the trades-people."

"And I daresay useful to others," said Lucian drily. "Now, Mrs. Bensusan, do you know if any lady was in the habit of passing through that passage at night?"

Before Mrs. Bensusan could answer the door was dashed open, and Rhoda, the red-headed, darted into the room.

"Don't answer, missus!" she cried shortly. "As you love me, mum, don't!"

CHAPTER XV

RHODA AND THE CLOAK

The one servant of Mrs. Bensusan was a girl of seventeen, who had a local fame in the neighbourhood on account of her sharp tongue and many precocious qualities. No one knew who her parents were, or where the fat landlady had picked her up; but she had been in the Jersey Street house some ten years, and had been educated and - in a manner - adopted by its mistress, although Mrs. Bensusan always gave her cronies to understand that Rhoda was simply and solely the domestic of the establishment.

Nevertheless, for one of her humble position, she had a wonderful power over her stout employer, the power of a strong mind over a weak one, and in spite of her youth it was well known that Rhoda managed the domestic economy of the house. Mrs. Bensusan was the sovereign, Rhoda the prime minister.

This position she had earned by dint of her own sharpness in dealing with the world. And the local tradesmen were afraid of Rhoda. "Mrs. Bensusan's devil," they called her, and never dared to give short weight, or charge extra prices, or pass off damaged goods as new, when Rhoda was the purchaser. On the contrary, No. 9 Jersey Street was supplied with everything of the best, promptly and civilly, at ordinary market rates; for neither butcher, nor baker, nor candlestick maker, was daring enough to risk Rhoda's tongue raging like a prairie fire over their shortcomings. Several landladies, knowing Rhoda's value, had tried to entice her from Mrs. Bensusan by offers of higher wages and better quarters, but the girl refused to leave her stout mistress, and so continued quite a fixture of the lodgings. Even in the city, Rhoda had been spoken of by clerks who had lived in Jersey Street, and so had more than a local reputation for originality.

This celebrated handmaid was as lean as her mistress was stout. Her hair was magnificent in quality and quantity, but, alas! was of the unpopular tint called red; not auburn, or copper hued, or the famous Titian color, but a blazing, fiery red, which made it look like a comic wig. Her face was pale and freckled, her eyes black - in strange contrast to her hair, and her mouth large, but garnished with an excellent set of white teeth.

Rhoda was not neat in her attire, perhaps not having arrived at the age of coquetry, for she wore a dingy grey dress much too short for her, a pair of carpet slippers which had been left by a departed lodger, and usually went about with her sleeves tucked up, and a resolute look on her sharp face. Such was the appearance of Mrs. Bensusan's devil, who entered to forbid her mistress confiding in Lucian.

"Oh, Rhoda!" groaned Mrs. Bensusan. "You bad gal! I believe as you've 'ad your ear to the keyhole."

"I 'ave!" retorted Rhoda defiantly. "It's been there for five minutes, and good it is for you, mum, as I ain't above listening. What do you mean, sir," she cried, turning on Lucian like a fierce sparrow, "by coming 'ere to frighten two lone females, and her as innocent as a spring chicken?"

"Oh!" said Lucian, looking at her composedly, "so you are the celebrated Rhoda? I've heard of you."

"Not much good, then, sir, if Miss Greeb was talking," rejoined the red-haired girl, with a sniff. "Oh, I know her."

"Rhoda! Rhoda!" bleated her mistress, "do 'old your tongue! I tell you this gentleman's a police."

"He ain't!" said the undaunted Rhoda. "He's in the law. Oh, I knows him!'

"Ain't the law the police, you foolish gal?"

"Of course it -" began Rhoda, when Lucian, who thought that she had displayed quite sufficient eccentricity, cut her short with a quick gesture.

"See here, my girl," he said sharply, "you must not behave in this fashion. I have reason to believe that the assassin of Mr. Vrain entered the house through the premises of your mistress."

"Lawks, what a 'orrible idear!" shrieked Mrs. Bensusan. "Good 'eavens, Rhoda, did you see the murdering villain?"

"Me? No! I never sawr nothing, mum," replied Rhoda doggedly.

Lucian, watching the girl's face, and the uneasy expression in her eyes, felt convinced she was not telling the truth. It was no use forcing her to speak, as he saw very plainly that Rhoda was one of those obstinate people whom severity only hardened. Much more could be done with her by kindness, and Denzil adopted this - to him - more congenial course.

"If Rhoda is bound by any promise, Mrs. Bensusan, I do not wish her to speak," he said indifferently, "but in the interests of justice I am sure you will not refuse to answer my questions."

"Lord, sir! I know nothing!" whimpered the terrified landlady.

"Will you answer a few questions?" asked Denzil persuasively.

Mrs. Bensusan glanced in a scared manner at Rhoda, who,

meanwhile, had been standing in a sullen and hesitating attitude. When she thought herself unobserved, she stole swift glances at the visitor, trying evidently to read his character by observation of his face and manner. It would seem that her scrutiny was favourable, for before Mrs. Bensusan could answer Lucian's question she asked him one herself.

"What do you want to know, sir?"

"I want to know all about Mr. Wrent."

"Why?"

"Because I fancy he has something to do with this crime."

"Lord!" groaned Mrs. Bensusan. "'Ave I waited on a murderer?"

"I don't say he is a murderer, Mrs. Bensusan, but he knows something likely to put us on the track of the criminal."

"What makes ye take up the case?" demanded Rhoda sharply.

"Because I know that Mr. Wrent came to board in this house shortly after Mr. Vrain occupied No. 13," replied Denzil.

"Who says he did?"

"Miss Greeb, my landlady, and she also told me that he left here two days after the murder."

"That's as true as true!" cried Mrs. Bensusan, "ain't it, Rhoda? We lost him 'cause he said he couldn't abide living near a house where a crime had been committed."

"Well, then," continued Lucian, seeing that Rhoda, without speaking, continued to watch him, "the coincidence of Mr. Wrent's stay with that of Mr. Vrain's strikes me as peculiar."

"You are a sharp one, you are!" said Rhoda, with an approving nod. "Look here, Mr. Denzil, would you break a promise?"

"That depends upon what the promise was."

"It was one I made to hold my tongue."

"About what?"

"Several things," said the girl shortly.

"Have they to do with this crime?" asked Lucian eagerly.

"I don't know. I can't say," said Rhoda; then suddenly her face grew black. "I tell you what, sir, I hate Mr. Wrent!" she declared.

"Oh, Rhoda!" cried Mrs. Bensusan. "After the lovely cloak he gave you!"

The red-haired girl looked contemptuously at her mistress; then, without a word, darted out of the room. Before Lucian could conjecture the reason of her strange conduct, or Mrs. Bensusan could get her breath again - a very difficult operation for her - Rhoda was back with a blue cloth cloak, lined with rabbit skins, hanging over her arm. This she threw down at the feet of Lucian, and stamped on it savagely with the carpet slippers.

"There's his present!" she cried angrily, "but I wish I could dance on him the same way! I wish - I wish I could hang him!"

"Can you?" demanded Lucian swiftly, taking her in the moment of wrath, when she seemed disposed to speak.

"No!" said Rhoda shortly. "I can't!"

"Do you think he killed Mr. Vrain?"

"No, I don't!"

"Do you know who did?"

"Blest if I do!"

"Does Mr. Wrent?" asked Denzil meaningly.

The girl wet her finger and went through a childish game. "That's wet," she said; then wiping the finger on her dingy skirt, "that's dry. Cut my throat if I tell a lie. Ask me something easier, Mr. Denzil."

"I don't understand you," said Lucian, quite puzzled.

"Rhoda! Rhoda! 'Ave you gone crazy?" wailed Mrs. Bensusan.

"Look here," said the girl, taking no notice of her mistress, "do you want to know about Mr. Wrent?"

"Yes, I do."

"And about that side passage as you talked of to the missis?"

"Yes."

"Then I'll answer yer questions, sir. You'll know all I know."

"Very good," said Lucian, with an approving smile, "now you are talking like a sensible girl."

"Rhoda! You ain't going to talk bad of Mr. Wrent?"

"It ain't bad, and it ain't good," replied Rhoda. "It's betwixt and between."

"Well, I must 'ear all. I don't want the character of the 'ouse took away," said Mrs. Bensusan, with an attempt at firmness.

"That's all right," rejoined Rhoda reassuringly, "you can jine in yerself when y' like. Fire away, Mr. Denzil."

"Who is Mr. Wrent?" asked Lucian, going straight to the point.

"I don't know," replied Rhoda; and henceforth the examination proceeded as though the girl were in the witness-box and Lucian counsel for the prosecution.

Q. When did he come to Jersey Street?

A. At the end of July, last year.

Q. When did he go away?

A. The morning after Boxing Day.

Q. Can you describe his appearance?

A. He was of the middle height, with a fresh complexion, white hair, and a white beard growing all over his face. He was untidy about his clothes, and kept a good deal to his own room among a lot of books. I don't think he was quite right in his head.

Q. Did he pay his rent regularly?

A. Yes, except when he was away. He would go away for a week at a time.

Q. Was he in this house on Christmas Eve?

A. Yes, sir. He came back two days before Christmas.

Q. Where had he been?

A. I don't know; he did not say.

Q. Did he have any visitors?

A. He did. A tall, dark man and a lady.

Q. What was the lady like?

A. A little woman; I never saw her face, as she always kept her veil down.

Q. What kind of a veil did she wear?

A. A black gauze veil with velvet spots.

Q. Did she come often to see Mr. Wrent?

A. Yes. Four or five times.

Q. When did she call last?

A. On Christmas Eve.

Q. At what hour?

A. She came at seven, and went away at eight. I know that because she had supper with Mr. Wrent.

Q. Did she leave the house?

A. Yes. I let her out myself.

Q. Did you ever hear any conversation between them?

A. No. Mr. Wrent took care of that. I never got any chance of listening at keyholes with him. He was a sharp one, for all his craziness.

Q. What was the male visitor like?

A. He was tall and dark, with a black moustache.

Q. Do you think he was a foreigner?

A. I don't know. I never heard him speak. Mr. Wrent let him out, as usual.

Q. When did he visit Mr. Wrent last?

A. On Christmas Eve. He came with the lady.

Q. Did he stay to supper also?

A. No. He went away at half-past seven. Mr. Wrent let him out, as usual.

Q. Did he go away altogether?

A. I - I - I am not sure! (here the witness hesitated).

Q. Why did Mr. Wrent give you the cloak?

A. To make me hold my tongue about the dark man.

Q. Why?

A. Because I saw him in the back yard.

Q. On what night?

A. On the night of Christmas Eve, about half-past eight.

CHAPTER XVI

MRS. VRAIN AT BAY

"You saw the dark man in the back yard on Christmas Eve?" repeated Lucian, much surprised by this discovery.

"Yes, I did," replied Rhoda decisively, "at half-past eight o'clock. I went out into the yard to put some empty bottles into the shed, and I saw the man standing near the fence, looking at the back of No. 13. When he heard me coming out he rushed past me and out by the side passage. The moon was shining, and I saw him as plain as plain."

"Did he seem afraid?"

"Yes, he did; and didn't want to be seen, neither. I told Mr. Wrent, and he promised me a cloak if I held my tongue. He said the dark man was waiting in the yard until the lady had gone, when he was coming in again."

"But the lady, you say, went at eight, and you saw the man half an hour later?"

"That's it, sir. He told me a lie, for he never came in again to see Mr. Wrent."

"But already the dark man had seen the lady?"

"Yes. He came in with her at seven, and went away at

half-past."

Lucian mechanically stooped down and picked up the fur cloak. He was puzzled by the information given by Rhoda, and did not exactly see what use to make of it. Going by the complexion of the man who had lurked in the back yard, it would appear that he was Count Ferruci; while the small stature of the woman, and the fact that she wore a velvet-spotted veil, indicated that she was Lydia Vrain; also the pair had been in the vicinity of the haunted house on the night of the murder; and, although it was true both were out of the place by half-past eight, yet they might not have gone far, but had probably returned later - when Rhoda and Mrs. Bensusan were asleep - to murder Vrain, between the hours of eleven and twelve on the same night.

This was all plain enough, but Lucian was puzzled by the account of Mr. Wrent. Who, he asked himself repeatedly, who was this grey-haired, white-bearded man who had so often received Lydia, who had on Christmas Eve silenced Rhoda regarding Ferruci's presence in the yard, by means of the cloak, and who - it would seem - possessed the key to the whole mystery?

Rhoda could tell no more but that he had stayed six months with Mrs. Bensusan, and had departed two days after the murder; whereby it would seem that his task having been completed, he had no reason to remain longer in so dangerous a neighbourhood. Yet four months had elapsed since his departure, and Denzil, after some reflection, asked Mrs. Bensusan a question or two regarding this interval.

"Has Mr. Wrent returned here since his departure?" he demanded.

"Lawks! no, sir!" wheezed Mrs. Bensusan, shaking her head. "I've never set eyes on him since he went. 'Ave you, Rhoda?" Whereat the girl shook her head also, and watched Lucian with an intensity of gaze which somewhat discomposed him.

"Did he owe you any money when he went, Mrs. Bensusan?"

"No, sir. He paid up like a gentleman. I always thought well of Mr. Wrent."

"Rhoda doesn't seem to share your sentiments," said Denzil drily.

"No, I don't!" cried the servant, frowning. "I hated Mr. Wrent!"

"Why did you hate him?"

"Never you mind, sir," retorted Rhoda grimly. "I hated him."

"Yet he bought you this cloak."

"No, he didn't!" contradicted the girl. "He got it from the lady!"

"What!" cried Lucian sharply. "Are you sure of that?"

"I can't exactly swear to it," replied Rhoda, hesitating, "but it was this way: The lady wore a cloak like that, and I admired it awful. She had it on when she came, Christmas Eve, and she didn't wear it when I let her out, and the next day Mr. Wrent gave it to me. So I suppose it is the same cloak."

"And did the lady go out into the cold winter weather without the cloak?"

"Yes; but she had a long cloth jacket on, sir, so I don't s'pose she missed it."

"Was the lady agitated when she went out?"

"I don't know. She held her tongue and kept her veil down."

"Can you tell me anything more?" asked Lucian, anxious to

make the examination as exhaustive as possible.

"No, Mr. Denzil," answered Rhoda, after some thought, "I can't, except that Mr. Wrent, long before Christmas, promised me a present, and gave me the cloak then."

"Will you let me take this cloak away with me?"

"If you like," replied Rhoda carelessly. "I don't want it.'

"Oh, Rhoda!" wailed Mrs. Bensusan. "Your lovely, lovely rabbit skin!"

"I'll bring it back again," said Lucian hastily. "I only want to use it as evidence."

"Ye want to know who the lady is?" said Rhoda sharply.

"Yes, I do. Can you tell me?"

"No; but you'll find out from that cloak. I guess why you're taking it."

"You are very sharp, Rhoda," said Lucian, rising, with a good-humoured smile, "and well deserve your local reputation. If I find Mr. Wrent, I may require you to identify him; and Mrs. Bensusan also."

"I'll be able to do that, but missus hasn't her eyes much."

"Hasn't her eyes?" repeated Denzil, with a glance at Mrs. Bensusan's staring orbs.

"Lawks, sir, I'm shortsighted, though I never lets on. Rhoda, 'ow can you 'ave let on to the gentleman as I'm deficient? As to knowing Mr. Wrent, I'd do so well enough," said Mrs. Bensusan, tossing her head, "with his long white beard and white 'ead, let alone his black velvet skull-cap."

"Oh, he wore a skull-cap?"

"Only indoors," said Rhoda sharply, "but here I'm 'olding the door wide, sir, so if you've done, we're done."

"I'm done, as you call it, for the present," replied Denzil, putting on his hat, "but I may come again. In the meantime, hold your tongues. Silence on this occasion will be gold; speech won't even be silver."

Mrs. Bensusan laughed at this speech in a fat and comfortable sort of way, while Rhoda grinned, and escorted Lucian to the front door. She looked so uncanny, with her red hair and black eyes, that the barrister could not forbear a question.

"Are you English, my girl?"

"No, I ain't!" retorted Rhoda emphatically. "I'm of the gentle Romany."

"A gipsy!"

"So you Gorgios call us!" replied the girl, and shut the door with what seemed to be unnecessary violence. Lucian went off with the cloak over his arm, somewhat discomposed by this last piece of information.

"A gipsy!" he repeated. "Humph! Can good come out of Nazareth? I don't trust that girl much. If I knew why she hates Wrent, I'd be much more satisfied with her information. And who the deuce is Wrent?"

Lucian had occasion to ask himself this question many times before he found its answer, and that was not until afterwards. At the present moment he dismissed it from his mind as unprofitable. He was too busy reflecting on the evidence obtained in Jersey Street to waste time in conjecturing further events. On returning to his lodgings he sat down to consider what was best to be done.

After much reflection and internal argument, he decided to call upon Mrs. Vrain, and by producing the cloak, force her into confessing her share of the crime. Whether she had been the principal in the deed, or an accessory before the fact, Lucian could not determine; but he was confident that in one way or another she was cognizant of the truth; although this she would probably conceal, as its revelation would likely be detrimental to her own safety.

At first Denzil intended to see Diana before visiting Mrs. Vrain, in order to relate all he had learned, and find out from her if the cloak really belonged to the widow. But on second thoughts he decided not to do so.

"I can tell her nothing absolutely certain about the matter," he said to himself, "as I cannot be sure of anything until I force Mrs. Vrain to confess. Diana," so he called her in his discourse to himself, "Diana will probably know nothing about the ownership of the cloak, as it seems new, and was probably purchased by Lydia during the absence of Diana in Australia. No, I have the address of Mrs. Vrain, which Diana gave me. It will be best to call on her, and by displaying the cloak make her acknowledge her guilt.

"With such evidence she cannot deny that she visited Wrent; and was in the vicinity of the house wherein her husband was murdered on the very night the crime was committed. Also she must state Ferruci's reason for hiding in the back yard, and tell me plainly who Wrent is, and why he helped the pair of them in their devilish plans. I am doubtful if she will speak; but altogether the evidence I have collected inculpates her so strongly that it will be quite sufficient grounds upon which to obtain a warrant for her arrest. And sooner than risk that, I expect she will tell as much as she can to exculpate herself - that is, if she is really innocent. If she is guilty," Lucian shrugged his shoulders, "then I cannot guess what course she will take."

Mrs. Vrain, with her father to protect her, had established

herself in a small but luxurious house in Mayfair, and was preparing to enjoy herself during the coming season. Although her husband had met with a terrible death scarcely six months before, she had already cast off her heavy mourning, and wore only such millinery indications of sorrow as suited with her widowed existence.

Ferruci was a constant visitor at the house; but although Lydia was now free, and wealthy, she by no means seemed ready to marry the Italian. Perhaps she thought, with her looks and riches, she might gain an English title, as more valuable than a Continental one; and in this view she was supported by her father. Clyne had no other desire than to see his beloved Lydia happy, and would willingly have sacrificed everything in his power to gain such an end; but as he did not like Ferruci himself, and saw that Lydia's affections towards him had cooled greatly, he did not encourage the idea of a match between them.

However, these matters were yet in abeyance, as Lydia was too diplomatic to break off with so subtle a man as the Count, who might prove a dangerous enemy were his love turned to hate, and Mr. Clyne was quite willing to remain on friendly terms with the man so long as Lydia chose that such friendship should exist. In short, Lydia ruled her simple father with a rod of iron, and coaxed Ferruci - a more difficult man to deal with - into good humour; so she managed both of them skilfully in every way, and contrived to keep things smooth, pending her plunge into London society. For all her childish looks, Lydia was uncommonly clever.

When Lucian's card was brought in, Mrs. Vrain proved to be at home, and as his good looks had made a deep impression on her, she received him at once. He was shown into a luxuriously furnished drawing-room without delay, and welcomed by pretty Mrs. Vrain herself, who came forward with a bright smile and outstretched hands, looking more charming than ever.

"Well, I do call this real sweet of you," said she gaily. "I guess it is about time you showed up. But you don't look well, that's a fact. What's wrong?"

"I'm worried a little," replied Lucian, confounded by her coolness.

"That's no use, Mr. Denzil. You should never be worried. I guess I don't let anything put me out."

"Not even your husband's death?"

"That's rude!" said Lydia sharply, the colour leaving her cheek. "What do you mean? Have you come to be nasty?"

"I came to return you this," said Denzil, throwing the cloak which he had carried on his arm before the widow.

"This?" echoed Mrs. Vrain, looking at it. "Well, what's this old thing got to do with me?"

"It's yours; you left it in Jersey Street!"

"Did I? And where's Jersey Street?"

"You know well enough," said Lucian sternly. "It is near the place where your husband was murdered."

Mrs. Vrain turned white. "Do you dare to say -" she began, when Denzil cut her short with a hint at her former discomposure.

"The stiletto, Mrs. Vrain! Don't forget the stiletto!"

"Oh, God!" cried Lydia, trembling violently. "What do you know of the stiletto?"

CHAPTER XVII

A DENIAL

"What do you know of the stiletto?" repeated Mrs. Vrain anxiously.

She had risen to her feet, and, with an effort to be calm, was holding on to the near chair. Her bright colour had faded to a dull white hue, and her eyes had a look of horror in their depths which transformed her from her childish beauty into a much older and more haggard woman than she really was. It seemed as though Lucian, by some necromantic spell, had robbed her of youth, vitality, and careless happiness. To him this extraordinary agitation was a proof of her guilt; and hardening his heart so as not to spare her one iota of her penalty - a mercy she did not deserve - he addressed her sternly:

"I know that a stiletto purchased in Florence by your late husband hung on the library wall of Berwin Manor. I know that it is gone!"

"Yes! yes!" said Lydia, moistening her white, dry lips, "it is gone; but I do not know who took it."

"The person who killed your husband."

"I feared as much," she muttered, sitting down again. "Do you know the name of the person?"

"As well as you do yourself. The name is Lydia Vrain!"

"I!" She threw herself back on the chair with a look of profound astonishment on her colourless face. "Mr. Denzil," she stammered, "is - is this - is this a jest?"

"You will not find it so, Mrs. Vrain."

The little woman clutched the arms of her chair and leaned forward with her face no longer pale, but red with rage and indignation. "If you are a gentleman, Mr. Denzil, I guess you won't keep me hanging on like this. Let us get level. Do you say I killed Mark?"

"Yes, I do!" said Lucian defiantly. "I am sure of it."

"On what grounds?" asked Mrs. Vrain, holding her temper back with a visible effort, that made her eyes glitter and her breath short.

"On the grounds that he was killed with that stiletto and -"

"Go slow! How do you know he was killed with that stiletto?"

"Because the ribbon which attached it to the wall was found in the Geneva Square house, where your husband was killed. Miss Vrain recognised it."

"Miss Vrain - Diana! Is she in England?"

"Not only in England, but in London."

"Then why hasn't she been to see me?"

Denzil did not like to answer this question, the more so as Lydia's sudden divergence from the point of discourse rather disconcerted him. It is impossible to maintain dignity in making a serious accusation when the person against whom it is made thinks so little of it as to turn aside to discuss a point of etiquette in connection with another woman.

Seeing that her accuser was silent and confused, Lydia recovered her tongue and colour, and the equability of her temper. It was, therefore, with some raillery that she continued her speech:

"I see how it is," she said contemptuously, "Diana has called you into her councils in order to fix this absurd charge on to me. Afraid to come herself, she sends you as the braver person of the partnership. I congratulate you on your errand, Mr. Denzil."

"You can laugh as much as you like, Mrs. Vrain, but the matter is more serious than you suppose."

"Oh, I am sure that my loving stepdaughter will make it as serious as possible. She always hated me."

"Pardon me, Mrs. Vrain," said Lucian, colouring with annoyance, "but I did not come here to hear you speak ill of Miss Vrain."

"I know that! She sent you here to speak ill *of* me and do ill *to* me. Well, so you and she accuse me of killing Mark? I shall be glad to hear the evidence you can bring forward. If you can make your charge good I should smile. Oh, I guess so!"

Denzil noticed that when Mrs. Vrain became excited she usually spoke plain English, without the U. S. A. accent, but on growing calmer, and, as it were, recollecting herself, she adopted the Yankee twang and their curious style of expression and ejaculation. This led him to suspect that the fair Lydia was not a born daughter of the Great Republic, perhaps not even a naturalised citizeness, but had assumed such nationality as one attractive to society in Europe and Great Britain.

He wondered what her past really was, and if she and her father were the doubtful adventurers Diana believed them to be. If so, it might happen that Lydia would extricate herself out of her present unpleasant position by the use of past experience. To give her no chance of such dodging, Lucian rapidly detailed the evidence against her so that she would be hard put to baffle it. But in this estimate he quite underrated Lydia's nerve and capability of fence, let alone the dexterity with which she produced a satisfactory reply to each of his questions.

"We will begin at the beginning, Mrs. Vrain," he said soberly, "say from the time you drove your unfortunate husband out of his own house."

"Now, I guess that wasn't my fault," explained Lydia. "I wasn't in love with old man Mark, but I liked him well enough, for he was a real gentleman; and when that make-mischief Diana, who cocked her nose at me, set out for Australia, we got on surprisingly well. Count Ferruci came over to stay, as much at Mark's invitation as mine, and I didn't pay too much attention to him anyhow."

"Miss Tyler says you did!"

"Sakes!" cried Mrs. Vrain, raising her eyebrows, "have you been talking to that old stump? Well, just you look here, Mr. Denzil! It was Bella Tyler who made all the mischief. She thought Ercole was sweet on her, and when she found out he wasn't, she got real mad, and went to tell Mark that I was making things hum the wrong way with the Count. Of course Mark had a row with him, and, of course, I got riz - not having done anything to lie low for. We had a row royal, I guess, and the end of it was that Mark cleared out. I thought he would turn up again, or apply for a divorce, though he hadn't any reason to. But he did neither, and remained away for a whole year. While he was away I got quit of Ercole pretty smart, I can tell you, as I wanted to shut up that old maid's mouth. I never knew where Mark was, or guessed what became of him, until I saw that advertisement, and putting two and two together to make four, I called to see Mr. Link, where I found you running the circus."

"Why did you faint on the mention of the stiletto?"

"I told you the reason, and Link also."

"Yes, but your reason was too weak to -"

"Oh, well, you're right enough there," interrupted Lydia, smiling. "All that talk of nerves and grief wasn't true. I didn't give my real reason, but I will now. When I heard that the old man had been stabbed by a stiletto I remembered that the one on the library wall had vanished some time before the Christmas Eve on which Mark was killed. So you may guess I was afraid."

"For yourself?"

"I guess not; it wasn't any of my funeral. I didn't take the stiletto, nor did I know who had; but I was afraid you might think Ferruci took it. The stiletto was Italian, and the Count is Italian, so it struck me you might put two and two together and suspect Ercole. I never thought you'd fix on me," concluded Lydia, with a scornful toss of her head.

"As a matter of fact, I fixed on you both," said Lucian composedly.

"And for what reason? Why should I and the Count murder poor Mark, if you please? He was a fool and a bore, but I wished him no harm. I was sorry as any one when I heard of his death, and I offered a good reward for the catching of the mean skunk that killed him. If I had done so myself I wouldn't have been such a fool as to sharpen the scent of the hounds on my own trail."

"You were in town on Christmas Eve?" said Denzil, not choosing to explain the motives he believed the pair had for committing the crime.

"I was. What of that?"

"You were in Jersey Street, Pimlico, on that night."

"I was never in Pimlico in my life!" declared Lydia wrathfully, "and, as I said before, I don't know where Jersey Street is."

"Do you know a man called Wrent?"

"I never heard of him!"

"Yet you visited him in Jersey Street on Christmas Eve, between seven and eight o'clock."

"Did I, really?" cried Mrs. Vrain, ironically, "and how can you prove I did?"

"By that cloak," said Lucian, pointing to where it lay on a chair. "You wore that cloak and a velvet-spotted veil."

"I haven't worn a veil of that kind for over a year," said Lydia decisively, "though I admit I used to wear veils of that sort. You can ask my maid if I have any velvet-spotted veils in my wardrobe just now. As to the cloak - I never wear rabbit skins."

"You might as a disguise."

"Sakes alive, man, what should I want with a disguise? I tell you the cloak isn't mine. You can soon prove that. Find out who made it, and go and ask in the shop if I bought it."

"How can I find out who made it?" asked Denzil, who was beginning to feel that Lydia was one too many for him.

"Here! I'll show you!" said Lydia, and picking up the cloak she turned over the tab at the neck, by which it was hung up. At the back of this there was a small piece of tape with printed black letters. "Baxter & Co., General Drapers, Bayswater," she read out, throwing down the cloak contemptuously. "I don't go to a London suburb for my frocks; I get them in Paris."

"Then you are sure this cloak isn't yours?" asked Lucian, much perplexed.

"No! I tell you it isn't! Go and ask Baxter & Co. if I bought it. I'll go with you, if you like; or better still," cried Mrs. Vrain, jumping up briskly, "I can take you to see some friends with whom I stayed on Christmas Eve. The whole lot will tell you that I was with them at Camden Hill all the night."

"What! Can you prove an alibi?"

"I don't know what you call it," retorted Lydia coolly, "but I can prove pretty slick that I wasn't in Pimlico."

"But - Mrs. Vrain - your friend - Ferruci was there!"

"Was he? Well, I don't know. I never saw him that time he was in town. But if you think he killed Mark you are wrong. I do not believe Ercole would kill a fly, for all he's an Italian."

"Do you think he took that stiletto?"

"No, I don't!"

"Then who did?"

"I don't know. I don't even know when it was taken. I missed it after Christmas, because that old schoolma'am told me it was gone."

"Old schoolma'am!"

"Well, Bella Tyler, if you like that better," retorted Mrs. Vrain. "Come, now, Mr. Denzil, I'm not going to let you go away without proving my - what do you call it? - alibi. Come with me right along to Camden Hill."

"I'll come just to satisfy myself," said Lucian, picking up the cloak, "but I am beginning to feel that it is unnecessary."

"You think I am innocent? Well," drawled Lydia, as Lucian nodded, "I think that's real sweet of you. I mayn't be a saint, but I'm not quite the sinner that Diana of yours makes me out."

"Diana of mine, Mrs. Vrain?" said Lucian, colouring.

The little woman laughed at his blush.

"Oh, I'm not a fool, young man. I see how the wind blows!" And with a nod she vanished.

CHAPTER XVIII

WHO BOUGHT THE CLOAK?

Mrs. Vrain sacrificed the vanity of a lengthy toilette to a natural anxiety to set herself right with Lucian, and appeared shortly in a ravishing costume fresh from Paris. Perhaps by arraying herself so smartly she wished to assure Denzil more particularly that she was a lady of too much taste to buy rabbit-skin cloaks in Bayswater: or perhaps - which was more probable - she was not averse to ensnaring so handsome a young man into an innocent flirtation.

The suspicion she entertained of Lucian's love for Diana only made Lydia the more eager to fascinate him on her own account. A conceit of herself, a hatred of her stepdaughter, and a desire to wring admiration out of a man who did not wish to bestow it. These were the reasons which led Mrs. Vrain to be particularly agreeable to the barrister. When the pair were ensconced in a swift hansom, and rolling rapidly towards Camden Hill, she began at once to prosecute her amiable designs.

"I guess you'll not mind being my best boy for the day," she said, with a coquettish glance. "You can escort me, first of all, to the Pegalls, and afterwards we can drive to Baxter & Co.'s in Bayswater, so that you can assure yourself I didn't buy that cloak."

"I am much obliged for the trouble you are taking, Mrs.

Vrain," replied the young man, avoiding with some reserve the insinuating glances of his pretty companion. "We shall do as you suggest. Who are the Pegalls, may I ask?"

"My friends, with whom I stopped on Christmas Eve," rejoined Mrs. Vrain. "A real good, old, dull English family, as heavy as their own plum puddings. Mrs. Pegall's a widow like myself, and I daresay she buys her frocks in the Bayswater stores. She has two daughters who look like barmaids, and ought to be, only they ain't smart enough. We had a real Sunday at home on Christmas Eve, Mr. Denzil. Whist and weak tea at eight, negus and prayers and bed at ten. Poppa wanted to teach them poker, and they kicked like mad at the very idea; but that was when he visited them before, I guess."

"Not the kind of family likely to suit you, I should think," said Lucian, regarding the little free-lance with a puzzled air.

"I guess not. Lead's a feather to them for weight. But it's a good thing to have respectable friends, especially in this slow coach of an old country, where you size everybody up by the company they keep."

"Ah!" said Lucian pointedly and - it must be confessed - rather rudely, "so you have found the necessity of having respectable friends, however dull?"

"That's a fact," acknowledged Mrs. Vrain candidly. "I've had a queer sort of life with poppa - ups and downs, and flyings over the moon, I guess."

"You are not American?" said Denzil suddenly.

"Sakes! How do you figure that out?"

"Because you are too pronouncedly Amurrican to be American."

"That's an epigram with some truth in it," replied Lydia

coolly. "Oh, I'm as much a U. S. A. article as anything else. We hung out our shingle in Wyoming, Wis., for a considerable time, and a girl who tickets herself Yankee this side flies high. But I guess I'm not going to give you my history," concluded Mrs. Vrain drily. "I'm not a Popey nor you a confessor."

"H'm! You've been in the South Seas, I see."

"There's no telling. How do you know?"

"The natives there use the word Popey to designate a Roman Catholic."

"You are as smart as they make 'em, Mr. Denzil. There's no flies about you; but I'm not going to give myself away. Ask poppa, if you want information. He's that simple he'll tell you all."

"Well, Mrs. Vrain, keep your own secret; it is not the one I wish to discover. By the way, you say your father was at Camden Hill on Christmas Eve?"

"I didn't say so, but he was," answered Lydia quietly. "He was not very well - pop can't stand these English winters - and wrote me to come up. But he was so sick that he left the Pegalls' about six o'clock."

"That was the letter which upset you."

"It was. I see old Bella Tyler kept her eyes peeled. I got the letter and came up at once. I've only got one parent left, and he's too good to be shoved away in a box underground while fools live. But here we are at the Pegalls'. I hope you'll like the kind of circus they run. Campmeetings are nothing to it."

The dwelling of the respectable family alluded to was a tolerably sized house of red brick, placed in a painfully neat garden, and shut in from the high road by a tall and jealous fence of green-painted wood. The stout widow and two stout spinster daughters, who made up the inmates, quite deserved Mrs. Vrain's epithet of "heavy." They were aggressively healthy, with red cheeks, black hair, and staring black eyes devoid of expression; a trio of Dutch dolls would have looked more intellectual. They were plainly and comfortably dressed; the drawing-room was plainly and comfortably furnished; and both house and inmates looked thoroughly respectable and eminently dull. What such a hawk as Mrs. Vrain was doing in this Philistine dove-cote, Lucian could not conjecture; but he admired her tact in making friends with a family whose heavy gentility assisted to ballast her somewhat light reputation; while the three of their brains in unison could not comprehend her tricks, or the reasons for which they were played.

"At all events, these three women are too honest to speak anything but the truth," thought Lucian while undergoing the ordeal of being presented. "So I'll learn for certain if Mrs. Vrain was really here on Christmas Eve."

The Misses Pegall and their lace-capped mamma welcomed Lucian with heavy good nature and much simpering, for they also had an eye to a comely young man; but the cunning Lydia they kissed and embraced, and called "dear" with much zeal. Mrs. Vrain, on her part, darted from one to the other like a bird, pecking the red apples of their cheeks, and cast an arch glance at Lucian to see if he admired her talent for manoeu-vering. Then cake and wine, port and sherry, were produced in the style of early Victorian hospitality, from which epoch Mrs. Pegall dated, and all went merry as a marriage bell, while Lydia laid her plans to have herself exculpated in Lucian's eyes without being inculpated in those of the family.

"We have just come up from our place in Somerset," explained Mrs. Pegall, in a comfortable voice. "The girls wanted to see the sights, so I just said, 'we'll go, dears, and perhaps we'll get a glimpse of the dear Queen.' I'm sure she has no more loyal subjects than we three."

"Are you going out much this year, dear Mrs. Vrain?" asked Beatrice Pegall, the elder and plainer of the sisters.

"No, dear," replied Lydia, with a sigh, putting a dainty handkerchief to her eyes. "You know what I have lost."

The two groaned, and Miss Cecilia Pegall, who was by way of being very religious in a Low Church way, remarked that "all flesh was grass," to which observation her excellent mamma rejoined: "Very true, dear, very true." And then the trio sighed again, and shook their black heads like so many mandarins.

"I should never support my grief," continued Lydia, still tearful, "if it was not that I have at least three dear friends. Ah! I shall never forget that happy Christmas Eve!"

"Last Christmas Eve, dear Mrs. Vrain?" said Cecilia.

"When you were all so kind and good," sobbed Lydia, with a glance at Lucian, to see that he noticed the confirmation. "We played whist, didn't we?"

"Four rubbers," groaned Mrs. Pegall, "and retired to bed at ten o'clock, after prayers and a short hymn. Quite a carol that hymn was, eh, dears?"

"And your poor pa was so bad with his cough," said Beatrice, "I hope it is better. He went away before dinner, too! Do say your pa is better!"

"Yes, dear, much better," said Lydia, and considering it was four months since Christmas Eve, Lucian thought it was time Mr. Clyne recovered.

"He enjoyed his tea, though," said Cecilia. "Mr. Clyne always says there is no tea like ours."

"And no evenings," cried Lydia, who was very glad there were not.

"Poppa and I are coming soon to have a long evening - to play whist again."

"But, dear Mrs. Vrain, you are not going?"

"I must, dears," with a kiss all round. "I have such a lot to do, and Mr. Denzil is coming with me, as poppa wants to consult him about some law business. He's a barrister, you know."

"I hope Mr. Denzil will come and see us again," said Mrs. Pegall, shaking hands with Lucian. A fat, puffy hand she had, and damp.

"Oh, delighted! delighted!" said Denzil hurriedly.

"Cards and tea, and sensible conversation," said Beatrice seriously, "no more."

"You forget prayers at ten, dear," rejoined Cecilia in low tones.

"We are a plain family, Mr. Denzil. You must take us as we are."

"Thank you, Mrs. Pegall, I will."

"Good-bye, dears," cried Lydia again, and with a final peck all round she skipped out and into the hansom, followed by her escort.

"Damn!" said Mrs. Vrain, when the cab drove away in the direction of Bayswater. "Oh, don't look so shocked, Mr. Denzil. I assure you I am not in the habit of swearing, but the extreme respectability of the Pegalls always makes me wish to relieve my feelings by going to the other extreme. What do you think of them?"

"They seem very good people, and genuine."

"And very genteel and dull," retorted Lydia. "Like

Washington, they can't tell a lie for a red cent; so you can believe I was there with poppa on Christmas Eve, only he went away, and I stayed all night."

"Yes, I believe it, Mrs. Vrain."

"Then I couldn't have been in Jersey Street or Geneva Square, sticking Mark with the stiletto?"

"No! I believe you to be innocent," said Lucian gravely. "In fact, I really don't think it is necessary to find out about this cloak at Baxter & Co.'s. I am assured you did not buy it."

"I guess I didn't, Mr. Denzil; but you want to know who did, and so do I. Well, you need not open your eyes. I'd like to know who killed Mark, also; and you say that cloak will show it?"

"I didn't say that; but the cloak may identify the woman I wrongfully took for you. She may have to do with the matter."

Lydia shook her pretty head. "Not she. Mark was as respectable as the Pegall gang; there's no woman mixed up in this matter."

"But I saw the shadow of a woman on the blind of No. 13!"

"You don't say! In Mark's sitting-room? Well, I should smile to know he was human, after all. He was always so precious stiff!"

Something in Mrs. Vrain's light talk of her dead husband jarred on the feelings of Lucian, and in some displeasure he held his peace. In no wise abashed, Lydia feigned to take no notice of this tacit reproof, but chatted on about all and everything in the most frivolous manner. Not until they had entered the shop of Baxter & Co. did she resume attention to business.

"Here," she said to the smiling shopwalker, "I want to know by whom this cloak was sold, and to what person."

The man examined the cloak, and noted a private mark on it, which evidently afforded him some information not obtainable by the general public, for he guided Lucian and his companion to a counter behind which stood a brisk woman with sharp eyes. In her turn she also examined the cloak, and departed to refresh her memory by looking at some account book. When she returned it was to intimate that the cloak had been bought by a man.

"A man!" repeated Lucian, much astonished. "What was he like?"

"A dark man," replied the brisk shopwoman, "dark hair, dark eyes, and a dark moustache. I remember him well, because he was a foreigner."

"A foreigner?" repeated Lydia in her turn. "A Frenchman?"

"No, madam - an Italian. He told me as much."

"Sakes alive!" cried Mrs. Vrain. "You are right, Mr. Denzil. It's Ferruci sure enough!"

CHAPTER XIX

THE DEFENCE OF COUNT FERRUCI

"It is quite impossible!" cried Mrs. Vrain distractedly. "I can't believe it nohow!"

The little woman was back again in her own drawing-room, talking to Lucian about the discovery which had lately been made regarding Ferruci's purchase of the cloak. Mrs. Vrain having proved her own innocence by the evidence of the Pegall family, was now trying to persuade both herself and Denzil that the Count could not be possibly implicated in the matter. He had no motive to kill Vrain, she said, a statement with which Lucian at once disagreed.

"I beg your pardon, Mrs. Vrain, he had two motives," said the barrister quickly. "In the first place, he was in love, and wished to marry you; in the second, he was poor, and wanted money. By the death of your husband he hoped to gain both."

"He has gained neither, as yet," replied Lydia sharply. "I like Ercole well enough, and at one time I was almost engaged to him. But he has a nasty temper of his own, Mr. Denzil, so I shunted him pretty smart to marry Mark Vrain. I wouldn't marry him now if he dumped down a million dollars at my feet to-morrow. Besides, poppa don't like him at all. I've got my money, and I've got my freedom, and I don't fool away either the one or the other on that Italian dude!"

"Is the Count acquainted with these sentiments?" asked Lucian drily.

"I guess so, Mr. Denzil. He asked me to marry him two months after Mark's death, and I just up and told him pretty plain how the cat jumped."

"In plain English, you refused him?"

"You bet I did!" cried Lydia vigorously. "So you see, Mr. Denzil, he could not have killed Mark."

"Why not? He did not know your true mind until two months after the murder."

"That's a fact, anyhow," commented Mrs. Vrain. "But what the mischief made him buy that rabbit-skin cloak?"

"I expect he bought it for the woman I mistook for you."

"And who may she be?"

"That is just what I wish to find out. This woman who came to Jersey Street so often wore this cloak; therefore, she must have obtained it from the Count. I'll make him tell me who she is, and what she has to do with this crime."

"Do you think she has anything to do with it?" said Mrs. Vrain doubtfully.

"I am certain. It must have been her shadow I saw on the blind."

"And the man's shadow was the Count's?" questioned Lydia.

"I think so. He bought the cloak for the woman, visited the man Wrent at Jersey Street, and was seen by the servant in the back yard. He did not act thus without some object, Mrs. Vrain, you may be sure of that."

"Sakes!" said Lydia, with a weary sigh. "I ain't sure of anything save that my head is buzzing like a sawmill. Who is Wrent, anyhow?"

"I don't know. An old man with white beard and a skull-cap of black velvet."

"Ugh!" said Mrs. Vrain, with a shiver. "Mark used to wear a black skull-cap, and the thought of it makes me freeze up. Sounds like a judge of your courts ordering a man to be lynched. Well, Mr. Denzil, it seems to me as you'd best hustle Ercole. If he knows who the woman is - and he wouldn't buy cloaks for her if he didn't - he'll know who this Wrent is. I guess he can supply all information."

"Where does he live?"

"Number 40, Marquis Street, St. James's. You go and look him up, while I tell poppa what a mean white he is. I guess poppa won't let him come near me again. Pop's an honest man, though he ain't no Washington."

"Suppose I find out that he killed your husband?" asked Lucian, rising.

"Then you'd best lynch him right away," replied Lydia without hesitation. "I draw the line at murder - some!"

The barrister was somewhat disgusted to hear Mrs. Vrain so coolly devote her whilom admirer to a shameful death. However, he knew that her heart was hard and her nature selfish; so there was little use in showing any outward displeasure at her want of charity. She had cleared herself from suspicion, and evidently cared not who suffered, so long as she was safe and well spoken of. Moreover, Lucian had learned all he wished about her movements on the night of the crime, and taking a hasty leave, he went off to Marquis Street for the purpose of bringing Ferruci to book for his share in the terrible business. However, the Count proved to be from home, and would not be back, so the servant said, until late that night.

Denzil therefore left a message that he would call at noon the next day, and drove from St. James's to Kensington, where he visited Diana. Here he detailed what he had learned and done from the time he had visited Mrs. Bensusan up to the interview with Lydia. Also he displayed the cloak, and narrated how Mrs. Vrain had cleared herself of its purchase.

To all this Diana listened with the greatest interest, and when Lucian ended she looked at him for some moments in silence. In fact, Diana, with all her wit and common sense, did not know how to regard the present position of affairs.

"Well, Miss Vrain," said Lucian, seeing that she did not speak, "what do you think of it all?"

"Mrs. Vrain appears to be innocent," said Diana in a low voice.

"Assuredly she is! The evidence of the Pegall family - given in all innocence - proves that she could not have been in Geneva Square or in Jersey Street on Christmas Eve."

"Then we come back to my original belief, Mr. Denzil. Lydia did not commit the crime herself, but employed Ferruci to do so."

"No," replied Denzil decidedly. "Whether the Italian is guilty or not, Mrs. Vrain knows nothing about it. If she were cognisant of his guilt she would not have risked going with me to Baxter & Co., and letting me discover that Ferruci had bought the cloak. Nor would she so lightly surrender a possible accomplice as she has done Ferruci. Whatever can be said of Mrs. Vrain's conduct - and I admit that it is far from perfect - yet I must say that she appears, by the strongest evidence, to be totally innocent and ignorant. She knows no more about the matter than her father does."

"Well," said Diana, unwilling to grant her stepmother too much grace, "we must give her the benefit of the doubt. What about Ferruci?"

"So far as I can see, Ferruci is guilty," replied Lucian. "To clear himself he will have to give the same proof as Mrs. Vrain. Firstly, he will have to show that he was not in Jersey Street on Christmas Eve; secondly, he will have to prove that he did not buy the cloak. But in the face of the servant's evidence, and the statement of the shopwoman, he will find it difficult to clear himself. Yet," added Lucian, remembering his failure with Lydia, "it is always possible that he may do so."

"It seems to me, Mr. Denzil, that your only chance of getting at the truth is to see the Italian."

"I think so myself. I will see him to-morrow."

"Will you take Mr. Link with you?"

"No, Miss Vrain. As I have found out so much without Link, I may as well proceed in the matter until his professional services are required to arrest Count Ferruci. By the way, I have never seen that gentleman. Can you describe his appearance to me?"

"Oh, as far as looks go there is no fault to be found with him," answered Diana. "He is a typical Italian, tall, slender, and olive complexioned. He speaks English very well, indeed, and appears to be possessed of considerable education. Certainly, to look at him, and to speak with him, you would not think he was a villain likely to murder a defenceless old man. But if he did not kill my poor father, I know not who did."

"I'll call on him to-morrow at noon," said Lucian, "and later on I shall come here to tell you what has passed between us."

This remark brought the business between them to a close, but Lucian would fain have lingered to engage Diana in lighter conversation. Miss Vrain, however, was too much disturbed by the news he had brought her to indulge in frivolous talk. Her mind, busied with recollections of her deceased father, and anxiously seeking some means whereby to avenge his death, was ill attuned to encourage at the moment the aspirations which she knew Lucian entertained.

The barrister, therefore, sighed and hinted in vain. His Dulcinea would have none of him or his courting, and he was compelled to retire, as disconsolate a lover as could be seen. To slightly alter the saying of Shakespeare, "the course of true love never does run smooth," but there were surely an unusual number of obstacles in the current of Denzil's desires. But as he consoled himself with reflecting that the greater the prize the harder it is to win, so it behooved him to do his devoir like a true knight.

The next day, at noon, Lucian, armed for the encounter with the evidence of Rhoda and of the cloak, presented himself at the rooms which Count Ferruci temporarily inhabited in Marquis Street. He not only found the Italian ready to receive him, but in full possession of the adventure of the cloak, which, as he admitted, he had learned from Lydia the previous evening. Also, Count Ferruci was extremely indignant, and informed Lucian that he was easily able to clear himself of the suspicion. While he raged on in his fiery Italian way, Denzil, who saw no chance of staying the torrent of words, examined him at his leisure.

Ercole Ferruci was, as Diana had said, a singularly handsome man of thirty-five. He was dark, slender, and tall, with dark, flashing eyes, a heavy black moustache, and an alert military look about him which showed that he had served in the army. The above description savours a trifle of the impossible hero of a young lady's dream; and, as a matter of fact, Ferruci was not unlike that ideal personage. He had all the looks and graces which women admire, and seemed honest and fiery enough in a manly way - the last person, as Lucian thought, to gain his aims by underhand ways, or to kill a helpless old man. But Lucian, legally experienced in human frailty, was not to be put off with voluble conversation and outward graces. He wished for proofs of innocence, and these he tried to obtain as soon as Ferruci drew breath in his fiery harangue.

"If you are innocent, Count," said Lucian, in reply to the fluent, incorrect English of the Italian, "appearances are against you. However, you can prove yourself innocent, if you will."

"Sir!" cried Ferruci, "is not my word good?"

"Not good enough for an English court," replied Lucian coldly. "You say you were not in Jersey Street on Christmas Eve. Who can prove that?"

"My friend - my dear friend, Dr. Jorce of Hampstead, sir. I was with him; oh, yes, sir, he will tell you so."

"Very good! I hope his evidence will clear you," replied the more phlegmatic Englishman. "And this cloak?"

"I never bought the cloak! I saw it not before!"

"Then come with me to the shop in Bayswater, and hear what the girl who sold it says."

"I will come at once!" cried Ferruci hastily, catching up his cane and hat. "Come, then, my friend! Come! What does the woman say?"

"That she sold the cloak to a tall man - to a dark man with a moustache, and one who told her he was Italian."

"Bah!" retorted the Count, as they hailed a hansom. "Is all that she can say? Why, all we Italians are supposed to be tall and dark, and wear moustaches. Your common people in England never fancy one of us can be fair."

"You are not fair," replied Lucian drily, "and your looks correspond to the description."

"True! Oh, yes, sir! But that description might describe a dozen of my countrymen. And, Mr. Denzil," added the Count, laughing, "I do not go round about saying to common people that I am an Italian. It is not my custom to explain."

Lucian shrugged his shoulders, and said no more until they entered the shop in Bayswater. As he knew from the previous visit where the saleswoman was located, he led the Count rapidly to the place. The girl was there, as brisk and businesslike as ever. She looked up as they approached, and came forward to serve them, with a swift glance at both.

"I am sorry to trouble you again," said Lucian ceremoniously, "but you told me yesterday that you sold a blue cloak, lined with rabbit skin, to an Italian gentleman, and -"

"And am I the gentleman?" interrupted Ferruci. "Did I buy a cloak?"

"No," replied the shopwoman, after a sharp glance. "This is not the gentleman who bought the cloak."

CHAPTER XX

A NEW DEVELOPMENT

"You see, Mr. Denzil," said Ferruci, turning triumphantly to Lucian, "I did not buy this cloak; I am not the Italian this lady speaks of."

Lucian was extremely astonished at this unexpected testimony in favour of the Count, and questioned the shopwoman sharply. "Are you certain of what you say?" he asked, looking at her intently.

"Yes, I am, sir," replied the girl stiffly, as though she did not like her word doubted. "The gentleman who bought the cloak was not so tall as this one, nor did he speak English well. I had great difficulty in learning what he wanted."

"But you said that he was dark, with a moustache - and -"

"I said all that, sir; but this is not the gentleman."

"Could you swear to it?" said Lucian, more chagrined than he liked to show to the victorious Ferruci.

"If it is necessary, I could, sir," said the shopwoman, with the greatest confidence. And after so direct a reply, and such certain evidence, Denzil had nothing to do but retire from an awkward position as gracefully as he could.

"And now, sir," said Ferruci, who had followed him out of the shop, "you come with me, please."

"Where to?" asked Lucian gloomily.

"To my friend - to my rooms. I have shown I did not buy the cloak you speak of. Now we must find my friend, Dr. Jorce, to tell you I was not at Jersey Street when you say."

"Is Dr. Jorce at your rooms?"

"I asked him to call about this time," said Ferruci, glancing at his watch. "When Mrs. Vrain speak to me of what you say I wish to defend myself, so I write last night to my friend to talk with you this day. I get his telegram saying he would come at two hours."

Lucian glanced in his turn at his watch. "Half-past one," he said, beckoning to a cab. "Very good, Count, we will just have time to get back to your place."

"And what you think now?" said Ferruci, with a malicious twinkle in his eyes.

"I do not know what to think," replied Lucian dismally, "save that it is a strange coincidence that *another* Italian should have bought the cloak."

The Count shrugged his shoulders as they got into the hansom, but he did not speak until they were well on their way back to Marquis Street. He then looked thoughtfully at his companion. "I do not believe coincidence," he said abruptly, "but in design."

"What do you mean, Count? I do not quite follow you."

"Some one who knows I love Mrs. Vrain wish to injure me," said the Italian rapidly, "and so make theirself like me to buy that cloak. Ah! you see? But he could not make himself as tall as me. Oh, yes, sir, I am sure it is so."

"Do you know any one who would disguise himself so as to implicate you in the murder?"

"No." Ferruci shook his head. "I cannot think of one man - not one."

"Do you know a man called Wrent?" asked Lucian abruptly.

"I do not, Mr. Denzil," said Ferruci at once. "Why do you ask?"

"Well, I thought he might be the man to disguise himself. But no," added Lucian, remembering Rhoda's account of Wrent's white hair and beard, "it cannot be him. He would not sacrifice his beard to carry out the plan; in fact he could not without attracting Rhoda's attention."

"Rhoda! Wrent! What strange names you talk of!" cried Ferruci vivaciously.

"No stranger than that of your friend Jorce."

Ferruci laughed. "Oh, he is altogether most strange. You see."

It was as the Italian said. Dr. Jorce - who was waiting for them in the Count's room - proved to be a small, dried-up atom of a man, who looked as though all the colour had been bleached out of him. At first sight he was more like a monkey than a man, owing to his slight, queer figure and agile movements; but a closer examination revealed that he had a clever face, and a pair of most remarkable eyes. These were of a steel-grey hue, with an extraordinary intensity of gaze; and when he fixed them on Lucian at the moment of introduction the young barrister felt as though he were being mesmerised.

For the rest, Jorce was dressed sombrely in black cloth, was extremely voluble and vivacious, and impressed Lucian with the idea that he was less a fellow mortal than a changeling from fairyland. Quite an exceptional man was Dr. Jorce, and, as the Italian said, "most strange."

"My good friend," said Ferruci, laying his stern hand on the shoulder of this oddity, "this gentleman wishes you to decide a - what do you say? - bet?"

"A bet!" cried the little doctor in a deep bass voice, but with some indignation. "Do I understand, Count, that you have brought me all the way from my place in Hampstead to decide a bet?"

"Ah, but sir, it is a bet most important," said Ferruci, with a smile. "This Mr. Denzil declares that he saw me in Pim - Pim - what?"

"In Pimlico," said Lucian, seeing that Ferruci could not pronounce the word. "I say that the Count was in Pimlico on Christmas Eve."

"You are wrong, sir," said Jorce, with a wave of his skinny hand. "My friend, Count Ferruci, was in my house at Hampstead on that evening."

"Was he?" remarked Lucian, astonished at this confident assertion. "And at what time did he leave?"

"He did not leave till next morning. My friend the Count remained under my roof all night, and left at twelve o'clock on Christmas morning."

"So you see," said Ferruci airily to Lucian, "that I could not have done what you think, as that was done - by what you said - between eleven and twelve on that night."

"Was the Count with you at ten o'clock on that evening?" asked Denzil.

"Certainly he was; so you have lost your bet, Mr. Denzil. Sorry to bring you such bad fortune, but truth is truth, you know."

"Would you repeat this statement, if I wished?"

"Why not? Call on me at any time. 'The Haven, Hampstead'; that will always find me."

"Ah, but I do not think it will be necessary for Mr. Denzil to call on you, sir," interposed the Count rapidly. "You can always come to me. Well, Mr. Denzil, are you satisfied?"

"I am," replied Lucian. "I have lost my bet, Count, and I apologise. Good-day, Dr. Jorce, and thank you. Count Ferruci, I wish you good-bye."

"Not even *au revoir*?" said Ferruci mockingly.

"That depends upon the future," replied Lucian coolly, and forthwith went away in low spirits at the downfall of his hopes. Far from revealing the mystery of Vrain's death, his late attempts to solve it had resulted in utter failure. Lydia had cleared herself; Ferruci had proved himself innocent; and Lucian could not make up his mind what was now to be done.

In this dilemma he sought out Diana, as, knowing from experience that where a man's logic ends a woman's instinct begins, he thought she might suggest some way out of the difficulty. On arriving at the Royal John Hotel he found that Diana was waiting for him with great impatience; and hardly giving herself time to greet him, she asked how he had fared in his interview with Count Ferruci.

"Has that man been arrested, Mr. Denzil?"

"No, Miss Vrain. I regret to say that he has not been arrested. To speak plainly, he has, so far as I can see, proved himself innocent."

"Innocent! And the evidence against him?"

"Is utterly useless. I brought him face to face with the woman who sold the cloak, and she denies that Ferruci bought it."

"But she said the buyer was an Italian."

"She did, and dark, with a moustache. All the same, she did not recognise the Count. She says the buyer was not so tall, and spoke worse English."

"Ferruci could make his English bad if he liked."

"Probably; but he could not make his stature shorter. No, Miss Vrain, I am afraid that our Italian friend, in spite of the evidence against him, did not buy the cloak. That he resembles the purchaser in looks and nationality is either a coincidence or -"

"Or what?" seeing that Lucian hesitated.

"Or design," finished the barrister. "And, indeed, the Count himself is of this opinion. He believes that some one who wished to get him into trouble personated him."

"Has he any suspicions as to whom the person may be?"

"He says not, and I believe him; for if he did suspect any particular individual he certainly would gain nothing by concealment of the fact."

"H'm!" said Diana thoughtfully, "so that denial of the saleswoman disposes of the cloak's evidence. What about the Count's presence in Jersey Street on Christmas Eve?"

"He was not there!"

"But Rhoda, the servant, saw him both in the house and in the back yard!"

"She saw a dark man, with a moustache, but she could not say that he was a foreigner. She does not know Ferruci, remember. The man she saw must have been the same as the purchaser of the cloak."

"Where does Ferruci say he was?"

"At Hampstead, visiting a friend."

"Oh! And what does the friend say?"

"He declares that the Count was with him on Christmas Eve and stayed all night."

"That is very convenient evidence for the Count, Mr. Denzil. Who is this accommodating friend?"

"A doctor called Jorce."

"Can his word be trusted?"

"So far as I can judge from his looks and a short acquaintance, I should say so."

"It was half-past eight when the servant saw the dark man run out of the yard?"

"Yes!"

"And at half-past eight Ferruci was at Hampstead in the house of Dr. Jorce?"

"Not that I know of," said Lucian, remembering that he had asked Jorce the question rather generally than particularly, "but the doctor declared that Ferruci was with him at ten o'clock on that evening, and did not leave him until next morning; so as your father was killed between eleven and twelve, Ferruci must be innocent."

"It would seem so, if this doctor is to be believed," muttered Diana reflectively, "but judging by what you have told me, there is nothing to show that Ferruci was *not* in Pimlico at eight-thirty, and was *not* the man whom the servant saw."

"Well, certainly he could get from Pimlico to Hampstead in an hour and a half. However, the main point about all this evidence is, that neither Ferruci nor Lydia Vrain killed your father."

"No! no! that seems clear. Still! still! they know about it. Oh, I am sure of it. It must have been Ferruci who was in Pimlico on that night. If so, he knows who Wrent is, and why he stayed in Jersey Street."

"Perhaps, although he denies ever hearing the name of Wrent. But I would not be surprised if the man who could solve the mystery is -"

"Who? - who?"

"Doctor Jorce himself. I feel sure of it."

CHAPTER XXI

TWO MONTHS PASS

Unwilling to give up prosecuting the Vrain case while the slightest hope remained of solving its mystery, Lucian sought out Link, the detective, and detailed all the evidence he had collected since the constituted authorities had abandoned the matter. Although Mrs. Vrain and Ferruci had exculpated themselves entirely, Denzil thought that Link, with his professional distrust and trained sense of ferreting out secrets, might discern better than himself whether such exculpations were warranted by circumstances.

Link heard all that Denzil had to tell him with outward indifference and inward surprise; for while unwilling, through jealousy of an amateur, to flatter the barrister by a visible compliment, yet he silently admitted that Denzil had made his discoveries and profited by them with much acuteness. What annoyed him, however, was that the young man had pushed his inquiries to the uttermost limit; and that there was no chance of any glory accruing to himself by prosecuting them further. Still, on the possibility that something might come of it, he went over the ground already traversed by the amateur detective.

"You should have told me of your intentions when Miss Vrain spoke to you in the first instance," he said to Lucian by way of rebuke. "As it is, you have confused the clues so much that I do not know which one to take."

"It seems to me that I have pursued each clue until fate or circumstance clipped it short," retorted Lucian, nettled by this injustice. "Mrs. Vrain has defended herself successfully, much in the same way as Count Ferruci has done. Your only chance of getting at the truth lies in discovering Wrent; and unless Rhoda helps you there, I do not see how you can trace the man."

"I am of a different opinion," said Link, lying freely to conceal his doubts of success in the matter. "As you have failed through lack of experience, I shall attempt to unravel this skein."

"You attempted to do so before, and gave it up because of the tangle," said Lucian with quiet irony. "And unless you discover more than I have done, you will dismiss the matter again as impossible. So far as I can see, the mystery of Vrain's death is more of a mystery than ever, and will never be solved."

"I'll make one last attempt to unriddle it, however," answered Link, with a confidence he was far from feeling, "but, of course - not being one of your impossible detectives of fiction - I may fail."

"You are certain to fail," said Lucian decisively, and with this disheartening prophecy he left Link to his task of - apparently - spinning ropes of sand.

Whether it was that Link was so doubtful of the result as to extend little energy in the search, or whether he really found the task impossible of accomplishment, it is difficult to say, but assuredly he failed as completely as Lucian predicted. With outward zeal he set to work; interviewed Lydia and the Italian, to make certain that their defence was genuine; examined the Pegall family, who were dreadfully alarmed by their respectability being intruded upon by a common detective, and obtained a fresh denial from Baxter & Co.'s saleswoman that Ferruci was the purchaser of the cloak. Also he cross-questioned Mrs. Bensusan and her sharp handmaid in the most exhaustive manner, and did his best to trace out the mysterious Wrent who had so much to do with the matter. He even called on Dr. Jorce at Hampstead, to satisfy himself as to the actual time of Ferruci's arrival in that neighbourhood on Christmas Eve. But here he received a check, for Jorce had gone abroad on his annual holiday, and was not expected back for a month.

In fact, Link did all that a man could do to arrive at the truth, only to find himself, at the end of his labours, in the same position as Lucian had been. Disgusted at this result, he threw up his brief, and called upon Diana and Denzil, with whom he had previously made an appointment, to notify them of his inability to bring the matter to a satisfactory conclusion.

"There is not the slightest chance of finding the assassin of Mr. Vrain," said Link, after he had set forth at length his late failures. "The more I go into the matter the more I see it."

"Yet you were so confident of doing more than I," said Lucian quietly.

Link turned sulkily, after the fashion of a bad loser.

"I did my best," he retorted gloomily. "No man can do more. Some crimes are beyond the power of the law to punish for sheer lack of proof. This is one of them; and, so far as I can see, this unknown assassin will be punished on Judgment Day - not before."

"Then you don't think that Signor Ferruci is guilty?" said Diana.

"No. He has had nothing to do with the matter; nor has Mrs. Vrain brought about the death in any way."

"You cannot say who killed my father?"

"Not for certain, but I suspect Wrent."

"Then why not find Wrent?" asked Diana bluntly.

"He has hidden his trail too well," began Link, "and - and -"

"And if you did find him," finished Denzil coolly, "he might prove himself guiltless, after the fashion of Mrs. Vrain and Ferruci."

"He might, sir; there is no knowing. But since you think I have done so little, Mr. Denzil, let me ask you who it is you suspect?"

"Dr. Jorce of Hampstead."

"Pooh! pooh!" cried Link, with contempt. "He didn't kill the man - how could he, seeing he was at Hampstead on that Christmas Eve midnight, as I found out from his servants?"

"I don't suspect him of actually striking the blow," replied Lucian, "but I believe he knows who did."

"Not he! Dr. Jorce has too responsible a position to mix himself up in a crime from which he gains no benefit."

"Why! what position does he hold?"

"He is the owner of a private lunatic asylum. Is it likely that a man like him would commit a murder?"

"Again I deny that he did commit the crime; but I am certain, from the very fact of his friendship with Ferruci, that he knows more than he chooses to tell. Why should the Italian be intimate with the owner of a private asylum - with a man so much beneath him in rank?"

"I don't know, sir. But if you suspect Dr. Jorce you had better see him when he comes back from his holidays - in a month."

"Where is he now?"

"In Italy, and the Count has gone with him."

Diana and Lucian looked at one another, and the former spoke: "That is strange," she said. "I agree with Mr. Denzil, it is peculiar, to say the least of it, that an Italian noble should make a bosom friend of a man so far inferior to him in position. Don't you think so yourself, Mr. Link?"

"Madam," said Link gravely, "I think nothing about it, save that you will never find out the truth. I have tried my best, and failed; and I am confident enough in my own power to say that where I have failed no one else will succeed. Miss Vrain, Mr. Denzil, I wish you good-day."

And with this bragging speech, which revealed the hurt vanity of the man, Mr. Link took his departure. Lucian held his peace, for in the face of this desertion of a powerful ally he did not know what to say. Diana walked to the sitting-room window and watched Link disappear into the crowd of passers-by. At that she heaved a sigh, for with him - she thought - went every chance of learning the truth, since if he, an experienced person in such matters, turned back from the quest, there could assuredly be no help in any one not professional, and with less trained abilities.

Then she turned to Lucian.

"There is nothing more to be done, I suppose," said she, sighing again.

"I am afraid not," replied Lucian dismally, for he was quite of her opinion regarding the desertion of the detective.

"Then I must leave this unknown assassin to the punishment of God!" said Diana quietly. "And I can only thank you for all you have done for me, Mr. Denzil, and say" - she hesitated and blushed, then added, with some emphasis - "say *au revoir*."

"Ah!" ejaculated Denzil, with an indrawn breath of relief, "I

am glad you did not say good-bye."

"I don't wish to say it, Mr. Denzil. I have not so many friends in the world that I can afford to lose so good a one as yourself."

"I am content," said Lucian softly, "that you should think of me as your friend - for the present."

His meaning was so unmistakable that Diana, still blushing, and somewhat confused, hastened to prevent his saying more at so awkward a moment. "Then as my friend I hope you will come and see me at Berwin Manor."

"I shall be delighted. When do you go down?"

"Within a fortnight. I must remain that time in town to see my lawyer about the estate left by my poor father."

"And see Mrs. Vrain?"

"No," replied Diana coldly. "Now that my father is dead, Mrs. Vrain is nothing to me. Indirectly, I look upon her as the cause of his death, for if she had not driven both of us out of our own home, my father might have been alive still. I shall not call on Mrs. Vrain, and I do not think she will dare to call on me."

"I'm not so sure of that," rejoined Lucian, who was well acquainted with the lengths to which Mrs. Vrain's audacity would carry her; "but let us dismiss her, with all your other troubles. May I call on you again before you leave town?"

"Occasionally," replied Diana, smiling and blushing; "and you will come down to Berwin Manor when I send you an invitation?"

"I should think so," said Denzil, in high glee, as he rose to depart; "and now I will say -"

"Good-bye?" said Miss Vrain, holding out her hand.

"No. I will use your own form of farewell - *au revoir*."

Then Lucian went out from the presence of his beloved, exulting that she had proved so kind as not to dismiss him when she no longer required his services. In another woman he would not have minded such ingratitude, but had Diana banished him thus he would have been miserable beyond words. Also, as Lucian joyfully reflected, her invitation to Berwin Manor showed that, far from wishing to lose sight of him, she desired to draw him into yet closer intimacy. There could be nothing but good resulting from her invitation and his acceptance, and already Denzil looked forward to some bright summer's day in the green and leafy country, when he should ask this goddess among women to be his wife. If encouragement and looks and blushes went for anything, he hardly doubted the happy result.

In the meantime, while Lucian dreamed his dreams, Diana, also dreaming in her own way, remained in town and attended to business. She saw her lawyers, and had her affairs looked into, so that when she went to Bath she was legally installed as the mistress of Berwin Manor and its surrounding acres. As Lucian hinted, Lydia did indeed try to see her stepdaughter. She called twice, and was refused admission into Diana's presence. She wrote three times, and received no reply to her letters; so the consequence was that, finding Diana declined to have anything to do with her in any way whatsoever, she became very bitter. This feeling she expressed to Lucian, whom she one day met in Piccadilly.

"As if I had done anything," finished Lydia, after a recital of all her grievances. "I call it real mean. Don't you think so, Mr. Denzil?"

"If you ask me, Mrs. Vrain," said Lucian stiffly, "I think you and Miss Vrain are better apart."

"Of course you defend her. But I guess I can't blame you, as I know what you are driving at."

"What about Signor Ferruci?" asked Denzil, parrying.

"Oh, we are good friends still, but nothing more. As he proved that he did not kill Mark, I've no reason to give him his walking-ticket. But," added Mrs. Vrain drily, "I guess you'll be married to Diana before I hitch up 'longside Ercole."

"How do you know I shall marry Miss Vrain?" asked Lucian, flushing.

"If you saw your face in a glass, you wouldn't ask, I guess. Tomatoes ain't in it for redness. I won't dance at your wedding, and I won't break my heart, either," and with a gay nod Mrs. Lydia Vrain tripped away, evidently quite forgetful of the late tragedy in her life.

CHAPTER XXII

AT BERWIN MANOR

The heritage of Diana lay some miles from Bath, in a pleasant wooded valley, through which meandered a placid and slow-flowing stream. On either side of this water stretched broad meadow lands, flat and fertile, as well they might be, seeing they were of rich black loam, and well drained, withal. To the right these meadows were bounded by forest lands, the trees of which grew thickly up and over the ridge, and on the space where wood met fields was placed the manor, a quaint square building of Georgian architecture, and some two centuries old.

Against the green of the trees its warm walls of red brick and sloping roof of bluish slate made a pleasant spot of colour. There stretched a terrace before it; beneath the terrace a flower garden and orchard; and below these the meadow lands, white with snow in winter, black in spring, with ridgy furrows, and golden with grain in the hot days of summer. Altogether a lovely and peaceful spot, where a man could pass pleasant days in rural quiet, a hermitage of rest for the life-worn and heart-weary.

Here, towards the end of summer, came Lucian, to rest his brain after the turmoil of London, and to court his mistress under the most favourable circumstances. Diana had established herself in her ancestral home with a superannuated governess as a chaperon, for without such a guardianship she could hardly have invited the barrister to visit her. Miss

Fergus Hume

Priscilla Barbar was a placid, silver-haired old dame, who, having taught Diana for many years, had returned, now that the American Mrs. Vrain had departed, to spend the rest of her days under the roof of her dear pupil.

She took a great fancy to Lucian, which was just as well, seeing what was the object of his visit, and complacently watched the growing attachment between the handsome young couple, who seemed so suited to one another. But her duties as chaperon were nominal, for when not pottering about the garden she was knitting in a snug corner, and when knitting failed to interest her she slumbered quietly, in defiance of the etiquette which should have compelled her to make a third in the conversation of her young friends.

As for Lucian and his charming hostess, they found that they had so many tastes in common, and enjoyed each other's society so much, that they were hardly ever apart. Diana saw with the keen eyes of a woman that Lucian was in love with her, and let it be seen in a marvellously short space of time, and without much difficulty, that she was in love with him.

But even after Lucian had been at the manor a fortnight, and daily in the society of Diana, he spoke no word of love. Seeing how beautiful she was, and how dowered with lands and rents and horses, he began to ask himself whether it was not rather a presumption on his part to ask her to share his life. He had only three hundred a year - six pounds a week - and a profession in which, as yet, he had not succeeded; so he could offer her very little in exchange for her beauty, wealth, and position.

The poor lover became quite pale with fruitless longing, and his spirits fell so low that good Miss Priscilla one day drew him aside to ask about his health.

"For," said she, "if you are ill in body, Mr. Denzil, I know of some remedies - old woman's medicines you will call them, no doubt - which, with the blessing of God, may do you good."

"Thank you, Miss Barbar, but I am not ill in body - worse luck!" and Lucian sighed.

"Why worse luck, Mr. Denzil?" said the old lady severely. "That is an ungrateful speech to Providence."

"I would rather be ill in body than ill in mind," explained Denzil, blushing, for in some ways he was younger than his years.

"And are you ill in mind?" asked Miss Priscilla, with a twinkle in her eyes.

"Alas! yes. Can you cure me?"

"No. For that cure I shall hand you over to Diana."

"Miss Priscilla!" And Lucian coloured again, this time with vexation.

"Oh, Mr. Denzil," laughed the governess, "because I am old you must not imagine that I am blind. I see that you love Diana."

"Better than my life!" cried the devoted lover with much fervour.

"Of course! That is the usual romantic answer to make. Well, why do you not tell Diana so, with any pretty additions your fancy suggests?"

"She might not listen to me," said this doubting lover dolefully.

"Very true," replied his consoler. "On the other hand, she might. Besides, Mr. Denzil, however much the world may have altered since my youth, I have yet to learn that it is the lady's part to propose to the gentleman."

"But, Miss Barbar, I am poor!"

"What of that? Diana is rich."

"Don't I know it? For that very reason I hesitate to ask her."

"Because you are afraid of being called a fortune-hunter, I suppose," said the old lady drily. "That shows a lack of moral courage which is not worthy of you, Mr. Denzil. Take an old woman's advice, young man, and put your fortunes to the test. Remember Montrose's advice in the song."

"You approve of my marrying Diana - I mean Miss Vrain?"

"From what I have seen of you, and from what Diana has told me about you, I could wish her no better husband. Poor girl! After the tragical death of her father, and her wretched life with that American woman, she deserves a happy future."

"And do you think - do you really think that she - that she - would be happy with - with me?" stammered Lucian, hardly daring to believe Miss Priscilla, whose acquaintance with him seemed too recent to warrant such trust.

The wise old woman laughed and nodded.

"Ask her yourself, my dear," she said, patting his hand. "She will be able to answer that question better than I. Besides, girls like to say 'yea' or 'nay,' themselves."

This seemed to be good advice, and certainly none could have been more grateful to the timid lover. That very night he made up his mind to risk his fortunes by speaking to Diana. It was no easy matter for the young man to bring himself to do so, for cool, bold, and fluent as he was on ordinary occasions, the fever of love rendered him shy and nervous. The looks of Diana acted on his spirits as the weather does on a barometer. A smile made him jocund and hilarious, a frown abashed him almost to gloom. And in the April weather of her presence he was as variable as a weather-cock. It is, therefore, little to be wondered at that one ordinarily daring should tremble to ask a question which might be answered in the negative. True, Miss Barbar's partisanship heartened him a trifle, but he still feared for the result. Cupid, as well as conscience, makes cowards of us all - and Lucian was a doubting lover.

Towards the end of his stay Miss Priscilla - as usual - fell asleep one evening after dinner, and Diana, feeling the house too warm, stepped out into the garden, followed by Lucian. The sun had just set behind the undulating hills, and the clear sky, to the zenith, was of a pale rose colour, striped towards the western horizon with lines of golden cloud. In the east a cold blue prevailed, and here and there a star sparkled in the arch of the sky.

The garden was filled with floating shadows, which seemed to glide into it from the dark recesses of the near woods, and in a copse some distance away a nightingale was singing to his mate, and filling the silence with melody. The notes fluted sweetly through the still air, mingling with the sigh of the rising wind and the musical splashing of the fountain. This shot up a pillar of silvery water to a great height, and in descending sprinkled the near flower beds with its cold spray. All was inexpressibly beautiful to the eye and soothing to the ear - a scene and an hour for love. It might have been the garden of the Capulets, and those who moved in it - the immortal lovers, as yet uncursed by Fate.

"Only three more days," sighed Lucian as he walked slowly down the path beside Diana, "and then that noisy London again."

"Perhaps it is as well," said Diana, in her practical way. "You would rust here. But is there any need for you to go back so soon?"

"I must - for my own peace of mind."

Diana started and blushed at the meaning of his tone and words.

Then she recovered her serenity and sat down on an old stone seat, near which stood a weather-beaten statue of Venus. Seeing that she kept silent in spite of his broad hint, Lucian - to bring matters to a crisis - resolved to approach the subject in a mythological way through the image of the goddess.

"I am sorry I am not a Greek, Miss Vrain," he said abruptly.

"Why?" asked Diana, secretly astonished by the irrelevancy of the remark.

Lucian plucked a red rose from the bush which grew near the statue and placed it on the pedestal.

"Because I would lay my offering at the feet of the goddess, and touch her knees to demand a boon."

"What boon would you ask?" said Diana in a low voice.

"I would beseech that in return for my rose of flowers she would give me the rose of womanhood."

"A modest request. Do you think it would be granted?"

"Do you?" asked Lucian, picking up the rose again.

"How can I reply to your parables, or read your dark sayings?" said Diana, half in earnest, half in mirth.

"I can speak plainer if you permit it."

"If - if you like!"

The young man laid the rose on Diana's lap. "Then in return for my rose give me - yourself!"

"Mr. Denzil!" cried Diana, starting up, whereby the flower fell to the ground. "You - you surprise me!"

"Indeed, I surprise myself," said Lucian sadly. "That I should dare to raise my eyes to you is no doubt surprising."

"I don't see that at all," exclaimed Diana coldly. "I like to be woo'd like a woman, not honoured like a goddess."

"You are both woman and goddess! But - you are not angry?"

"Why should I be angry?"

"Because I - I love you!"

"I cannot be angry with - with - shall we say a compliment."

"Oh, Diana!"

"Wait! wait!" cried Miss Vrain, waving back this too eager lover. "You cannot love me! You have known me only a month or two."

"Love can be born in an hour," cried Lucian eagerly. "I loved you on the first day I saw you! I love you now - I shall love you ever!"

"Will you truly love me ever, Lucian?"

"Oh, my darling! Can you doubt it? And you?" He looked at her hopefully.

"And I?" she repeated in a pretty mocking tone, "and I?" With a laugh, she bent and picked up the flower. "I take the rose and I give you -"

"Yourself!" cried the enraptured lover, and the next moment he was clasping her to his breast. "Oh, Diana, dearest! Will you really be my wife?"

"Yes," she said softly, and kissed him.

For a few moments the emotions of both overcame them too much to permit further speech; then Diana sat down and made Lucian sit beside her.

"Lucian," she said in a firm voice, "I love you, and I shall be your wife - when you find out who killed my poor father!"

"It is impossible!" he cried in dismay.

"No. We must prosecute the search. I have no right to be happy while the wretch who killed him is still at large. We have failed hitherto, but we may succeed yet! and when we succeed I shall marry you."

"My darling!" cried Lucian in ecstasy; and then in a more subdued tone: "I'll do all I can to find out the truth. But, after all, from what point can I begin afresh?"

"From the point of Mrs. Vrain," said Diana unexpectedly.

"Mrs. Vrain!" cried the startled Lucian. "Do you still suspect her?"

"Yes, I do!"

"But she has cleared herself on the most undeniable evidence."

"Not in my eyes," said Diana obstinately. "If Mrs. Vrain is innocent, how did she find out that the unknown man murdered in Geneva Square was my father?"

"By his assumption of the name of Berwin, which was mentioned in the advertisement; also from the description of the body, and particularly by the mention of the cicatrice on the right cheek, and of the loss of the little finger of the left hand."

Diana started. "I never heard that about the little finger," she said hurriedly. "Are you sure?"

"Yes. I saw myself when I knew your father as Berwin, that he had lost that little finger."

"Then, Lucian, you did *not* see my father!"

"What!" cried Denzil, hardly able to credit her words.

"My father never lost a finger!" cried Diana, starting to her feet. "Ah, Lucian, I now begin to see light. That man who called himself Berwin, who was murdered, was not my father. No, I believe - on my soul, I believe that my father, Mark Vrain, is alive!"

CHAPTER XXIII

A STARTLING THEORY

When Diana declared that her father yet lived, Lucian drew back from her in amazement, for of all impossible things said of this impossible case this saying of hers was the strangest and most incredible. Hitherto, not a suspicion had entered his mind but that the man so mysteriously slain in Geneva Square was Mark Vrain, and, for the moment, he thought that Diana was distraught to deny so positive a fact.

"It is impossible," said he, shaking his head, "quite impossible. Mrs. Vrain identified the corpse, and so did other people who knew your father well."

"As to Mrs. Vrain," said Diana contemptuously, "I quite believe she would lie to gain her own ends. And it may be that the man who was murdered was like my father in the face, but -"

"He had the mark on his cheek," interrupted Lucian, impatient of this obstinate belief in the criminality of Lydia.

"I know that mark well," replied Miss Vrain. "My father received it in a duel he fought in his youth, when he was a student in a German university; but the missing finger." She shook her head.

"He might have lost the finger while you were in Australia," suggested the barrister.

"He might," rejoined Diana doubtfully, "but it is unlikely. As to other people identifying the body, they no doubt did so by looking at the face and its scar. Still, I do not believe the murdered man was my father."

"If not, why should Mrs. Vrain identify the body as that of her husband?"

"Why? Because she wanted to get the assurance money."

"She may have been misled by the resemblance of the dead man to your father."

"And who provided that resemblance? My dear Lucian, I would not be at all surprised to learn that there was conspiracy as well as murder in this matter. My father left his home, and Lydia could not find him. I quite believe that. As she cannot prove his death, she finds it impossible to obtain the assurance money; so what does she do?"

"I cannot guess," said Lucian, anxious to hear Diana's theory.

"Why, she finds a man who resembles my father, and sets him to play the part of the recluse in Geneva Square. She selects a man in ill health and given to drink, that he may die the sooner; and, by being buried as Mark Vrain, give her the money she wants. When you told me of this man Berwin's coughing and drinking, I thought it strange, as my father had no consumptive disease when I left him, and never, during his life, was he given to over-indulgence in drink. Now I see the truth. This dead man was Lydia's puppet."

"Even granting that this is so, which I doubt, Diana, why should the man be murdered?"

"Why?" cried Diana fiercely. "Because he was not dying quickly enough for that woman's purpose. She did not kill him herself, if her alibi is to be credited, but she employed Ferruci to murder him."

"You forget Signor Ferruci also proved an alibi."

"A very doubtful one," said Miss Vrain scornfully. "You did not ask that Dr. Jorce the questions you should have done. Go up to London now, Lucian, see him at Hampstead, and find out if Ferruci was at his house at eight o'clock on Christmas Eve. Then I shall believe him guiltless; till then, I hold him but the creature and tool of Lydia."

"Jorce declares that Ferruci was with him at the house when the murder was committed?"

"Can you believe that? Ferruci may have made it worth the while of this doctor to lie. And even granting that much, the presence of Ferruci at the Jersey Street house shows that he knew what was going to take place on that night, and perhaps arranged with another man to do the deed. Either way you look at it, he and Lydia are implicated."

"I tell you it is impossible, Diana," said Lucian, finding it vain to combat this persistent belief. "All this plotting of crime is such as is found in novels, not in real life -"

"In real life," cried Diana, taking the words out of his mouth, "more incredible things take place than can be conceived by the most fantastic imagination of an author. Look at this talk of ours - it began with words of love and marriage speeches, and it ends with a discussion of murder. But this I say, Lucian, that if you love me, and would have me marry you, you must find out the truth of these matters. Learn if this dead man is my father - for from what you have told me of the lost finger I do not believe that he is. Hunt down the assassin, and discover if he is whom I believe him to be - Ferruci himself; and learn, if you can, what Lydia has to do with all these evil matters. Do this, and I am yours. Refuse, and I shall not marry you!"

"You set me a hard task," said Lucian, with a sigh, "and I hardly know how to set about it."

"Be guided by me," replied Diana. "Go up to London and put an advertisement in the papers offering a reward for the discovery of my father. He is of medium height, with grey hair, and has a clean-shaven face, with a scar on it -"

"You describe the dead man, Diana."

"But he has not lost a finger," continued Diana, as though she had not heard him. "If my father, for fear of Lydia, is in hiding, he will come to you or me in answer to that advertisement."

"But he must have seen the report of his death by violence in the papers, if indeed he is alive," urged Lucian, at his wit's end.

"My father is weak in the head, and perhaps was afraid to come out in the midst of such trouble. But if you put in the advertisement that I - his daughter - am in England, he will come to me, for with me he knows he is safe. Also call on Dr. Jorce, and find out the truth about Signor Ferruci."

"And then?"

"Then when you have done these two things we shall see what will come of them. Promise me to do what I ask you."

"I promise," said Lucian, taking her hand, "but you send me on a wild-goose chase."

"That may be, Lucian, but my heart - my presentiment - my - instinct - whatever you like to call it - tells me otherwise. Now let us go inside."

"Shall we tell Miss Barbar of our engagement?" asked Denzil timidly.

"No; you will tell no one of that until we learn the truth of thisconspiracy. When we do, Lucian, you will find that my father is not dead but is alive, and will be at our wedding."

"I doubt it - I doubt it."

"I am sure of it," answered Diana, and slipping her hand within the arm of her lover she walked with him up to the house. It was the strangest of wooings.

Miss Barbar, with a true woman's interest in love affairs, was inclined to congratulate them both when they entered, deeming - as the chance had been so propitious - that Lucian had proposed. But Diana looked so stern, and Lucian so gloomy, that she held her peace.

Later on, when her curiosity got the better of her desire not to offend her pupil, she asked if Denzil had spoken.

"Yes," replied Diana, "he has spoken."

"And you have refused him?" cried the old lady in dismay, for she did not relish the idea that Lucian should have lost by her counsel.

"No; I have not refused him."

"Then you have said 'yes,' my dear!"

"I have said sufficient," replied Diana cautiously. "Please do not question me any further, Miss Barbar. Lucian and I understand one another very well."

"She calls him by his Christian name," thought the wise old dame, "that is well. She will not speak of her happiness, that is ill," and in various crafty ways Miss Barbar tried to learn how matters actually stood between the pair.

But if she was skilful in asking questions, Diana was equally skilful in baffling them, and Miss Barbar learned nothing more than her pupil chose to tell her, and that was little enough. To perplex her still further, Lucian departed for London the next day, with a rather disconsolate look on his handsome face, and gave his adviser no very satisfactory explanation at parting.

So Miss Barbar was forced to remain in ignorance of the success or failure of her counsel, and could by no means discover if the marriage she was so anxious to bring about was likely to take place. And so ended Denzil's visit to Berwin Manor.

In the meantime, Lucian went back to London with a heavy heart, for he did not see how he was to set about the task imposed on him by Diana. At first he thought it would be best to advertise, as she advised, but this he considered would do no good, as if Vrain - supposing him to be alive and in hiding - would not come out at the false report of his murder, he certainly would not appear in answer to an advertisement that might be a snare.

Then Lucian wondered if it would be possible to have the grave opened a second time that Diana might truly see if the corpse was that of her father or of another man. But this also was impossible, and - to speak plainly - useless, for by this time the body would not be recognisable; therefore, it would be of little use to exhume the poor dead man, whomsoever he might be, for the second time. Finally, Lucian judged it would be wisest of all to call on Dr. Jorce, and find out why he was friendly with Ferruci, and how much he knew of the Italian's doings.

While the barrister was making up his mind to this course he was surprised to receive a visit from no less a person than Mr. Jabez Clyne, the father of Lydia.

The little man, usually so bright and merry, now looked worried and ill at ease. Lucian - so much as he had seen of him - had always liked him better than Lydia, and was sorry to see him so downcast. Nor when he learned the reason was he better pleased. Clyne told it to him in a roundabout way.

"Do you know anything against Signor Ferruci?" he asked, when the first greetings were over.

"Very little, and that bad," replied Denzil shortly.

"Do you refer to the horrible death of my son-in-law?"

"Yes, I do, Mr. Clyne. I believe Ferruci had a hand in it, and if you bring him here I'll tell him so."

"Can you prove it?" asked Clyne eagerly.

"No. As yet, Ferruci has proved that he was not in Geneva Square on the night of the crime - or rather," added Lucian, correcting himself, "at the hour when the murder was committed."

Clyne's face fell. "I wish you could discover if he is guilty or not," he said. "I am anxious to know the truth."

"Why?" asked Lucian bluntly.

"Because if he is guilty, I don't want my daughter to marry a murderer."

"What! Is Mrs. Vrain going to marry him?"

"Yes," said the little man disconsolately, "and I wish she wasn't."

"So do I - for her own sake. I thought she did not like him. She said as much to me."

"I can't make her out, Mr. Denzil. She grew tired of him for a time, but now she has taken up with him again, and nothing I can say or do will stop the marriage. I love Lydia beyond words, as she is my only child, and I don't want to see her married to a man of doubtful reputation like Ferruci. So I thought I'd call and see if you could help me."

"I can't," replied Lucian. "As yet I have found out nothing likely to implicate Ferruci in the crime."

"But you may," said Clyne hopefully.

Lucian shrugged his shoulders.

"If I do, you shall know at once," he said.

CHAPTER XXIV

LUCIAN IS SURPRISED

Although Denzil received Mr. Clyne with all courtesy, and promised to aid him, if he could, in breaking off the marriage with Ferruci, by revealing his true character to Mrs. Vrain, he by no means made a confidant of the little man, or entrusted him with the secret of his plans. Clyne, as he well knew, was dominated in every way by his astute daughter, and did he learn Lucian's intentions, he was quite capable - through sheer weakness of character - of revealing the same to Lydia, who, in her turn - since she was bent upon marrying Ferruci - might retail them to the Italian, and so put him on his guard.

Denzil, therefore, rid himself of the American by promising to tell him, on some future occasion, all that he knew about Ferruci. Satisfied with this, Clyne departed in a more cheerful mood, and, apparently, hoped for the best.

After his departure, Lucian again began to consider his idea of calling on Jorce regarding the alibi of Ferruci. On further reflection he judged that, before paying the visit to Hampstead, it might be judicious to see Rhoda again, and refresh his memory in connection with the events of Christmas Eve. With this idea he put on his hat, and shortly after the departure of Clyne walked round to Jersey Street.

On ringing the bell, the door was opened by Rhoda in person, looking sharper and more cunning than ever. She informed him that he could not see Mrs. Bensusan, as that good lady was in bed with a cold.

"I don't want to see your mistress, my girl," said Lucian quickly, to stop Rhoda from shutting the door in his face, which she seemed disposed to do. "I desire to speak with you."

"About that there murder?" asked Rhoda sharply. Then in reply to the nod of Lucian she continued: "I told you all I knew about it when you called before. I don't know nothing more."

"Can you tell me the name of the dark man you saw in the yard?"

"No, I can't. I know nothing about him."

"Did you ever hear Mr. Wrent mention his name?"

"No, sir. He called and he went, and I saw him in the back yard at 8.30. I never spoke to him, and he never spoke to me."

"Could you swear to the man if you saw him?"

"Yes, I could. Have you got him with you?" asked Rhoda eagerly.

"Not at present," answered Lucian, rather surprised by the vindictive expression on the girl's face. "But later on I may call upon you to identify him."

"Do you know who he is?" asked the servant quickly.

"I think so."

"Did he kill that man?"

"Possibly," said Denzil, wondering at these very pointed questions. "Why do you ask?"

"I have my reasons, sir. Where is my cloak?"

"I will return it later on; it will probably be used as evidence."

Rhoda started. "Where?" she demanded, with a frown.

"At the trial."

"Do you think they'll hang the person who killed Mr. Vrain?"

"If the police catch him, and his guilt is proved, I am sure they will hang him."

The girl's eyes flashed with a wicked light, and she clasped and unclasped her hands with a quick, nervous movement. "I hope they will," she said in a low, rapid voice. "I hope they will."

"What!" cried Lucian, with a step forward. "Do you know the assassin?"

"No!" cried Rhoda, with much vehemence. "I swear I don't, but I think the murderer ought to be hanged. I know - I know - well, I know something - see me to-morrow night, and you'll hear."

"Hear what?"

"The truth," said this strange girl, and shut the door before Lucian could say another word.

The barrister, quite dumbfounded, remained on the step looking at the closed door. So important were Rhoda's words that he was on the point of ringing again, to interview her once more and force her to speak. But when he reflected that Mrs. Bensusan was in bed, and that Rhoda alone could reopen the door - which from her late action it was pretty evident she would not do - he decided to retire for the present. It was little use to call in the police, or create trouble by forcing his way into the house, as that might induce Rhoda to run away before giving her evidence. So Lucian departed, with the intention of keeping the next night's appointment, and hearing what Rhoda had to say.

"The truth," he repeated, as he walked along the street. "Evidently she knows who killed this man. If so, why did she not speak before, and why is she so vindictive? Heavens! If Diana's belief should be a true one, and her father not dead? Conspiracy! murder! this gypsy girl, that subtle Italian, and the mysterious Wrent! My head is in a whirl. I cannot understand what it all means. To-morrow, when Rhoda speaks, I may. But - can I trust her? I doubt it. Still, there is nothing else for it. I *must* trust her."

Talking to himself in this incoherent way, Lucian reached his rooms and tried to quiet the excitement of his brain caused by the strange words of Rhoda. It was yet early in the afternoon, so he took up a book and threw himself on the sofa to read for an hour, but he found it quite impossible to fix his attention on the page. The case in which he was concerned was far more exciting than any invention of the brain, and after a vain attempt to banish it from his mind he jumped up and threw the book aside.

Although he did not know it, Lucian was suffering from a sharp attack of detective fever, and the only means of curing such a disease is to learn the secret which haunts the imagination. Rhoda, as she stated - rather ambiguously, it must be confessed - could reveal this especial secret touching the murder of Vrain; but, for some hidden reason, chose to delay her confession for twenty-four hours. Lucian, all on fire with curiosity, found himself unable to bear this suspense, so to distract his mind and learn, if possible, the true relationship existing between Ferruci and Jorce, he set out for Hampstead to interview the doctor.

"The Haven," as Jorce, with some humour, termed his private asylum, was a red brick house, large, handsome, and commodious, built in a wooded and secluded part of

Hampstead. It was surrounded by a high brick wall, over which the trees of its park could be seen, and possessed a pair of elaborate iron gates, opening on to a quiet country lane. Externally, it looked merely the estate of a gentleman.

The grounds were large, and well laid out in flower gardens and orchards; and as it was Dr. Jorce's system to allow his least crazy patients as much liberty as possible, they roamed at will round the grounds, giving the place a cheerful and populated look. The more violent inmates were, of course, secluded; but these were well and kindly treated by the doctor. Indeed, Jorce was a very humane man, and had a theory that more cures of the unhappy beings under his charge could be effected by kindness than by severity.

His asylum was more like a private hotel with paying guests than an establishment for the retention of the insane, and even to an outside observer the eccentricities of the doctor's family - as he loved to call them - were not more marked than many of the oddities possessed by people at large. Indeed, Jorce was in the habit of saying that "There were more mad people in the world than were kept under lock and key," and in this he was doubtless right. However, the kindly and judicious little man was like a father to those under his charge, and very popular with them all. Anything more unlike the popular conception of an asylum than the establishment at Hampstead can scarcely be imagined.

When Lucian arrived at "The Haven," he found that Jorce had long since returned from his holiday, and was that day at home; so on sending in his card he was at once admitted into the presence of the local potentate. Jorce, looking smaller and more like a fairy changeling than ever, was evidently pleased to see Lucian, but a look on his dry, yellow face indicated that he was somewhat puzzled to account for the visit. However, preliminary greetings having passed, Lucian did not leave him long in doubt.

"Dr. Jorce," he said boldly, and without preamble, "I have

called to see you about that alibi of Signor Ferruci's."

"Alibi is a nasty word, Mr. Denzil," said Jorce, looking sharply at his visitor.

"Perhaps, but it is the only word that can be used with propriety."

"But I thought that I was called on to decide a bet."

"Oh, that was Count Ferruci's clever way of putting it," responded Lucian, with a sneer. "He did not wish you to know too much about his business."

"H'm! Perhaps I know more than you think, Mr. Denzil."

"What do you mean, sir?" cried Lucian sharply.

"Softly, Mr. Denzil, softly," rejoined the doctor, waving his hand. "I shall explain everything to your satisfaction. Do you know why I went to Italy?"

"No; no more than I know why you went with Signor Ferruci," replied Lucian, recalling Link's communication.

"Ah!" said Jorce placidly, "you have been making inquiries, I see. But you are wrong in one particular. I did not go to Italy with Ferruci - I left him in Paris, and I went on myself to Florence to find out the true character of the man."

"Why did you wish to do that, doctor?"

"Because I had some business with our mutual friend, the Count, and I was not altogether pleased with the way in which it was conducted. Also, my last interview with you about that bet made me suspicious of the man. Over in Florence I learned sufficient about the Count to assure me that he is a bad man, with whom it is as well to have as little to do as possible. I intended to return at once with this information and call on you, Mr. Denzil. Unfortunately, I fell ill of an attack of typhoid fever in Florence, and had to stay there these two months."

"I am sorry," said Lucian, noting that the doctor did look ill, "but why did you not send on your information to me?"

"It was necessary to see you personally, Mr. Denzil. I arrived back a few days ago, and intended writing to you when I recovered from the fatigue of the journey. However, your arrival saves me the trouble. Now I can tell you all about Ferruci, if you like."

"Then tell me, Doctor, if you spoke truly about that alibi?"

"Yes, I did. Count Ferruci was with me that night, and stayed here until the next morning."

"What time did he arrive?"

"About ten o'clock, or, to be precise," said Jorce, "about ten-thirty."

"Ah!" cried Lucian exultantly, "then Ferruci must have been the man in the back yard!"

"What do you mean by that?" asked Jorce in a puzzled tone.

"Why, that Count Ferruci has had to do with a crime committed some months ago in Pimlico. A man called Mark Vrain was murdered, as you may have seen in the papers, Doctor, and I believe Ferruci murdered him."

"If I remember rightly," said Jorce with calmness, "the man in question was murdered shortly before midnight on Christmas Eve. If that is so, Ferruci could not have killed him, because, as I said before, he was here at half-past ten on that night."

"I don't say he actually killed the man," explained Lucian

eagerly, "but he certainly employed some one to strike the blow, else what was he doing in the Jersey Street yard on that night? You can say what you like, Dr. Jorce, but that man is guilty of Mark Vrain's death."

"No," replied Jorce coolly, "he's not, for the simple reason that Vrain is not dead."

"Not dead?" repeated Lucian, recalling Diana's belief.

"No! For the last few months Mark Vrain, under the name of Michael Clear, has been in this asylum!"

CHAPTER XXV

A DARK PLOT

"So Vrain is alive, after all!" was Lucian's comment on the speech of Jorce, "and he is here under your charge? Jove! it's wonderful! Diana was right, after all!"

"Diana? Who is Diana?" queried Jorce, then held up his hand to stop his visitor from replying. "Wait! I know! Vrain mentioned his daughter Diana."

"Yes, she is the daughter of Vrain, and she believes her father to be alive."

"On what grounds?"

"Because the dead man, whom, until lately, she believed to be Mr. Vrain, had one of his little fingers missing. That fact came to her knowledge only a week ago. When it did, she declared that the deceased could not be her father."

"H'm!" said Jorce thoughtfully, "I am quite in the dark as to why Mr. Vrain was put under my charge."

"Because Ferruci wished to marry his widow."

"I see! Ferruci substituted another man for my patient and had him killed."

"Evidently," replied Lucian; "but I am almost as much in the dark as you are, Dr. Jorce. Tell me how Vrain came to be placed here, and, exchanging confidence for confidence, I'll let you know all I have discovered since the death of the man in Geneva Square who called himself Berwin."

"That is a fair offer," replied Jorce, clearing his throat, "and one which I willingly accept. I do not wish you to think that I am in league with Signor Ferruci. What I did was done honestly. I am not afraid of telling my story."

"I am sure of that," said Lucian heartily. "I guessed that Ferruci had not trusted you altogether, from the time he feigned that your evidence was needed only to decide a bet."

"Trust me!" echoed Jorce, with scorn. "He never trusted me at all. He is too cunning for that. However, you shall hear."

"I'm all attention, Doctor."

"A week before last Christmas, Signor Ferruci called to see me, and explained that he was interested in a gentleman called Michael Clear, whom he had met some years before in Italy. Clear, he said, had been most intimate with him, but later on had indulged so much in the morphia habit that their friendship had terminated with high words. Afterwards, Clear had returned to England, and Ferruci lost sight of him for some months. Then he visited England, and one day found Clear in the street, looking ill and wretched. The man had become a confirmed morphiamaniac, and the habit had weakened his brain. The Count pitied the poor creature, according to his own story, and took him to his home, the whereabouts of which Clear was happily able to remember."

"Where is the house?" asked Lucian, taking out his pocketbook.

"Number 30, St. Bertha's Road, Bayswater," replied Jorce; and when the barrister, for his private information, had made a note of the address, he continued: "It then appeared that Clear was married. The wife told Ferruci that she was afraid of her husband, who, in his fits of drink - for he drank likewise - often threatened to kill her. They had lost their money, and the poor woman was at her wit's end what to do. Ferruci explained to me that out of friendship he was most anxious to befriend Clear, and stated that Mrs. Clear wished to get her husband cured. He proposed, therefore, to put Clear into my asylum, and pay on behalf of the wife."

"A very ingenious and plausible plan," said Lucian. "Well, Doctor, and what did you say?"

"I agreed, of course, provided the man was certified insane in the usual way. Ferruci then departed, promising to bring Mrs. Clear to see me. He brought her late on Christmas Eve, at ten -"

"Ah!" interrupted Lucian, "did she wear a black gauze veil with velvet spots?"

"She did, Mr. Denzil. Have you met her?"

"No, but I have heard of her. She was the woman who visited Wrent in Jersey Street. No doubt Ferruci was waiting for her in the back yard."

"Who is Wrent?" asked Jorce, looking puzzled.

"Don't you know the name, Doctor?"

"No."

"Did Mrs. Clear never mention it?"

"Never."

"Nor Ferruci?"

"No. I never heard the name before," replied Jorce complacently.

"Strange!" said Denzil reflectively. "Yet Wrent seems to be at the bottom of the whole plot. Well, never mind, just now. Please continue, my dear Doctor. What did Mrs. Clear say?"

"Oh, she repeated Ferruci's story, amplified in a feminine fashion. She was afraid of Michael, who, when excited with morphia or drink, would snatch up a knife to attempt her life. Twice she had disarmed him, and now she was tired and frightened. She was willing for him to go into my asylum since Count Ferruci had so kindly consented to bear the expense, but she wished to give him one more chance. Then, as it was late, she stayed here all night. So did the Count, and on Christmas Day they went away."

"When did they come back?"

"About a fortnight later, and they brought with them the man they both called Michael Clear."

"What is he like?"

"An old man with a white beard."

"Is he mad?" asked Lucian bluntly.

"He is not mad now, only weak in the head," replied Jorce professionally, "but he was certainly mad when he arrived. The man's brain is wrecked by morphia."

"Not by drink?"

"No; although it suited Mrs. Clear and Ferruci to say so. But Clear, as I may call him, was very violent, and quite justified Mrs. Clear's desire to sequester him. She told me that he often imagined himself to be other people. Sometimes he would feign to be Napoleon; again the Pope; so when he, a week after he was in the asylum, insisted that he was Mark Vrain, I put it down to his delusion."

"But how could you think he had come by the name, Doctor?"

"My dear sir, at that time the papers were full of the case and its mystery, and as we have a reading-room in this asylum, I fancied that Clear had seen the accounts, and had, as a delusion, called himself Vrain. Afterwards he fell into a kind of comatose state, and for weeks said very little. He was most abject and frightened, and responded in a timid sort of way to the name of Clear. Naturally this confirmed me in my belief that his calling himself Vrain was a delusion. Then he grew better, and one day told me that his name was Vrain. Of course, I did not believe him. Still, he was so persistent about the matter that I thought there might be something in it, and spoke to Ferruci."

"What did he say?"

"He denied that the man's name was anything but Clear. That the wife and two doctors - for the poor soul had been duly certified as insane - had put him into the asylum; and altogether persisted so strongly in his original story that I thought it was absurd to put a crazy man's delusion against a sane man's tale. Besides, everything regarding the certificate and sequestrating of Clear had been quite legal. Two doctors - and very rightly, too - had certified to the insanity of the man; and his wife - as I then believed Mrs. Clear to be - had consented to his detention."

"What made you suspicious that there might be something wrong?" asked Lucian eagerly.

"My visit to meet you, at Ferruci's request, to prove the alibi," responded Jorce. "I thought it was strange, and afterwards, when a detective named Mr. Link, called, I thought it was stranger still."

"But you did not see Link?"

"No. I was in Italy then, but I heard of his visit. In Florence I heard from a most accomplished gossip the whole story of Mr. Vrain's marriage and the prior engagement of Mrs. Vrain to Ferruci. I guessed that there might be some plot, but I could not quite understand how it was carried out, save that Vrain - as I then began to believe Clear to be - had been placed in my asylum under a false name. On my return I intended to see you, when I was laid up in Florence with the fever. Now, however, that we have met, tell me so much of the story as you know. Afterwards we shall see Mr. Vrain."

Lucian was willing enough to show his confidence in Jorce, the more so as he needed his help. Forthwith he told him all he knew, from the time he had met Michael Clear, *alias* Mark Berwin, *alias* Mark Vrain, in Geneva Square, down to the moment he had presented himself for information at the gates of "The Haven." Doctor Jorce listened with the greatest attention, his little face puckered up into a grim smile, and shook his head when the barrister ended his recital.

"A bad world, Mr. Denzil, a bad world!" he said, rising. "Come with me, and I'll take you to see my patient."

"But what do you think of it all?" said Denzil, eager for some comment.

"I'll tell you that," rejoined Jorce, "when you have heard the story of Mr. Vrain."

In a few minutes Lucian was led by his guide into a pleasant room, with French windows opening on to a wide verandah, and a sunny lawn set round with flowers. Books were arranged on shelves round the walls, newspapers and magazines were on the table, and near the window, in a comfortable chair, sat an old man with a volume in his hand. As Jorce entered he stood up and shuffled forward with a senile smile of delight. Evidently - and with reason, poor soul - he considered the doctor his very good friend.

"Well, well!" said the cheery Jorce, "and how are you to-day, Mr. Vrain?"

"I feel very well," replied Vrain in a soft, weak voice. "Who is this, Doctor?"

"A young friend of mine, Mr. Vrain. He wishes to hear your story."

"Alas! alas!" sighed Vrain, his eyes filling with tears, "a sad story, sir."

The father of Diana was of middle height, with white hair, and a long white beard which swept his chest. On his cheek Lucian saw the cicatrice of which Diana had spoken, and mainly by which the dead man had been falsely identified as Vrain. He was very like Clear in figure and manner; but, of course, the resemblance in the face was not very close, as Clear had been clean shaven, whereas the real Vrain wore a beard. The eyes were dim and weak-looking, and altogether Lucian saw that Vrain was not fitted to battle with the world in any way, and quite weak enough to become the prey of villains, as had been his sad fate.

"My name is Mark Vrain, young sir," said he, beginning his story without further preamble. "I lived in Berwin Manor, Bath, with my wife Lydia, but she treated me badly by letting another man love her, and I left her. Oh, yes, sir, I left her. I went away to Salisbury, and was very happy there with my books, but, alas! I took morph -"

"Vrain!" said Jorce, holding up his finger, "no!"

"Of course, of course," said the old man, with a watery smile, "I mean I was very happy there. But Signor Ferruci, a black-hearted villain" - his face grew dark as he mentioned the name - "found me out and made me come with him to London. He kept me there for months, and then he brought me here."

"Kept you where, Mr. Vrain?" asked Lucian gently.

The old man looked at him with a vacant eye. "I don't know," he said in a dull voice.

"You came here from Bayswater," hinted Jorce.

"Yes, yes, Bayswater!" cried Vrain, growing excited. "I was there with a woman they called my wife. She was not my wife! My wife is fair, this woman was dark. Her name was Maud Clear: my wife's name is Lydia."

"Did Mrs. Clear say you were her husband, Michael?"

"Yes. She called me Michael Clear, and brought me to stay with the doctor. But I am not Michael Clear!"

CHAPTER XXVI

THE OTHER MAN'S WIFE

As soon as Lucian arrived back in his rooms he sat down at his desk and wrote a long letter to Diana, giving a full account of his extraordinary discovery of her father in Jorce's asylum, and advising her to come up at once to London.

When he posted this - which he did the same night - he sighed to think it was not a love letter. He could have covered reams of paper with words of passion and adoration; he could have poured out his whole soul at the feet of his divinity, telling her of his love, his aspirations, his hopes and fears. No doubt, from a common-sense view, the letter would have been silly enough, but it would have relieved his mind and completed his happiness of knowing that he loved and was beloved.

But in place of writing thus, he was compelled by his promise to Diana to pen a description of his late discovery, and interesting as the case was now growing, he found it irksome to detail the incident of the afternoon. He wished to be a lover, not a detective.

So absent-minded and distraught was Lucian, that Miss Greeb, who had long suspected something was wrong with him, spoke that very evening about himself. She declared that Lucian was working too hard, that he needed another rest, although he had just returned from the country, and recommended a sleeping draught. Finally she produced a letter which had just arrived, and as it was in a female hand, Miss Greeb watched its effect on her admired lodger with the keen eyes of a jealous woman. When she saw him flush and seize it eagerly, casting, meanwhile, an impatient look on her to leave the room, she knew the truth at once, and retired hurriedly to the kitchen, where she shed floods of tears.

"I might have guessed it," gasped Miss Greeb to a comfortable cat which lay selfishly before the fire. "He's far too good-looking not to be snapped up. He'll be leaving me and setting up house with that other woman. I only hope she'll do for him as well as I have done. I wonder if she's beautiful and rich. Oh, how dreadful it all is!" But the cat made no comment on this tearful address - not as much as a mew. It rolled over into a warmer place and went to sleep again. Cats are particularly selfish animals.

Two days afterwards Miss Greeb opened the door to a tall and beautiful lady, who asked for Mr. Denzil, and was shown into his sitting-room. With keen instinct, Miss Greeb decided that this was the woman who had taken possession of Lucian's heart, and being a just little creature, in spite of her jealousy, was obliged to admit that the visitor was as handsome as a picture. Then, seeing that there was no chance for her beside this splendid lady, she consoled herself with a dismal little proverb, and looked forward to the time when it would be necessary to put a ticket in the parlour window. Meanwhile, to have some one on whose bosom she could weep, Miss Greeb went round to see Mrs. Bensusan, leaving Diana in possession of Lucian, and the cat sole occupant of the kitchen.

In the drawing-room, on the front floor, Diana, with her eyes shining like two stars, was talking to Lucian. She had come up at once on receipt of his letter; she had been to Hampstead, she had seen her father, and now she was telling Lucian about the visit.

"He knew me at once, poor dear," she said rapidly, "and asked me if I had been out, just as if I'd left the house for a visit and come back. Ah!" - she shook her head and sighed - "I am afraid he'll never be quite himself again."

"What does Jorce think?"

"He says that father can be discharged as cured, and is going to see about it for me. Of course, he will never be quite sane, but he will never be violent so long as morphia and drugs of that sort are kept from him. As soon as he is discharged I shall take him back to Bath, and put him in charge of Miss Barbar; then I shall return to town, and we must expose the whole conspiracy!"

"Conspiracy?"

"What else do you call it, Lucian? That woman and Ferruci have planned and carried it out between them. They put my father into the asylum, and made another man pass as him, in order to get the assurance money. As their tool did not die quickly enough, they killed him."

"No, Diana. Both Lydia and Ferruci have proved beyond all doubt that they were not in Pimlico at the hour of the death. I believe they contrived this conspiracy, but I don't believe they murdered Clear."

"Well, we shall see what defence they make. But one thing is certain, Lucian - Lydia will have to disgorge the assurance money."

"Yes, she certainly will, and I've no doubt the Assurance Company will prosecute her for fraud in obtaining it. I shall see Ferruci to-morrow and force him to confess his putting your father in the asylum."

"No!" said Diana, shaking her head. "Don't do that until you have more evidence against him."

"I think the evidence of Jorce is strong enough. I suppose you mean the evidence of Mrs. Clear?"

"Yes; although for her own sake I don't suppose she will speak."

Lucian nodded. "I thought of that also," he said, "and yesterday I went to St. Bertha Street, Bayswater, to see her. But I found that she had moved, and no one knew where she was. I expect, having received her price for the conspiracy, she has left London. However, I put an advertisement in the papers, saying if she called on me here she would hear of something to her advantage. It is in the papers this morning."

"I doubt if she will call," said Diana seriously. "What about the promised revelation of Rhoda?"

"I believe that girl is deceiving me," cried Lucian angrily. "I went round to Jersey Street, as she asked me, and only saw Mrs. Bensusan, who said that Rhoda was out and would not be back for some time. Then I had to wait for you here and tell you all about your father, so the thing slipped my memory. I have not been near the place since, but I'll go round there to-night. Whatever is Miss Greeb thinking of?" cried Lucian, breaking off quickly. "That front door bell has been ringing for at least five minutes!"

To Diana's amusement, Lucian went and shouted down the stairs to Miss Greeb, but as no reply came, and the bell was still ringing furiously, he was obliged to open the door himself. On the step there stood a little woman in a tailor-made brown frock, a plainly trimmed brown straw hat with a black gauze velvet-spotted veil. At once Denzil guessed who she was.

"You are Mrs. Clear?" he said, delighted that she had replied so quickly to his advertisement, for it had only that morning appeared in the newspapers.

"Yes, I am," answered the woman, in a quick, sharp voice. "Are you the L. D. who advertised for me?"

"Yes. Come upstairs. I have much to say to you."

"Diana," said Lucian, on entering the room with his prize, "let me introduce you to Mrs. Clear."

"Mrs. Clear! Are you the wife of the man who was murdered in the house opposite?"

Mrs. Clear uttered a cry of astonishment, and turned as if to retreat. But Denzil was between her and the door, so she saw that there was nothing for it but to outface the situation. As though she found it difficult to breathe, she threw up her veil, and Diana beheld a thin white face with two brilliant black eyes.

"This is a trap," said Mrs. Clear, hoarsely, looking from the one to the other. "Who are you?"

"I," said Lucian, politely, "I am the man who met your husband before -"

"My husband! I have my husband in an asylum. You can't have met him!"

"You are telling a falsehood," said Diana fiercely. "The gentleman in the asylum of Dr. Jorce is not your husband, but my father!"

"Your father? And who are you?"

"I am Diana Vrain."

Mrs. Clear gave a screech, and dropped back on to the sofa, staring at Diana with wide-open and terrified eyes.

"And now, Mrs. Clear, I see you realise the situation," Lucian said coldly. "You must confess your share in this conspiracy."

"What conspiracy?" she interrupted furiously.

"The putting of Mr. Vrain into an asylum, and the passing off of your husband, Michael Clear, as him."

"I don't know anything about it."

"Come, now, you talk nonsense! If you refuse to speak I'll have you arrested at once."

"Arrest me!" She bounded off the sofa with flashing eyes.

"Yes, on a charge of conspiracy. It is no use your getting angry, Mrs. Clear, for it won't improve your position. We - that is, this lady and myself - wish to know, firstly, how your husband came to be masquerading as Mr. Vrain; secondly, where we can find the man called Wrent, who employed your husband; and thirdly, Mrs. Clear, we wish to know, and the law wishes to know, who killed your husband."

"I don't know who killed him," said the woman, looking rather afraid, "but I believe Wrent did."

"Who is Wrent?"

"I don't know."

"You don't know many things," said Diana, taking part in the conversation, "but you must tell us what you do know, otherwise I shall call in a policeman and have you arrested."

"You can't prove anything against me."

"I think I can," said Lucian in the most cheerful manner. "I can prove that you were in No. 13 of this Square, seeing your husband, for I found on the fence dividing the back yard of that house from one in Jersey Street a scrap of a veil such as you wear. Also the landlady and servant can prove that you called on Mr. Wrent several times, and were with him on the night of the murder. Then there is the evidence of your cloak, which you left behind, and which Wrent gave to the servant

Rhoda. Also the evidence of Signor Ferruci -"

"Ferruci! What has he said about me?"

Lucian saw that revenge might make the woman speak, so he lied in the calmest manner to get at the truth. "Ferruci says that he contrived the whole conspiracy."

"So he did," said Mrs. Clear, with a nod.

"And took you to 'The Haven,' at Hampstead, on Christmas Eve."

"That's true. He took me from Wrent's house in Jersey Street. You need not go on, Mr. L. D. I admit the whole business."

"You do?" cried Lucian and Diana together.

"Yes, if only to spite that old villain Wrent, who has not paid me the money he promised."

Before Lucian and Miss Vrain could express their pleasure at Mrs. Clear coming to this sensible conclusion, the door opened suddenly, and little Miss Greeb, in a wonderful state of agitation, tripped in.

"Oh, Mr. Denzil! I've just been to Mrs. Bensusan's, and Rhoda's run away!"

"Run away!"

"Yes! She hasn't been back all day, and left a note for Mrs. Bensusan saying she was going to hide, because she was afraid."

CHAPTER XXVII

A CONFESSION

Now, indeed, Lucian had his hands full. Rhoda, the red-headed servant of Mrs. Bensusan, had run away on the plea that she was afraid of something - what she did not explain in the note she left behind her, and it was necessary that she should be discovered, and forced into confessing what she knew of the conspiracy and murder. Mrs. Clear, not having been paid her hush money, had betrayed the confidence and misdeeds of Ferruci, thereby revealing an extent of villainy for which neither Diana nor Lucian was prepared. Now the Count had to be seen and brought to book for his doings, Lydia informed that her husband was in the asylum, and Vrain himself had to be released in due form from his legal imprisonment. How Lucian, even with the assistance of Diana, could deal with all these matters, he did not know.

"Why not see Mr. Link?" suggested Diana, when Mrs. Clear had departed, after making a clean breast of the nefarious transactions in which she had been involved. "He may take the case in hand again."

"No doubt," responded Denzil drily, "but I am not very keen to hand it over to him, seeing that he has abandoned it twice. Again, if I call in the police, it is all over with Lydia and the Count. They will be arrested and punished."

"For the murder of Clear?"

"Perhaps, if it can be proved that they have anything to do with it; certainly for the conspiracy to get the assurance money by the feigned death of your father."

"Well," said Diana coldly, "and why should they not receive the reward of their deeds?"

"Quite so; but the question is, do you wish any scandal?"

Diana was silent. She had not looked at the matter from this point of view. It was true what Lucian said. If the police took up the case again, Lydia and her accomplice would be arrested, and the whole sordid story of their doings would be in the papers.

Diana was a proud woman, and winced at the idea of such publicity. It would be as well to avoid proceeding to such extremities. If the assurance money was returned by Lydia, she would be reduced to her former estate, and by timely flight might escape the vengeance of the defrauded company. After all, she was the wife of Vrain, and little as Diana liked her, she did not wish to see the woman who was so closely related to the wronged man put in prison; not for her own sake, but for the sake of the name she so unworthily bore.

"I leave it in your hands," said Diana to Lucian, who was watching her closely.

"Very good," replied Denzil. "Then I think it will be best for me to see Ferruci first, and hear his confession; afterwards call on Mrs. Vrain, and learn what she has to say. Then -"

"Well," said Diana, curiously, "what then?"

"I will be guided by circumstances. In the meantime, for the sake of your name, we had better keep the matter as quiet as possible."

"Mrs. Clear may speak out."

"Mrs. Clear won't speak," said Denzil grimly. "She will keep quiet for her own sake; and as Rhoda has left Jersey Street, there will be no danger of trouble from that quarter. First, I'll see Lydia and the Count, to get to the bottom of this conspiracy; then I'll set the police on Rhoda's track, that she may be arrested and made to confess her knowledge of the murder."

"Do you think she knows anything?"

"I think she knows everything," replied Lucian with emphasis. "That is why she has run away. If we capture her, and force her to speak, we may be able to arrest Wrent."

"Why Wrent?" asked Diana.

"Have you forgotten what Mrs. Clear said? I agree with her that he is the assassin, although we can't prove it as yet."

"But who is Wrent?"

"Ah!" said Lucian, significantly, "that is just what I wish to find out."

The upshot of this interview was that early the next morning Denzil went to the chambers of Ferruci, in Marquis Street, and informed the servant that he wanted particularly to see the Count.

At first the Italian, being still in bed - for he was a late riser – did not incline to grant his visitor an interview; but on second thoughts he ordered Lucian to be shown into the sitting-room, and shortly afterwards joined him there wrapped in a dressing-gown. He welcomed the barrister with a smiling nod, and having some instinct that Lucian came on an unpleasant errand, he did not offer him his hand. From the first the two men were on their guard against one another.

"Good-morning, sir," saidFerruci in his best English. "May I ask why you take me from my bed so early?"

"To tell you a story."

"About my friend Dr. Jorce saying I was with him on that night?" sneered the Count.

"Partly, and partly about a lady you know."

Ferruci frowned. "You speak of Mrs. Vrain?"

"No," replied Lucian coolly. "I speak of Mrs. Clear."

At the mention of this name, which was the last one he expected to hear his visitor pronounce, the Italian, in spite of his coolness and cunning, could not forbear a start.

"Mrs. Clear?" he repeated. "And what do you know of Mrs. Clear?"

"As much as Dr. Jorce could tell me, Count."

Ferruci's brow cleared. "Then you know I pay for keeping her miserable husband with my friend," he said composedly. "It is for her sake I am so kind."

"Rather it is for your own you are so cunning."

"Cunning! A most strange word for my goodness," said the Count coolly.

"The most fit word, you mean," replied Lucian, impatient of this fencing. "It is no use beating about the bush, Count. I know that the man you keep in the asylum is not Clear, but Mark Vrain."

"La! la! la! You talk great humbug. Mr. Vrain is dead and buried!"

"He is not dead," answered Lucian resolutely, "and the man who was buried under his name is Michael Clear, the husband of the woman who told me all."

Ferruci, who had been pacing impatiently up and down the room, stopped short, with a nervous laugh.

"This is most amusing," he said, with an emotion he could not conceal despite his self-control. "Mrs. Clear told you all, eh? She told you what, my friend?"

"That is the story I have come to tell you," replied Lucian sharply.

"Very good," said Ferruci, with a shrug. "I wait to hear this pretty story," and with a frown he threw himself into a chair near Lucian. Apparently he saw that he was found out, for it took him all his time to keep his voice from trembling and his hands from shaking. The man was not a coward, but being thus brought face to face with a peril he little expected, it was scarcely to be wondered at that he felt shaken and nervous. Moreover, he knew little about the English law, and hardly guessed how his misdeeds would be punished. Still, he did not surrender on the spot, but listened quietly to Lucian's story, in the hope of seeing some way of escape from his awkward position.

"The other day I went to Dr. Jorce's asylum," said Lucian slowly, "and there I discovered - it matters not how - that your friend Clear was Mr. Vrain; also I learned that he had been placed in the asylum by you and Mrs. Clear. Jorce gave me her address in Bayswater, but when I went there I could not find her; she had left. I then put an advertisement in all the papers, stating that if she called on me she would hear of something to her advantage. Now, Count, it appears that Mrs. Clear was in the habit of looking into the papers to see if there was any message from yourself, or your friend Wrent, so she saw my advertisement at once, and came in person to reply to it."

"One moment, Mr. Denzil," said Ferruci politely. "I know no one called Wrent, and he is not my friend."

"We'll come to that hereafter," answered Lucian, with a shrug. "In the meantime I'll proceed with my story, which I see interests you very much. Well, Count, it seems that Michael Clear was an actor, who bore a strong resemblance to Mr. Vrain, save that he had not a scar on his face. Vrain, at Bath, was always clean shaven; now he wears a long white beard, but that is neither here nor there. Clear had a moustache, but when that was shaved off he looked exactly like Vrain. For purposes of your own, which you can easily guess, you made the acquaintance of this man, a profligate and a drunkard, and proposed, for a certain sum of money to be paid to his wife, that he, Michael Clear, should personate Vrain and live in the Silent House in Geneva Square, under the name of Berwin. You knew that Clear was slowly dying of consumption and drink, so you trusted that he would die as Vrain; that Mrs. Vrain - who I believe is in the plot - would recognise the corpse by the description in the newspapers; and that, when Clear was buried as Vrain, she would get the assurance money and marry you."

"That is clever," said the Count, with a sneer.

"But is it true?"

"You know best," answered Lucian, coolly. "However, all turned out as you expected, for Clear died as Vrain - or rather was murdered at your command, as he did not die quickly enough - his body was recognised by Mrs. Vrain, buried as her husband, and she got the assurance money. The only thing that remains for your conspiracy to be entirely successful is that Mrs. Vrain should marry you; and - as I was told by Mr. Clyne - that has pretty well been arranged."

"Do you think, then, that Clyne would let his daughter marry a man who has done all this?" said Ferruci, who was now very pale.

"I don't believe Clyne knows anything about it," replied Lucian coldly. "You and Mrs. Vrain made up this pretty plot between you. Vrain himself told me how you decoyed him from Salisbury, and took him to Mrs. Clear's, in Bayswater, where he passed as her husband, although, as she confesses, she kept him as a kind of prisoner."

"But this is wrong," cried Ferruci, trying to laugh. "This is most foolish. How would a man, of his own will, pass as the husband of a woman he knew not?"

"A sane man would not; but none knew better than you, Count, that Vrain was not sane, and that you dosed him with drugs, and let Mrs. Clear keep him locked up in her house until you put him in the asylum. Vrain was a puppet in your hands, and you locked him up in an asylum a fortnight after the man who personated him was murdered. You intended to marry Mrs. Vrain and keep her wretched husband in that asylum all his life."

"The best place for a lunatic," said Ferruci.

"Ah!" cried Lucian. "Then you admit that that Vrain was mad?"

"I admit nothing, not even that he is alive. If what you say is true," said the Italian, cunningly, "how came it that the murdered man had the scar on his cheek? He might have been like Vrain, eh, but not so much."

"Mrs. Clear explained that," replied Lucian quickly. "You made that scar, Count, with vitriol, or some such stuff. You don't know chemistry for nothing, I see."

"I am quite ignorant of chemistry," said Ferruci sullenly.

"Jorce heard a different story in Florence."

"In Florence! Did Jorce ask about me there?" said the Count

in alarm.

"He did, and heard some strange tales, Count. Come, now, it is no use your trying to evade this matter further. Jorce can prove that you put Vrain into his asylum under the name of Clear. Miss Vrain can prove that the so-called Clear is her father, and Mrs. Clear - who has turned Queen's evidence - has exposed the whole of your conspiracy. The game's up, Count."

Ferruci sprang from his seat and began to walk hastily up and down the room. He looked haggard and pale, and years older, as he recognised his position, for he saw very plainly that he was trapped, and that nothing remained to him but flight. But how to fly? He stopped opposite to Lucian.

"What do you intend to do?" he demanded in a hoarse voice.

"Have you arrested, along with Mrs. Vrain," replied Lucian, making this threat to force Ferruci into defending himself or confessing.

"Mrs. Vrain is innocent - she knows nothing about this conspiracy, as you call it. I planned the whole thing myself."

"You admit, then, that the so-called Vrain was really Michael Clear?"

"Yes. I got him to personate the man Vrain, so that I could get the assurance money when I married Lydia. I chose Clear because he was like Vrain. I made the scar on the cheek, and I thought he would die soon, being consumptive."

"And you killed him?"

"No! No! I swear I did not kill him!"

"Did you not take that stiletto from Berwin Manor?"

"No! I never did! I am telling the truth! I do not know who killed Clear."

"Did you not visit Wrent in Jersey Street?"

"Yes. I was the man Rhoda saw in the back yard. I was waiting for Mrs. Clear, to take her to Hampstead; and in the meantime I thought I would climb over the fence and see Clear. But the girl saw me, so I ran away, and joined Mrs. Clear up the road. I was not aware at the time that the woman who saw me was Rhoda. Afterwards I went to Hampstead with Mrs. Clear, to see Jorce."

"Did you buy the cloak?"

"I did. That girl in Baxter & Co.'s told a lie for me. I was warned by Mrs. Vrain that you had made questions about the cloak, so I went to the girl and told her you were a jealous husband, and paid her to say it was not I who bought the cloak. She did so, quite ignorant of the real reason I wished her to deny knowing me."

"Why did you buy the cloak?" asked Lucian, satisfied with this explanation.

"I bought it for Wrent. He asked me to buy it, but what he wanted it for I do not know. He had it some days before Christmas, and, I believe, gave it to Mrs. Clear, and afterwards to the girl Rhoda. But of this I am not sure."

"Who is Wrent?" asked Denzil, reserving the most important question for the last.

"Wrent?" said Ferruci, smiling in a sneering way. "Ah! you wish to know who Wrent is? Well, excuse me for a few minutes, and I'll bring you something to show who he is."

With a nod to Lucian he passed into his bedroom, leaving the barrister much astonished. He thought that Ferruci was Wrent himself, and had gone away to resume the disguise of wig and beard. While he pondered thus the Count reappeared, carrying a small bottle in his hand.

"Mr. Denzil," said he, with a ghastly smile, "I have played a bold game, and, thanks to a woman's treachery, I have lost. I hoped to get twenty thousand pounds and a charming wife; but I have gained nothing but poverty and a chance of imprisonment; but I am of noble birth, and I will not survive my dishonour. You wish to know who Wrent is - you shall never know."

He raised the bottle to his lips before Lucian, motionless with horror, could rush forward, and the next moment Count Ercole Ferruci was lying dead on the floor.

CHAPTER XXVIII

THE NAME OF THE ASSASSIN

That afternoon London was ringing with the news of Ferruci's suicide; but no paper could give any reason for the rash act. This inability was due to the police, who, anxious to capture those concerned in the conspiracy to obtain the assurance money of the Sirius Company, kept everything they could out of the papers, lest Lydia and Wrent should be put on their guard, and so escape.

Lucian had been forced to report the death of Ferruci to the authorities. Now the case was out of his hands again, and in those of Link, who blamed the young barrister severely for not having brought him into the matter before. The detective was always more prone to blame than to praise.

"But what could I do?" cried Lucian angrily. "You threw up the case twice! You said the assassin of Clear - or, as you thought, Vrain - would never be discovered!"

"I did my best, and failed," retorted Link, who did not like his position. "You have had better luck and have succeeded."

"My luck has been sheer hard work, Link. I was not so faint-hearted as you, to draw back at the first check."

"Well, well, the whole truth hasn't been discovered yet, Mr. Denzil. As you have found out this conspiracy, I may learn who the assassin is."

"We know that already. The assassin is Wrent."

"You have yet to prove that."

"I?" said Lucian, with disdain. "I prove nothing. I wash my hands of the whole affair. You are a detective; let me see what you will make of a case which has baffled you twice!" and Denzil, with rage in his heart, went off, laughing at the discomfiture of Link.

At that moment the detective hated his successful rival with his whole heart.

Lucian took a hansom to the Royal John Hotel in Kensington, where Diana, in a great state of alarm, was reading the evening papers, which contained short notices of Ferruci's death. On seeing her lover, she hurried forward anxiously and caught him by the hand.

"Lucian, I am so glad you have come!" she cried, leading him to a chair. "I sent messages both to Geneva Square and Sergeant's Inn, but you were neither at your lodgings nor in your office."

"I was better employed, my dear," said Lucian, with a weary sigh, for he was quite worn out with fatigue and anxiety. "I have been with Link, telling him about Ferruci's death, and being blamed as the cause of it."

"You blamed! And why?" said Diana, with just indignation.

"Because I forced Ferruci to confess the truth, and when he saw that there was every chance of his being put into jail for his villainy, he went to his bedroom and took poison. You know, Mrs. Clear said the man was something of a chemist, so I suppose he prepared the poison himself. It was very swift in its action, for he dropped dead before I could recover my presence of mind."

"Lucian! this is terrible!" cried Diana, wringing her hands.

"You may well say that," he replied gloomily. "Now the whole details of the case will be in the papers, and that unfortunate woman will be arrested."

"Lydia! And what will her father say? It will break his heart!"

"Perhaps; but he must take the consequences of having brought up his daughter so badly. Still," added Lucian, reflectively, "I do not believe that Lydia is so guilty as Wrent. That scoundrel seems to be at the bottom of the affair. Ferruci and he contrived and carried out the whole thing between them, and a precious pair of villains they are."

"Will Wrent be arrested?"

"If he can be found; but I fancy the scoundrel has made himself scarce out of fright. Since he left Jersey Street, after the murder, he has not been heard of. Even Mrs. Clear does not know where he is. You know she has put advertisements in the papers in the cypher he gave her - according to the arrangement between them - but Wrent has not turned up."

"And Rhoda?"

"Rhoda is still missing. The police are getting warrants out for the servant, for Wrent, for Mrs. Clear, and for Lydia Vrain. Ferruci, luckily for himself and his family, has escaped the law by his own act. It was the wisest thing the scoundrel could do to kill himself and avoid dishonour. I must admit the man had pluck."

"It is terrible! terrible! What will be the end of it?"

"Imprisonment for the lot, I expect, unless they can prove that Wrent murdered Clear; then they will hang him. But now that

Fergus Hume

Ferruci is dead, I fancy Rhoda is the only witness who can prove Wrent's guilt. That is why she ran away. I don't wonder she was afraid to stay. But I feel quite worn out with all this, Diana. Please give me a biscuit and a glass of port; I have had nothing all day."

With a sigh, Diana touched the bell, and when the waiter made his appearance gave the order. She felt low-spirited and nervous, in spite of the discovery that her father was alive and well; and indeed the extraordinary events of the last few days were sufficient to upset the strongest mind.

Lucian was leaning back in his chair with closed eyes, for his head was aching with the excitement of the morning. Suddenly he opened them and jumped up. At the same time Diana threw open the door with an exclamation, and both of them heard the thin, high voice of a woman, who apparently was coming up the stairs.

"Never mind my name," said the voice, "I'll tell it to Miss Vrain myself. Take me to her at once."

"Lydia!" called Lucian, "and here? Great heavens! Why does she come here?"

Diana said nothing, but compressed her lips as Lydia, followed by the waiter with the biscuits and wine, came into the room. She was plainly and neatly dressed, and wore a heavy veil, but seemed greatly excited. She did not say a word, nor did Diana, until the waiter left the room and closed the door. Then she threw up her veil, revealing a haggard face and red eyes, swollen with weeping, and filled with an expression of terror.

"Sakes alive! isn't this awful?" she wailed, making a clutch at Miss Vrain's arm. "You've done it, this time, Diana. Ferruci's dead, and your father alive, and I'm not a widow, and my father away I don't know where! I was told that the police were after me, so I'm clearing out."

"Clearing out, Mrs. Vrain?" repeated Diana, stiffly.

"I should think so!" sobbed Lydia. "I don't want to stay and be put in gaol, though what I've done to be put in gaol for, I don't know."

"What?" cried Lucian indignantly. "You don't know - when this abominable conspiracy is -"

"I know nothing of the conspiracy," interrupted Lydia.

"Did you not get Ferruci to put your husband into an asylum?"

"I? I did nothing of the sort. I thought my husband was dead and buried until Ferruci told me the truth, and then I held my tongue until I could think of what to do. After Ercole died, his servant came round and told me all - he overheard the conversation you had with the Count, Mr. Denzil. I was never so astonished in my life as to hear about Mrs. Clear and her husband - and Mark alive - and - and - oh, Lord! isn't it dreadful? Give me a glass of wine, Diana, or I'll go right off in a dead faint!"

In silence Miss Vrain poured out a glass of port and handed it to her stepmother, who sipped it in a most tearful mood. Lucian looked at the wretched little woman without saying a word, and wondered if, indeed, she was as innocent as she made herself out to be. He thought that, after all, she might be ignorant of Ferruci's plots, although she had certainly benefited by them; but she was such a glib liar that he did not know how much to believe of her story. However, she had hitherto only given a general idea of her connection with the matter, so when she had finished her wine, and was somewhat calmer, Lucian begged her to be more explicit.

"Did you know - did you guess, or even suspect - that your husband was alive?"

"Mr. Denzil," said Lydia, with unusual solemnity, "as I'm a married woman, and not the widow I thought I was, I did not know that Mark was alive! I'm bad, I daresay, but I am not bad enough to shut a man up in a lunatic asylum and pretend he is dead, just to get money, much as I like it. What I did about identifying the corpse was done in good faith."

"You really thought it was my father's body?" questioned Diana doubtfully.

"I swear I did," responded Mrs. Vrain, emphatically. "Mark walked out of the house because he thought I was carrying on with Ferruci, which I wasn't. It was that Tyler cat who made the trouble between us, and Mark was so weak and silly - half crazy, I think, with his morphia and over-study - that he cleared right out, and I never knew where he had gone to. When I saw that notice about the murdered man in Geneva Square, who called himself Berwin, and was marked on the cheek, I thought he might be my husband. When the coffin was opened, I really believed I saw poor Mark's dead body. The face was just like his, and scarred in the same way."

"What about the missing finger, Mrs. Vrain? If I remember, you even gave a cause for its loss."

"Well, it was this way," replied Lydia, somewhat discomposed. "I knew that Mark hadn't lost a finger when he left, but Ferruci said that if I denied it the police might refuse to believe that the body was that of my husband. So, as I was sure it was Mark's corpse, I just said he had lost a finger out West. I didn't think there was any harm in saying so, as for all I knew he might have got it chopped off after leaving me. But the face of the dead man was - as I thought - Mark's, and he called himself Berwin, which, you know, Diana, is the name of the Manor, and the scar was on the cheek. I know now it was all contrived by Ercole; but then I was quite ignorant."

"When did you find out the truth?"

"After that cloak business. Ferruci came to me, and I told him what that girl at Baxter's had said, and insisted that he should tell me the truth. Well, he did, in order to force me to marry him, and then I told him to go and make it right with the girl, so that when Mr. Denzil went again she'd deny that Ercole had bought the cloak."

"She denied it, sure enough," said Lucian grimly. "Ferruci, before he died, told me he had bribed her to speak falsely. What more did the Count reveal to you, Mrs. Vrain? - the conspiracy?"

"Yes. He said he'd found Mark hiding at Salisbury, half mad with morphia, and had taken him up to Mrs. Clear's, where it seems he went mad altogether, so they locked him up as her husband in a lunatic asylum. Ferruci also told me that he had seen Michael Clear on the stage, and that as he was so like Mark, and was likely to die of drink and consumption, he got him to play the part of Mark in Geneva Square, under the name of Berwin. Mrs. Clear visited her husband there by climbing over a back fence, and getting down a cellar, somehow."

"I know that," said Lucian. "It was Mrs. Clear's shadow I saw on the blind. She was fighting with her husband, and when I rang the bell they were both so alarmed that they left the house by the back way and got into Jersey Street. Then Mrs. Clear went home, and the man himself came round into the Square by the front way. That was how I met him. I wondered how people were in the house during his absence. Mrs. Clear told me all."

"Did she say why her husband made you examine the house?" asked Diana.

"No. But I expect he made me do so that I should not have my suspicions about that back entrance. But, Mrs. Vrain, when Ferruci confessed that your husband was alive, why did you not tell it to the world?"

"Well, I'd got the assurance money, you see," said Lydia, with shrewd candour, "and I thought the company would make a fuss and take it back - as I suppose they will now. Ferruci wanted me to marry him, but I wasn't so bad as that. I did not want to commit bigamy. But I really held my tongue because Ferruci told me who killed Clear."

"He knew, then?" cried Lucian, "and denied it to me! Who killed the man?"

"Wrent did - the man who lived in Jersey Street."

"And who is at the bottom of the whole plot!" said Lucian furiously. "Do you know where he is to be found?"

"Yes," said Lydia boldly, "I do; but I'm not going to tell where he is!"

"Why not?"

"Because I don't want him punished."

"But I do," said Diana angrily. "He is a wretch who ought to suffer!"

"Very well," said Lydia, loudly and spitefully, "then make him suffer, for this Wrent is your own father! It was Mark who killed Michael Clear!"

CHAPTER XXIX

LINK SETS A TRAP

In the course of their acquaintance, Diana had put up with a great deal from the little American adventuress, owing to her position of stepmother, but when she heard her accusing the man she had ruined of murder, the patience of Miss Vrain gave way. She rose quickly, and walking over to where Lydia was shrinking in her chair, towered in righteous indignation above the shameless little woman.

"You lie, Mrs. Vrain!" she said in a low, distinct voice, with a flushed face and indignation in her eyes. "You know you lie!"

"I - I only repeat what Ferruci told me," whimpered Lydia, rather alarmed by the attitude of her stepdaughter. "I'm sure I hope Mark didn't kill the man, but Ercole said that he was in Jersey Street for that purpose."

"It is not true! My father was in the asylum at Hampstead!"

"Indeed he wasn't - not at the time Clear was killed!" protested Lydia. "He was not put into the asylum until at least two weeks after Christmas. Is that not so, Mr. Denzil?"

"It is so," assented Lucian gravely, "but even admitting so much, it is impossible to believe that Mr. Vrain was in Jersey Street. For many months before Christmas he was in charge of Mrs. Clear, at Bayswater."

"So Ercole said," replied Lydia, "but he used to get away from Mrs. Clear at times, and had to be brought back."

"He wandered when he got the chance," said Lucian, with hesitation. "I admit as much."

"Well, then, when he was not at Bayswater he used to live in Jersey Street as Wrent. Ferruci found him out there, and tried to get him to go back, and he took Mrs. Clear several times to the same place in order to persuade him to return to Bayswater. That was why Mrs. Clear visited Jersey Street. Oh, Mark played his part there as Mr. Wrent, I guess; there ain't no two questions about that," finished Lydia triumphantly. "He is the assassin, you bet!"

"I don't believe it!" cried Diana furiously. "Why, my father is too weak in the head to have the will, let alone the courage, to masquerade like that. He is like a child in leading-strings."

"That's his cunning, Diana. He's 'cute enough to pretend madness, so that he won't be hanged!"

"It is impossible that Vrain can be Wrent," said Lucian decidedly. "I agree with Miss Vrain; he is too weak and irresponsible to carry out such a deed. Besides, I don't see how you prove him guilty of the murder; you do not even know that he could enter the Silent House by the secret way."

"I don't know anything about it, except what Count Ferruci told me,"
said Lydia obstinately. "And he said that Vrain, as Wrent, killed Clear.
But you can easily prove if it's true or not."

"How can we prove it?" asked Diana coldly.

"By laying a trap for Mark. You know - at least Ercole told me, and I suppose Mrs. Clear told you - that she corresponded with Mark - Wrent, I mean – in the agony column of the

"By means of a cypher? Yes, I know that, but she hasn't received any answer yet."

"Of course not," replied Lydia, with triumph, "because Wrent - that's Mark, you know - is in the asylum, and can't answer her."

"This is all nonsense!" broke in Lucian, impatient of this cobweb spinning. "I don't believe a word of Ferruci's story. If Vrain lived in Jersey Street as Wrent, why should Mrs. Clear visit him?"

"To get him back to Bayswater."

"Nonsense! nonsense! And even admitting as much, why should Mrs. Clear, in the newspapers, correspond in cypher with a man whom she not only knows is in an asylum as her husband, but who can be seen by her at any time?"

"I quite agree with you, Lucian," cried Diana emphatically. "Count Ferruci told a pack of falsehoods to Mrs. Vrain! The thing is utterly absurd!"

"Oh, I guess I'm not so easily made a fool of as all that!" cried Lydia, firing up. "If you don't believe me, lay the trap I told you of. Let Mark go free out of the asylum; get Mrs. Clear, with her cypher and newspapers, to ask him to meet her in the house where Clear was murdered, and then you'll see if Mark won't turn up in his character of Wrent."

"He will not!" cried Diana vehemently. "He will not!"

"Mark, when he left me," went on the angry Lydia, "had plenty of hair, and was clean shaven. Now - as Ferruci told me, for I haven't seen him - he is bald, and wears a skull-cap of black velvet, and a white beard. After Ercole told me about Jersey Street I went there to ask that fat woman about Mark;

she said he had gone away two days after Christmas, and described him as an old man with a skull-cap and a white beard."

"Oh!" cried Lucian, for he recollected that Rhoda gave the same description.

"Ah! you know I speak the truth!" said Lydia, rising, "but I've had enough of all this. I've lost my money, and I don't suppose I'll go back to Mark. I've been treated badly all round, and I don't know what poppa will say. But I'm going out of London to meet him."

"You said you did not know where your father was!" cried Diana scornfully.

"I don't tell you everything, Diana," retorted Lydia, looking very wicked, "but, if you must know, poppa went over to Paris last week, and I'm going over there to meet him. He'll raise Cain for the way I've been treated."

"Well," said Lucian, as she prepared to take her leave, "I hope you'll get away."

"Do you intend to stop me, Mr. Denzil?" flashed out Mrs. Vrain, furiously.

"Not I; but I'll give you a hint - the railway stations will be watched by the police."

"For me?" said Lydia, with a scared expression. "Oh, sakes! it's awful! and I've done nothing. It's not my fault if I got the assurance money. I really thought that Mark was dead. But I'll try and get away to poppa; he'll put things right. Good-bye, Mr. Denzil, and Diana; you've done me a heap of harm, but I don't bear malice," and Mrs. Vrain rushed out of the room in a great hurry to escape the chance of arrest hinted at by Lucian. She had a sharp eye to her own safety.

Diana waited until the cab which Lydia had kept waiting was driving away, and then turned with an anxious expression on her face to look at Lucian. "My dear," she said, taking his arm, "what do you think of Lydia's accusation?"

"Against your father?" said Lucian. "Why, I don't believe it!"

"Nor do I; but it will be as well to set the trap she suggests; for if my father does not fall into it - and as he is not Wrent, I don't believe he will - the real man may keep the appointment with Mrs. Clear."

"Whosoever Wrent is, I don't think he'll come again to the Silent House," replied the barrister, shaking his head. "It would be thrusting his head into the lion's jaws. If he is in London he'll see the death of Ferruci described in the papers, and no doubt will guess that the game is up; so he'll keep away."

"Nevertheless, we'll do as Lydia suggests," said Diana obstinately. "You see Mr. Link and Mrs. Clear, and arrange about the cypher. Then my father is to be discharged as cured to-morrow, and I'll let him go out if he pleases. Of course, I'll follow him; then I'll be able to see if he goes to Pimlico."

"But, Diana, suppose he does go to the Silent House, and proves to be Wrent?"

"He won't do that, my dear. My father is no more Wrent than you are. I believe Lydia speaks in the full belief that he is; but Ferruci, for his own ends, lied to her. However, to trap the real man, let us do as Lydia suggests. The idea is a good one."

"Well, we'll try," said Lucian, with a sigh. "But I do hope, Diana, that this case will end soon. Every week there is some fresh development in a new direction, and I am getting quite bewildered over it."

"It will end with the capture of Wrent, the assassin."

"I hope so; and God grant Wrent does not prove to be your father!"

"There is no fear of that," said Diana gravely. "My father is insane more or less, but he is not a murderer. I am quite content to risk the trap suggested by that woman."

Lucian did not at once adopt the plan to net Wrent - whosoever he might be - invented by Lydia, and approved of by Diana. On the whole, he could not bring himself to believe that a weak-headed, foolish old creature like Vrain had masqueraded in Jersey Street as Wrent. Still there were certain suspicious incidents which fitted in very neatly with Ferruci's story. Mrs. Clear had stated that Vrain, when under her charge, escaped several times, and had remained away for several days, until brought back again by the Count. Again, the appearance of Wrent, as described by Rhoda, was precisely the same as the looks of Vrain when Lucian saw him in the Hampstead asylum; so it seemed that there might be some truth in the story.

"But it's impossible!" said Lucian to himself. "Vrain is half mad and incapable of conducting his own life, or arranging so cleverly to commit a crime. Also he had no money, and, had he lived in Jersey Street, would not have been able to pay Mrs. Bensusan. There is something more in the coincidence of this similarity of looks than meets the eye. I'll see Link and hear what he has to say on the subject. It's time he found out something."

The next day Lucian paid a visit to Link, but was not received very amiably by that gentleman, who proved to be in a somewhat bad temper. He was not altogether pleased with Lucian finding out more about the case than he had discovered himself, and also - to further ruffle his temper - the clever Lydia had given him the slip. He had called at her Mayfair house with a warrant for her arrest, only to find out that - having received timely warning from Ferruci's servant - she had fled. In vain the railway stations had been watched. Lydia, taking the hint given to her by Lucian, had baffled that peril by taking the Dover train at a station outside London.

Lucian heard what Link had to say on the subject, but did not reveal the fact that Lydia had paid a visit to Diana, or had gone to meet her father at Dover. He did not want to give the little woman up to justice, as he was beginning to believe her innocent; and that, in all truth, she had known nothing of the Ferruci-Wrent conspiracy.

Therefore, giving no information to Link as to the little woman's whereabouts, Denzil told - as coming from himself - his idea that Wrent might fall into a trap set for him in the Pimlico House by means of Mrs. Clear's cypher. Link listened to the tale attentively, and decided to adopt the idea.

"It is a good one," he admitted generously, "and I'm not jealous enough to cut off my nose to spite my face. You have had the better of me all through this case, Mr. Denzil, and we have had words over it; but I'll show you that I can appreciate your cleverness by adopting your plan."

"I am greatly obliged to you for your good opinion," said Lucian drily, for he saw with some humour that Link was only too anxious to benefit by the very cleverness of which he pretended to be so jealous. "And you will see Mrs. Clear?"

"Yes; I'll see her at once, and get her to invite Wrent to Pimlico by that cypher, with a threat that she will betray the whole plot if he does not come."

"I daresay he knows already that Mrs. Clear is a traitress?"

"Impossible!" replied Link quickly. "I have kept Mrs. Clear's name out of the papers. It is known that Ferruci is dead, and that Mrs. Vrain is likely to be arrested in connection with her supposed husband's murder. But the fact of Mrs. Clear putting the real Vrain into the asylum is not known, nor, indeed, anything about the woman. If Wrent thinks she'll tell tales,

Fergus Hume

he'll meet her in their own hunting grounds in Geneva Square, to make his terms. Hitherto he has not replied to her requests for money, but now he'll think she is driven into a corner, and will fix her up once and for all."

"Do you think that Wrent is Vrain?"

"Good Lord! no!" replied Link, staring. "What put that into your head?"

Lucian immediately told about the supposed connection between Vrain and Wrent, but, suppressing that it was Lydia's or Ferruci's idea, based his supposition on the fact of the resemblance between the two men. Link heard the theory with scorn, and scouted the idea that the two men could be one and the same.

"I've seen Vrain," said he. "The old man is as mad as a March hare and as silly as a child. He's in his dotage, and could not possibly carry out such a plan. But we can easily learn the truth."

"From whom?" asked Lucian.

"Ah, Mr. Denzil, you are not so clever as you think yourself," scoffed Link. "Why, from Mrs. Clear, to be sure. She visited at Jersey Street, and saw Wrent, and as Vrain was then with her in the character of her husband, she'll be able to tell us if they are two men or one person."

"You are right, Link. I never thought of that."

"He! he! Then I can still teach you something," replied Link, in high good humour at having for once scored off the too clever barrister, and forthwith went off to see Mrs. Clear.

How this interview with that lady sped, or what she told him, he refused to reveal to Lucian; but its result was that a cypher appeared in the agony column of the *Daily Telegraph*, calling upon Wrent to meet her in the Silent House in Pimlico, under the penalty of her telling the police all she knew if he did not come. In the same issue of the paper in which this message appeared there was a paragraph stating that Mrs. Vrain had been arrested at Dover.

CHAPTER XXX

WHO FELL INTO THE TRAP?

However closely one may study the fair sex, there is no understanding them in the least. No one can say how a woman will act in a given situation; for feminine actions are based less on logical foundations than on the emotion of the moment.

Diana had never liked Lydia; when the American girl became her stepmother she hated her, and not only said as much but showed in her every action that she believed what she said. She declared that she would be glad to see Lydia deprived of her money and put into jail! The punishment would be no more than she deserved.

Yet when these things came to pass; when, by the discovery that Vrain yet lived, Lydia lost her liberty; and when, as connected with the conspiracy, she was arrested on a criminal warrant and put into prison, Diana was the only friend she had. Miss Vrain declared that her stepmother was innocent, visited her in prison, and engaged a lawyer to defend her. Lucian could not forbear pointing out the discrepancy between Diana's past sentiments and her present actions; but Miss Vrain was quite ready with an excuse.

"I am only doing my duty," she said. "In herself I like Lydia as little as ever I did, but I think we have suspected her wrongly in being connected with this conspiracy, so I wish to help her if possible. And after all," added Diana, " she is my father's wife," as if that fact extenuated all.

"He has reason to know it," replied Lucian bitterly. "If it had not been for Lydia, your father would not have left his home for a lunatic asylum, nor would Clear have been murdered."

"I quite agree with you, Lucian; but some good has come out of this evil, for if things had not been as they are, you and I would never have met."

"Egad! that is true!" said Lucian, kissing her. "It's an ill wind that blows nobody any good."

So Diana played the part of a Good Samaritan towards her stepmother, and helped her to bear the evil of being thrust into prison. Lydia wrote to her father in Paris, but received no reply, and therefore was without a friend in the world save Diana. Later on she was admitted to bail, and Diana took her to the hotel in Kensington, there to wait for the arrival of Mr. Clyne. His absence and silence were both unaccountable.

"I hope nothing is wrong with poppa," wept Lydia. "As a rule, he is always smart in replying, and if he has seen about Ercole's death and my imprisonment in the papers, I'm sure he will be over soon."

While she was thus waiting for her father, and Link in every way was seeking evidence against her, Mrs. Clear received an answer to her message. In the same column of the *Daily Telegraph*, and in the same cypher, there appeared a message from Wrent that he would meet Mrs. Clear at No. 13 Geneva Square.

Link was delighted when Mrs. Clear showed him this, and rubbed his hands with much pleasure. Affairs were about to be brought to a crisis, and as Link was the moving spirit in the matter, his vanity was sufficiently gratified as to make him quite amiable.

"We've got him this time, Mr. Denzil," he said, with enthusiasm. "You and I and a couple of policemen will go down to that house in Geneva Square - by the front, sir, by the front."

"Mrs. Clear, also?" questioned Lucian, wishing to be enlightened on all points.

"No. She'll come in by the back, down the cellarway, as Wrent expects her to come. Then he'll follow in the same path and walk right into the trap."

"But won't the two be seen climbing over that fence in the daytime?" asked the barrister doubtfully.

"Who said anything about the daytime, Mr. Denzil? I did not, and Wrent knows too much to risk himself at a time that he can be seen from the windows of the adjacent houses. No! no! The meeting with Mrs. Clear is to take place in the front room at ten o'clock, when it will be quite dark. You, I, and the policemen will hide in what was the bedroom, and listen to what Wrent has to say to Mrs. Clear. We'll give him rope enough to hang himself, sir, and then pounce out and nab him."

"Well, he won't show much fight if he is Mr. Vrain."

"I don't believe he is Mr. Vrain," retorted the detective bluntly.

"I am doubtful of that, also," admitted Lucian, "but you know Vrain is now out of the asylum, and, for the time being, has been left to his own devices. The reply to the cypher did not appear until he was in that position. Supposing, after all, this mysterious Wrent proves to be this unhappy man?"

"In that case, he'll have to pay for his whistle, sir."

"You mean in connection with the conspiracy?"

"Yes, and perhaps with the murder of Clear; but we don't know if the so-called Wrent committed the crime. For such reason, Mr. Denzil, I wish to overhear what he says to Mrs. Clear. It is as well to give him enough rope to hang himself with."

"Can you trust Mrs. Clear?"

"Absolutely. She knows on which side her bread is buttered. Her only chance of getting free from her share of the matter is to turn Queen's evidence, and she intends to do so."

"What did she say about Vrain being Wrent?"

"Well, sir," said Link, putting his head on one side, and looking at Lucian with an odd expression, "you had better wait till the man's caught before I answer that question. Then, maybe, you won't require an answer."

"It is very probable I won't," replied Lucian drily. "What time am I to see you to-night?"

"I'll call for you at nine o'clock sharp, and we'll go across to the house at once. I have the key in my pocket now. Peacock gave it to me this morning. The scene will be quite dramatic."

"I hope it won't prove to be Vrain," said Lucian restlessly, for he thought how grieved Diana would be.

"I hope not," answered Link curtly, "but there's no knowing. However, if the old man does get into trouble he can plead insanity. His having been in the asylum of Jorce is a strong card for him to play. Good-day, Mr. Denzil. I'll see you to-night at nine o'clock sharp."

"Good-day," replied Lucian, and the pair parted for the time being.

Lucian did not go near Diana that day. In the first place, he did not wish to see Lydia, for whom he had no great love; and in the second, he was afraid to speak to Diana as to the possibility of her father being Wrent.

Diana, as a good daughter should, held firmly to the idea that her father could not behave in such a way; and as a sensible woman, she did not think that a man with so few of his senses about him could have acted the dual part with which he was credited without, in some measure, betraying himself.

Lucian was somewhat of this opinion himself, yet he had an uneasy feeling that Vrain might prove to be the culprit. The fact of Vrain's being often away from Mrs. Clear's house in Bayswater, and Wrent absent in the same way from Mrs. Bensusan's house in Jersey Street, appeared strange, and argued a connection between the two. Again, the resemblance between them was most extraordinary and unaccountable.

On the whole, Lucian was not satisfied in his mind as to what would be the end of the matter, and had he known Mrs. Clear's address he would have gone to question her about it. But only Link knew where the woman was to be found, and kept that information to himself - especially from Denzil. Now that he had the reins once more in his hands, he did not intend that the barrister should take them again.

Punctual to the minute, Link, in a state of subdued excitement, came to Lucian's rooms. Already he had sent his two policemen over to the house, into which he had instructed them to enter in the quietest and most unostentatious manner, and now came to escort the barrister across.

Lucian put on his hat at once, and the two walked out into the dark night, for dark it was, with no moon, few stars, and a great many clouds. A most satisfactory night for their purpose.

"All the better," said Link, casting a look round the deserted square; "all the better for our little game. I wish to secure this fellow as quietly as possible. Here's the door open - in with you, Mr. Denzil!"

According to instructions, a policeman had waited behind the closed door, and at the one sharp knock of his superior opened it at once so that the two slipped in as speedily as possible. Link had a dark-lantern, which he used carefully, so that no light could be seen from the window looking on to the square; and with his three companions he went into the back room which had formerly been used by Clear as a sleeping apartment. Here the two policemen stationed themselves in one corner; and Link, with Lucian, waited near the door leading into the sitting-room, so as to be ready for Mrs. Clear.

All was so dark and lonely and silent that Lucian's nerves became over-strained, and it was as much as he could do to prevent himself from trembling violently. In a whisper he conversed with Link.

"Have you heard anything of that girl Rhoda?" he asked.

"We have traced her to Berkshire," whispered Link. "She went back to her gypsy kinsfolk, you know. I dare say we'll manage to lay hands on her sooner or later."

"She is an accomplice of Wrent's, I believe."

"So do I, and I hope to make him confess as much to-night. Hush!"

Suddenly Link had laid his clasp on Lucian's wrist to command silence, and the next moment they heard the swish-swish of a woman's dress coming along the passage. She entered the sitting-room cautiously, moving slowly in the darkness, and stole up to the door behind which Lucian and the detective were hiding. The position of this she knew well, because it was opposite the window.

"Are you there?" whispered Mrs. Clear nervously.

"Yes," replied Link in the same tone. "Myself, Mr. Denzil, and two policemen. Keep the man in talk, and find out, if possible, if he committed the murder."

"I hope he won't kill me," muttered Mrs. Clear. "He will, if he knows I've betrayed him."

"That will be all right," said Link in a low, impatient voice. "We will rush out should he prove dangerous. Get over by the window, so that we can see a little of you and Wrent when you talk."

"No! no! Don't leave the door open! He'll see you!"

"He won't, Mrs. Clear. We'll keep back in the darkness. If he shows a light, we'll rush him before he can use a weapon or clear out. Get back to the window!"

"I hope I'll get through with this all right," said Mrs. Clear nervously. "It's an awful situation," and she moved stealthily across the floor to the window.

There was a faint gaslight outside, and the watchers could see her figure and profile black against the slight illumination. All was still and silent as the grave when they began their dreary watch.

The minutes passed slowly in the darkness, and there was an unbroken silence save for the breathing of the watchers and the restless movements of Mrs. Clear near the window. They saw her pass and repass the square of glass, when, unexpectedly, she paused, rigid and silent.

A stealthy step was ascending the distant stair, and pacing cat-like along the passage.

Lucian felt a tremor pass through his body as the steps of the murderer sounded nearer and clearer. They paused at the door, and then moved towards the window where Mrs. Clear was standing.

"Is that you?" said a low voice, which came weirdly out of the darkness.

"Yes. I have been waiting for the last half hour, Mr. Wrent," replied the woman in nervous tones. "I am glad you have come."

"I am glad, also," said the voice harshly, "as I wish to know why you propose to betray me."

"Because you won't pay me the money," said Mrs. Clear boldly. "And if you don't give it to me this very night I'll go straight and tell the police all about my husband."

"I'll kill you first!" cried the man with a snarl, and made a dash at the woman. With a cry for help she eluded him and sprang towards the bedroom door for protection. The next moment the four watchers were in the room wrestling with Wrent. When he felt the grip of their hands, and knew that he was betrayed, he cried out savagely, and fought with the strength of two men. However, he could do little against his four adversaries, and, worn out with the struggle, collapsed suddenly on to the dusty floor with a motion of despair.

"Lost! lost!" he muttered. "All lost!"

Breathing hard, Link slipped back the cover of the dark lantern and turned the light on to the face of the prisoner. Out of the darkness started a pale face with white hair and long white beard. Lucian uttered a cry.

"Mr. Vrain!" he said, shrinking back, "Mr. Vrain!"

"Look again," said Link, passing his hand rapidly over the face and head of the prostrate man. Denzil did look, and uttered a second cry more startling than the first. Wig and beard and venerable looks were all gone, and he recognised at once who

Fergus Hume

Wrent was.

"Jabez Clyne! - Jabez Clyne!" he exclaimed in astonishment.

"Yes!" cried Link triumphantly, "Jabez Clyne, conspirator and assassin!"

CHAPTER XXXI

A STRANGE CONFESSION

"I, Jabez Clyne, write this confession in my prison cell, of my own free will, and without coercion from any one; partly because I know that the evidence concerning my share in the Vrain conspiracy is strong against me, and partly because I wish to exonerate my daughter Lydia.

"She is absolutely innocent of all knowledge concerning the feigned death of her husband and his actual existence in a private lunatic asylum; and on the strength of this confession of mine - which will fix the guilt of the matter on the right persons - I demand that she shall be set free. It is not fair that she should suffer, for I and Ferruci planned and carried out the whole conspiracy. Well, Ferruci has punished himself, and soon the law will punish me, so it is only justice that Lydia should be discharged from all blame. On this understanding I set out the whole story of the affair - how it was thought of, how it was contrived, and how it was carried out. Now that Count Ferruci is dead, this confession can harm no one but myself, and may be the means of setting Lydia free. So here I begin my recital.

"I was always an unlucky man, and the end of my life proves to be as unfortunate as the beginning. I was born in London some fifty and more years ago, in a Whitechapel slum, of drunken and profligate parents, so it is little to be wondered at that my career has been anything but virtuous or respectable.

In my early childhood - if it may be called so - I was beaten and starved, set to beg, forced to thieve, and never had a kind word said to me or a kind deed done to me. No wonder I grew up a callous, hardened ruffian. As the twig is bent, so will the tree grow.

"Out of this depth of degradation I was rescued by a philanthropist, who had me fed and clothed and educated. I had at his hands every chance of leading a respectable life, but I did not want to become smug and honest. My early training was too strong for that, so after a year or two of enforced goodness I ran away to sea. The vessel I embarked on as a stowaway was bound for America. When I was discovered hiding among the cargo we were in mid-ocean, and there was nothing for it but to carry me to the States. Still, to earn my passage, I was made cabin-boy to a ruffianly captain, and once more tasted the early delights of childhood, viz., kicks, curses, and starvation. When the ship arrived in New York I was turned adrift in the city without a penny or a friend.

"It is not my purpose to describe my sufferings, as such description will do no good and interest nobody; particularly as the purpose of this confession is to declare the Vrain conspiracy and its failure; so I will pass over my early years as speedily as possible. To be brief: I became a newsboy, then a reporter; afterwards I went West and tried my luck in San Francisco, later on in Texas; but in every case I failed, and became poorer and more desperate than ever. In New Orleans I set up a newspaper and had a brief time of prosperity, when I married the daughter of a hotelkeeper, and for the time was happy.

"Then the Civil War broke out, and I was ruined. My wife died, leaving me with one child, whom I called Lydia, after her, but that child died also, and I was left alone. After the war I prospered again for a time, and married a woman with money. She also died, and left a daughter, and this child I again called Lydia, in memory of my first wife, who was the only woman I ever truly loved. I placed little Lydia in a convent for education, and devoted my second wife's money to that purpose; then I started out for the fifth or sixth time to make my fortune. Needless to say, I did not make it.

"I pass over a long period of distress and prosperity, hopes and fears. One day I was rich, the next poor; and Fate - or whatever malignant deity looked after my poor affairs - knocked me about most cruelly, tossed me up, threw me down, and at the end of a score of years left me comparatively prosperous, with an income, in English money, of L500 a year. With this I returned to Washington to seek Lydia, and found her grown up into a beautiful and clever girl. Her beauty gave me the idea that I might marry her well in Europe as an American heiress. So for Europe we started, and after many years of travel about the Continent we settled down in the Pension Donizetti in Florence. There Lydia was admired for her beauty and wit, and courted for her money! But save for my ten pounds a week, which we eked out in the most frugal manner, we had not a penny between us.

"It was in Florence that we met with Vrain and his daughter, who came to stay at the Pension. He was a quiet, harmless old gentleman, a trifle weak in the head, which his daughter said came from over-study, but which I discovered afterwards was due to habitual indulgence in morphia and other drugs. His daughter watched him closely, and - not having a will of his own by reason of his weak brain - he submitted passively to her guidance. I heard by a side wind that Vrain was rich, and had a splendid mansion in the country; so I hinted to Lydia that as it seemed difficult to get her a young husband, it would be better for her to marry a rich old one. At that time Lydia was in love with, and almost engaged to, Count Ercole Ferruci, a penniless Italian nobleman, who courted my pretty girl less for her beauty than for her supposed wealth. When I suggested that Lydia should marry Vrain, she refused at first to entertain the idea; but afterwards, seeing that the man was old and weak, she thought it would be a good thing as his wife to inherit his money, and then, as his widow, to marry Ferruci. I think, also, that the pointed dislike which Diana Vrain manifested for us both - although I am bound to say she hated Lydia more than she did me - had a great deal to do with my daughter marrying Vrain. However, the end of it was that Lydia broke off her engagement with Ferruci - and very mad he was at losing her - and married Mark Vrain in Florence.

"After the marriage the old man, who at that time was quite infatuated with Lydia, made a will leaving her his assurance money of L20,000, but the house near Bath, and the land, he left to Diana. I am bound to say that Lydia behaved very well in this matter, as she could have had all the money and land, but she was content with the assurance money, and did not rob Diana Vrain of her birthright. Yet Diana hated her, and still hates her; but I ask any one who reads this confession if my dear Lyddy is not the better woman of the two? Who dares to say that such a sweet girl is guilty of the crimes she is charged with?

"Well, the marriage took place, and we all journeyed home to Berwin Manor; but here things went from bad to worse. Old Vrain took again to his morphia, and nothing would restrain him; then Lydia and Diana fought constantly, and each wished the other out of the house. I tried to keep the peace, and blamed Lyddy - who is no saint, I admit - for the way in which she was treating Diana. With Miss Vrain I got on very well, and tried to make things easy for her; but in the end the ill-will between her and my Lydia became so strong that Diana left the house, and went out to Australia to live with some relatives.

"So Lydia and I and old Vrain were left alone, and I thought that everything would be right. So it would have been if Lydia had not put matters wrong again by inviting Ferruci over to stay. But she would insist upon doing so, and although I begged and prayed and commanded her not to have so dangerous a man in the house, she held her own; and in the face of my remonstrances, and those of her husband, Count Ferruci came to stay with us.

"From the moment he entered the house there was nothing but trouble. Vrain became jealous, and, mad with drugs he took, often treated Lydia with cruelty and violence, and she came to me for protection. I spoke to Vrain, and he insulted me, wishing to turn me out of the house; but for Lydia's sake I remained. Then a Miss Tyler came to stay, and falling in love with Count Ferruci, grew jealous of Lydia, and made trouble with Vrain. The end of it was that after a succession of scenes, in which the old man behaved like the lunatic he was, he left the house, and not one of us knew where he went to. That was the last Lydia saw of her husband.

"After that trouble I insisted that Count Ferruci should leave the house; also Miss Tyler. They both did, but came back at times to pay Lydia a visit. We tried to find Vrain, but could not, as he had vanished altogether. Ferruci, I saw, was in love with Lydia, and she with him, but neither the one nor the other hinted at a future marriage should Vrain die. I do not say that Lydia was a fond wife to Vrain, but he treated her so badly that he could not expect her to be; and I dare say I am the one to blame all through, as I made Lydia marry Vrain when she loved Ferruci. But I did it all for the best, so as to get money for my dear girl; and if it has turned out for the worst, my inordinate affection for my child is to blame. All I have done has been for Lydia's sake; all Ferruci did was for Lydia's sake, as he truly loved her; but I swear by all that I hold most holy that Lydia knew not how either of us was working to secure her happiness. Well, Ferruci is dead, and I am in jail, so we have paid in full for our wickedness.

"I had no idea of getting rid of Vrain until one day Ferruci took me aside and told me that he had found Vrain at Salisbury. He stated that the man was still taking morphia, but in spite of his excesses had so strong a constitution that it appeared he would live for many years. The Count then said that he loved Lydia dearer than life, and wished to marry her if Vrain could be got out of the way. I cried out against murder being done, as I never entertained such an idea for a moment; but Ferruci denied that he wished to harm the man. He wanted him put away in a lunatic asylum, and when I asked him how even then he could marry Lydia, he suggested his scheme of substituting a sickly and dying man for Vrain. The scheme - which was entirely invented by the Count - was as follows:

"Ferruci said that in a minor London theatre he had seen an actor called Clear, who was wonderfully like Vrain, save that he had no scar on the cheek, and had a moustache, whereas Vrain was always clean-shaved. He had made the acquaintance of the actor - Michael Clear was his full name - and of his wife. They proved to be hard up and mercenary, so Ferruci had no difficulty in gaining over both for his purpose. For a certain sum of money (which was to be paid to Mrs. Clear when her husband was dead and the Count, married to Lydia, was possessed of the assurance money) Clear agreed to shave off his moustache and personate Vrain. Ferruci, who was something of a chemist, created by means of some acid a scar on Clear's cheek like that on Vrain's, so that he resembled my son-in-law in every way save that he had lost one little finger.

"Ferruci wanted me to join him in the conspiracy so that I could watch Clear impersonating Vrain, while he himself kept his eye on the real Vrain, who was to be received into Mrs. Clear's house at Bayswater and passed off as her husband. All Mrs. Clear wanted was the money, as - long since wearied of her drunken husband - she did not care if he lived or died. Clear, on his part, knowing that he could not live long, was quite willing to play the part of Vrain on condition that he had plenty to eat and drink, and could live in idleness and luxury. His wishes in this direction cost us a pretty penny, as he bought everything of the best.

"To this plot I refused consent until I saw how Vrain was: so when Ferruci brought him from Salisbury - where he was hiding - to London, I had an interview with him. He proved to be so stupefied with drugs that he hardly knew me, so, seeing that my Lydia would get no good out of her life by being tied to such a husband, I determined that I would assist Ferruci, on the understanding, of course, that Vrain was to be well looked after in every way. We agreed that when Clear died, and his body was identified as Vrain's, that the real man should be put in an asylum, which was - and I am sure every one will agree with me - the best place for him.

"All this being arranged, I went out to look for a house in a secluded part of the town, in which Clear - under the name of Berwin - should live until he died as Vrain. I did not wish to see about the house in my new character, lest I should be recognised, if there was any trouble over the assurance money; to complicate matters, I determined to disguise myself as the real Vrain. Of course, Clear personated Vrain as Lydia had last seen him, that is, clean-shaven, and neat in his dress. But the real Vrain, neglecting his personal appearance, had cultivated a long, white beard, and wore a black velvet skull-cap to conceal a baldness which had come upon him. I disguised myself in this fashion, therefore, and went to Pimlico under the name of Wrent."

CHAPTER XXXII

THE CONFESSION (*Continued*)

"In Geneva Square, Pimlico, I found the house I wanted. It was No. 13, and was said to be haunted, as cries had been heard in it at night, and lights had been seen flitting from window to window when no one was in the house. I looked at it without entering, or calling on the landlord, and then I went into Jersey Street to see the back. The house in the same section with it was kept by a Mrs. Bensusan, who took in lodgers. Her rooms were vacant, and as it suited me very well that I should be a neighbour to Clear, I took the rooms. They proved - as I shall explain - better for our purpose than I was aware of.

"When I told Ferruci of my discovery, he gave Clear money and made him hire the house and furnish two rooms for himself. I supplied the money. In this way Clear, calling himself Berwin, which was the name of Vrain's house in the country, came to live in Pimlico. We also removed the real Vrain to Mrs. Clear's at Bayswater, and he passed as her husband. So weak were his brains, and so cowed was his spirit, that there was no difficulty in keeping him in the house, and the neighbours were told merely that Clear was ill.

"For my part, I took up my abode in Jersey Street under the name of Wrent, and met Clear outside on occasions when it was necessary for me to see him; but I never entered the house - for obvious reasons.

"I was constantly afraid lest Clear, in his drunken fits - for he was always more or less drunk - should reveal our secret, and I took as my bedroom an apartment in Mrs. Bensusan's out of the window of which I could overlook the back of No. 13. One night, when I was watching, I saw a dark figure glide into Mrs. Bensusan's yard and climb over the fence, only to disappear. I was terribly alarmed, and wondering what was wrong, I put on my clothes and hurried downstairs into the yard. Also I climbed over the fence into the yard of No. 13. Here I could not see where the figure had disappeared to, as the doors and windows at the back of the house were all locked. I could not conjecture who the woman was - for it was a woman I saw - who had entered, or why she had done so, or in what way she had gained admission.

"While I was thus thinking I saw the woman again. She apparently rose out of the earth, and after closing what appeared to be a trap-door, she made for the fence. I stopped her before she got there, and found to my surprise that she was a red-headed servant of Mrs. Bensusan's - a kind of gypsy, very clever, and - I think - with much evil in her. She was alarmed at being discovered, and begged me not to tell on her. For my own sake, I promised not to do so, but made her explain how she got into the house, and why she entered it. Then she told me an extraordinary tale.

"For some years, she said, she had been with Mrs. Bensusan, who had taken her from the gypsies to civilise her, and hating the restraint of civilised life, she had been in the habit of roaming about at night. Knowing that the house at the back was unoccupied, this Rhoda - for that is her name - climbed over the fence and tried to get into it, but found the doors and windows bolted and barred.

"Then one night she saw a kind of grated window amid the grass, and as this proved not to be bolted, she pulled it open. Taking a candle with her, she went on a voyage of discovery, and dropped through this hole some distance into a disused cellar. Only a cat could have got in safely, for the height was considerable; and, indeed, Rhoda did not risk that mode of entrance again, for, finding a ladder in the cellar, which, I presume, had been used to get at the higher bins of wine, she placed this against the aperture, and thus was enabled to ascend and descend without difficulty. Frequently by this means she entered the empty house, and went from room to room with her candle, singing gypsy songs as she wandered. So here I had found the ghost of No. 13, although I don't suppose this impish gypsy girl knew as much. She haunted the house just to amuse herself, when fat Mrs. Bensusan thought she was safe in bed.

"I asked Rhoda why she had entered the house on that particular night when I had caught her. She confessed that she had seen some articles of silver in Clear's rooms which she wished to steal; but on this occasion he had locked the door - a thing which he did not always do in his drunken humours - and so Rhoda was returning disappointed. After this confession I made her go back to her own house and promised to keep her secret. I also told her that if she held her tongue I would give her a present. For this purpose I made Ferruci buy me a cloak lined with rabbit skins, as Rhoda on her night excursions wanted something to keep her warm. When Ferruci gave it to me, and it was lying in my room, Mrs. Clear came one night to see me, and finding it cold, she borrowed the cloak to wrap round her. She kept it for some time, and brought it back on Christmas Eve, when I gave it next day to Rhoda. It was Ferruci who bought the cloak, not I; and it was purchased for Rhoda, not for Mrs. Clear.

"The next night I entered No. 13 by the cellarway, and found it of great advantage, as I could visit Clear without exciting suspicion, and so keep an eye on him. At first he was alarmed by my unexpected appearance, but when I showed him the secret way, he made use of it also. We used it only on dark nights, and it was for this reason that we were not noticed by the neighbours. It would never have done for any one of us to be seen climbing over the fence. Mrs. Clear once visited her husband, and had a quarrel with him about his drinking. It was her shadow and Clear's which Denzil saw on the blind. As soon as they heard his ring they both went out the back way, and in climbing hurriedly over the fence Mrs. Clear tore her veil. It was a portion of this which Denzil found.

"On that night, Clear, after leaving his wife, entered the square by the front, and so met with Denzil, much to the latter's surprise. I was very angry when Clear showed Denzil over the house; but he said that the young man was very suspicious, and he only showed him the house to prove that there was no one in it, and that he must have been mistaken about the shadows on the blind. Notwithstanding this explanation, I did not approve of Clear's act, nor, indeed, of his acquaintance with Denzil.

"For some months matters went on in this way. Clear remained in the Silent House, drinking himself to death; Mrs. Clear looked after Vrain in her Bayswater house; and I, in my old-man disguise, remained in Jersey Street, although at times I left there and went to see my daughter. All this time Lydia had no idea of what we were preparing. Then I began to grow wearied of the position, for Clear proved tougher than we anticipated, and showed no signs of dying. In despair, I thought I would give him the means to kill himself.

"Mind, I did not wish to murder him myself; but the man, when in his drinking fits, thought he was attacked by enemies, and when in a melancholic frame of mind, on recovery, would frequently hint at suicide. I therefore thought that if a weapon were left within his reach he might kill himself. I don't defend my conduct in this case, but surely this drunken scoundrel was better dead than alive. In choosing a weapon, I wished to select one that would implicate Ferruci rather than myself, in case there was any trouble over the matter; so I chose for my purpose a stiletto which hung by a parti-coloured ribbon on the walls of the library at Berwin Manor. I fancied that the stiletto, having been bought in Florence, and Ferruci coming from Florence, he, if anyone - should any of these facts come to light - would be credited with giving it to Clear.

"I took this stiletto from Berwin Manor some time before Christmas, and, bringing it up to town, I left it, on the day before Christmas, on the table in Clear's sitting-room. That was at nine o'clock in the night, and that was when I last saw him alive. Who killed him I know no more than any one else.

"On Christmas Eve I was ill, and wrote to Lydia to come up. She met me at the Pegalls', but as I felt ill, I left there at six o'clock, and Lydia stayed with the family all night. At seven o'clock Mrs. Clear came to me with Ferruci, and brought back the cloak which I gave afterwards to Rhoda. She wanted to see her husband again, but I refused to let her risk the visit. Ferruci came to tell me that he was arranging to place Vrain - who was becoming too violent to be restrained - in the private asylum of Dr. Jorce, at Hampstead. Mrs. Clear was to go with him, and we conversed about the matter.

"Ferruci went away first, as he desired to see Clear, and for that purpose waited about until it was darker, and went into the back yard shortly after eight o'clock. There he was seen by Rhoda as he was about to climb the fence, and, not knowing it was the girl, he took fright and ran out of the yard into Jersey Street. Here he found Mrs. Clear, who had left me and was waiting for him, and the pair went off to see Dr. Jorce at Hampstead. I believe they remained there all night.

"Left alone, I climbed over the fence about nine o'clock, and saw Clear. He was celebrating Christmas Eve by drinking heavily, and I was unable to bring him to reason. I therefore left the stiletto which I had brought with me on the table, and returned to my house in Jersey Street. I never saw him alive again. I went to bed and slept all night, so I was aware of nothing in connection with the death until late on Christmas Day. Then Mrs. Bensusan was told by Miss Greeb, the landlady of Denzil, that the tenant of No. 13 had been murdered. I fancied that he had killed himself in a fit of melancholia, with the stiletto I had left on his table; but I did not dare to go near the house to find this out.

"Afterwards I learned that the doctor who examined the body was of the opinion that Clear had been murdered; and, being afraid about the police taking up the case, I paid Mrs. Bensusan a week's rent and left her house two days after Christmas. I returned to Berwin Manor, and shortly afterwards Ferruci joined me there, as he had successfully incarcerated Vrain in the asylum under the name of Michael Clear.

"When the advertisement came out, it was I who hinted to Lydia that the dead man - seeing that he was called Berwin - might be her husband. We went up to town: Lydia identified the body of Clear as her husband in all innocence - for after death the man looked more like Vrain than ever; and in due time the assurance money was obtained.

"I do not think there is anything more to tell, save that I did not know that Mrs. Clear had betrayed me. I could not pay her the money, as I could not get it from Lydia. I told Lydia I was going to Paris, but in reality I was hunting for Rhoda, who had run away from Jersey Street. I fancied she might betray us, and wished to make things safe with her. Before I found her, however, I saw in the papers that Ferruci had committed suicide; also that Lydia - who had gone to Dover to meet me, thinking I was returning from Paris - had been arrested. Then I saw Mrs. Clear's advertisement saying she would betray me if I did not pay the money. I consented to meet her in order to implore her silence, and so fell into the clutches of the law.

"I may state that I did not kill Clear, as I never saw him after nine o'clock, and then he was alive. In spite of what the doctor said, I am still inclined to think he killed himself. Now I have made a clean breast of it - I am willing to be punished; but I hope Lydia will be set free, for whosoever is guilty, she is innocent. I have been an unlucky man, and I remain one at this moment when I sign myself for the last time, JABEZ CLYNE."

* * * * *

Needless to say, both Link and Denzil were greatly surprised at this confession, which revealed all things save the one they wished to know.

"What do you think of this idea of suicide?" asked Lucian.

"It is quite out of the question," replied the detective decidedly. "The doctor who examined the body said that it was impossible the man could have committed suicide. The position of the wound shows that; also the power of the stroke. No man could drive a stiletto so dexterously and strongly into the heart. Also the room was in confusion, which points to a struggle, and the stiletto is missing. It was not suicide, but murder, and I believe either Clyne or Ferruci killed the man."

"But Ferruci was not -"

"He was not there after ten," interrupted Link, "but he was there about eight. I dare say when Rhoda saw him he was coming back after having committed the deed, and Clyne says the stiletto was not there at the time just to screen him."

"It is of little use to screen the dead," said Lucian. "I think only one person can tell the truth about this murder, and that is Rhoda."

"I'm looking for her, Mr. Denzil."

This was easy saying, but harder doing, for weeks passed away, and in spite of all the efforts of the police Rhoda could not be found. Then one morning the detective, much excited, burst into Lucian's rooms waving a paper over his head.

"A confession!" he cried. "Another confession!"

"Of whom?" asked Lucian, surprised.

"Of Rhoda!" replied Link excitedly. "She has confessed! It was Rhoda who killed Michael Clear!"

CHAPTER XXXIII

WHAT RHODA HAD TO SAY

Of all the news concerning the truth of Clear's death, this was the last which Lucian expected to hear. He stood staring at the excited face of the detective in wide-eyed surprise, and for the moment could not find his voice.

"It is true, I tell you!" cried Link, sitting down and smoothing out the paper which he carried. "Rhoda, and none other, killed the man!"

"Are you sure, Link?"

"Of course I am. This," flourishing the paper, "is her dying confession."

"Her dying confession?" repeated the barrister blankly. "Is she dead, also?"

"Yes. It is a long story, Mr. Denzil. Sit down, and I'll tell it to you. As you have had so much to do with the beginning of the case, it is only fair that you should know the end, and a strange end it is."

Without a word Lucian sat down, feeling quite confused, for in no way could he guess how Clear had come by his death at the hands of Rhoda. He had suspected Lydia as guilty of the crime; he had credited Ferruci with its commission, and he had been certain of the guilt of Clyne, *alias* Wrent; but to discover that the red-headed servant was the culprit entirely bewildered him. She had no motive to kill the man; she had given evidence freely in the matter, and in all respects had acted as an innocent person. So this was why she had left Jersey Street? It was a fear of being arrested for the crime which had driven her into the wilds. But, as Lucian privately thought, she need not have fled, for - so far as he could see - beyond the startling announcement of Link, there was no evidence to connect her with the matter. It was most extraordinary.

"I see you are astonished," said Link, with a nod; "so was I. Of all folk, I least suspected that imp of a girl. The truth would never have been known, had she not confessed at the last moment; for even now I cannot see, on the face of it, any evidence - save her own confession - to inculpate her in the matter. So you see, Mr. Denzil, the mystery of this man's death, which we have been so anxious to solve, has not been explained by you, or discovered by me, but has been brought to light by chance, which, after all, is the great detective. You may well look astonished," repeated the man slowly; "I am - immensely."

"Let me hear the confession, Link!"

"Wait one moment. I'll tell you how it came to be made, and then I'll relate the story in my own fashion, as the way in which the confession is written is too muddled for you to understand clearly. Still, it shows plainly enough that Clyne, for all our suspicions, is innocent."

"And Rhoda, the sharp servant girl, guilty," said Lucian, reflectively. "I never should have thought that she was involved in the matter. How the deuce did she come to confess?"

"Well," said Link, clearing his throat as a preliminary to his narrative, "it seems that Mr. Bensusan, in a fit of philanthropy, picked up this wretched girl in the country. She belonged to some gypsies, but as her parents were dead, and the child a burden, the tribe were glad to get rid of her. Rhoda Stanley - that is her full name - was taken to London by Mrs. Bensusan, who tried to civilise her."

"I don't think she succeeded very well, Link. Rhoda, with her cunning ways and roaming about at night, was always a savage at heart. In spite of what Clyne says in his confession, I believe she took a delight in turning No. 13 into a haunted house with her shrieking and her flitting candles. How she must have enjoyed herself when she heard the talk about the ghost!"

"I have no doubt she did, Mr. Denzil, but even those delights wearied her, and she longed to get back to the free gypsy life. When she found - through you, sir - that the police wanted to know too much about Clear's death, she left Mrs. Bensusan in the lurch, and tramped off down to the New Forest, where she picked up again with her tribe."

"How did her mistress take her desertion?"

"Very much to heart, as she had treated the young savage very kindly, and ought to have received more gratitude. Perhaps when she hears how her adopted child wandered about at night, and ended by killing Clear, she will be glad she is dead and buried. Yet, I don't know. Women are wonderfully soft-hearted, and certainly Rhoda is thought no end of by that fat woman."

"Well! well!" said Lucian, impatient of this digression. "So Rhoda went back to her tribe?"

"Yes, sir; and as she was sharp, clever, and, moreover, came with some money which she had stolen from Mrs. Bensusan - for she added theft to ingratitude - she was received with open arms. With her gypsy cousins she went about in the true gypsy style, but, not being hardened to the outdoor life in wet weather, she fell ill."

"Civilisation made her delicate, I suppose," said Denzil grimly.

"Exactly; she was not fit for the tent life after having lived for so long under a comfortable roof. She fell ill with inflammation of the lungs, and in a wonderfully short space of time she died."

"When did she confess her crime?"

"I'm coming to that, sir. When she was dying she sent two gypsies to the nearest magistrate - who happened to be the vicar of the parish in which the tribe were then encamped - and asked him to see her on a matter of life and death. The vicar came at once, and when he became aware that Rhoda was the girl wanted in the Vrain case - for he had read all about her in the papers - he became very interested. He took down the confession of the wretched girl, had it signed by two witnesses and Rhoda herself, and sent it up to Scotland Yard."

"And this confession -"

"Here it is," said Link, pointing to the manuscript on the table; "but
it is too long to read, so I shall just tell you briefly what Rhoda confessed, and how she committed the crime."

"Go on! I am most anxious to hear, Link!"

"Well, Mr. Denzil, you know that Rhoda was in the habit of visiting No. 13 by night and amusing herself by wandering about the empty rooms, although I don't know what pleasure she found in doing so. It seems that when Clear became the tenant of the house, Rhoda was very angry, as his presence interfered with her midnight capers. However, on seeing his rooms - for Clear found her one night, and took her in to show them to her - she was filled with admiration, and with true gypsy instinct wanted to steal some of the ornaments. She tried to pocket a silver paper-knife on that very night Clear was so hospitable to her, but she was not sharp enough, and the man saw the theft. In a rage at her dishonesty he turned her out of the room, and swore that he would thrash her if she came into his presence again."

"Did the threat keep Rhoda away?"

"Not it. I am sure you saw enough of that wildcat to know nothing would frighten her. She certainly did not thrust herself personally on Clear, but whenever his back was turned she took to stealing things out of his room, when he was foolish enough to leave the door open. Clear was much enraged, and complained to Clyne - known to Rhoda as Wrent - who in his turn read the girl a sharp lecture.

"But having shown Clyne the cellarway into the house, Miss Rhoda knew too much, and laughed in Clyne's face. He did not dare to make her thefts public, or complain to Mrs. Bensusan, lest Rhoda should tell of the connection between him and the tenant of the Silent House, who passed under the name of Berwin. Therefore, he told Clear to keep his sitting-room door locked."

"A wise precaution, with that imp about," said Lucian. "I hope Clear was sensible enough to adopt it."

"Yes, and no. When he was sober he locked the door, and when drunk he left it open, and Rhoda looted at will. And now comes the more important part of the confession. You remember that Clyne left the stiletto from Berwin Manor on Clear's table?"

"Yes, with the amiable intention that the poor devil should kill himself. He left it on Christmas Eve, too - a pleasant time for a man to commit suicide!"

"Of course, the intention was horrible!" said Mr. Link, gravely. "Some people might think such an act incredible; but I have seen so much of the worst side of human nature that I am not surprised. Clyne was too cowardly to kill the man himself, so he thought to make Clear his own executioner by leaving the stiletto in his way. Well, sir, the weapon proved to be useful in the way it was intended by Clyne, for Clear was killed with that very weapon."

"And by Rhoda!" said Lucian, nodding. "I see! How did she get hold of it?"

"By accident. When Wrent - I mean Clyne - and Mrs. Bensusan went to bed on Christmas Eve, Rhoda thought she would have some of her devil dances in the haunted house; so she slipped out of bed and into the yard, and dropped down into the cellar, whence she went up to Clear's rooms."

"Was Clear in bed?"

"No; but he was in his bedroom, and, according to Rhoda, furiously drunk. You know that Clyne said the man had been drinking all day. On this night he had left his sitting-room door open, and the lamp burning. On the table was the silver-handled stiletto, with the ribbon; and when Rhoda peered into the room to see what she could pick up, she thought she would like this pretty toy. She stole forward softly and took the stiletto, but before she could get back to the door, Clear, who had been watching her, reeled out and rushed at her."

"Did she run away?"

"She couldn't. Clear was between her and the door. She ran round the room, upsetting everything, for she thought he would kill her in his drunken rage. Don't you remember, Mr. Denzil, how disorderly the room was? Well, Clear got Rhoda into a corner, and was going to strike her; she had the stiletto still in her hand, and held it point outward to save herself from the blow. She thought when he saw the weapon he would not dare to come nearer. However, either he did not see the stiletto, or was too drunk to feel fear, for he stumbled and fell forward, so that the dagger ran right into his heart. In a moment he fell dead, before he had time, as Rhoda says, to even utter a cry."

"So it was an accident, after all?" said Lucian.

"Oh, yes, quite an accident," replied Link, "and I can see very plainly how it took place. Of course, Rhoda was terrified at what she had done - although she really was not to blame - and leaving the dead man, ran away with the stiletto. She dropped the ribbon off it near the cellar door as she was running away, and there Mrs. Kebby found it."

"What did she do with the stiletto?"

"She had it in her room, and when she left Mrs. Bensusan she carried it with her down the country. In proof of the truth, she gave it to the vicar who wrote down her confession, and he sent it up with the papers to Scotland Yard. Queer case, isn't it?"

"Very queer, Link. I thought everybody was guilty but Rhoda."

"Ah!" said the detective, significantly, "it is always the least suspected person who is guilty. I could have sworn that Clyne was the man. Now it seems that he is innocent, so instead of hanging he will only be imprisoned for his share in the conspiracy."

"He may escape that way," said Lucian drily, "but, morally speaking, I regard him as more guilty than Rhoda."

CHAPTER XXXIV

THE END OF IT ALL

Two years after the discovery of Rhoda's guilt, Mr. and Mrs. Denzil were seated in the garden of Berwin Manor. It was a perfect summer evening, at the sunset hour, something like that evening when, in the same garden, almost at the same time, Lucian had asked Diana to be his wife. But between then and now twenty-four months had elapsed, and many things had taken place of more or less importance to the young couple.

The mystery of Clear's death had been solved; Lydia had been set free as innocent of crime; her father, found guilty of conspiracy to obtain the assurance money, had been condemned to a long term of imprisonment, and, what most concerned Lucian and Diana, Mark Vrain had really and truly gone the way of all flesh.

After the conclusion of the Vrain case Lucian had become formally engaged to Diana, but it was agreed between them that the marriage should not take place for some time on account of her father's health. After his discharge as cured from the asylum of Dr. Jorce, Miss Vrain had taken her father down to his own place in the country, and there tended him with the most affectionate solicitude, in the hope that he would recover his health. But the hope was vain, for by his over-indulgence in morphia, his worrying and wandering, and irregular mode of life, Vrain had completely shattered his health. He lapsed into a state of second childhood, and, being deprived of the drugs which formerly had excited him to a state of frenzy, sank into a pitiable condition. For days he would remain without speaking to any one, and even ceased to take a pleasure in his books. Finally his limbs became paralysed, and so he spent the last few months of his wretched life in a bath-chair, being wheeled round the garden.

Still, his constitution was so strong that he lived for quite twelve months after his return to his home, and died unexpectedly in his sleep. Diana was not sorry when he passed so easily away, for death was a merciful release of his tortured soul from his worn-out body. So Mark Vrain died, and was buried, and after the funeral Diana went abroad, with Miss Priscilla Barbar for a companion.

In the meantime, Lucian stayed in grimy, smoky London, and worked hard at his profession. He was beginning to be known, and in time actually received a brief or two, with which he did his best in court. Still, he was far from being the successful pleader he hoped to be, for law, of all professions, is one which demands time and industry for the attainment of any degree of excellence. It is rarely that a young lawyer can go to sleep and wake to find himself famous; he must crawl rather than run. With diligence and punctuality, and observance of every chance, in time the wished-for goal is reached, although that goal, in nine cases out of ten, is a very moderate distance off. Lucian did not sigh for a judgeship, or for a seat on the Woolsack; he was content to be a barrister with a good practice, and perhaps a Q.C.-ship in prospect. However, during the year of Diana's mourning he did so well that he felt justified in asking her to marry him when she returned. Diana, on her side, saw no obstacle to this course, so she consented.

"If you are not rich, my dear, I am," she said, when Lucian alleged his poverty as the only bar to their union, "and as money gives me no pleasure without you, I do not care to stay in Berwin Manor in lonely spinsterhood. I shall marry you whenever you choose."

And Lucian, taking advantage of this gracious permission, did choose to be married, and that speedily; so within two years after the final closing of the Vrain case they became man and wife. At the time they were seated in the garden, at the hour of sunset, they had only lately returned from their honeymoon, and were now talking over past experiences. Miss Priscilla, who had been left in charge of the Manor during their absence, had welcomed them back with much joy, as she looked upon the match as one of her own making. Now she had gone inside, on the understanding that two are company and three are none, and the young couple were left alone. Hand in hand, after the foolish fashion of lovers, they sat under a leafy oak tree, and the sunlight glowed redly on their happy faces. After a short silence Lucian looked at the face of his wife and laughed.

"What is amusing you, dear?" said Mrs. Denzil, with a sympathetic smile.

"My thoughts were rather pleasant than amusing," replied Lucian, giving the hand that lay in his a squeeze, "but I was thinking of Hans Andersen's tale of the Elder Mother Tree, and of the old couple who sat enjoying their golden wedding under the linden, with the red sunlight shining on their silver crowns."

"We are under an oak and wear no crowns," replied Diana in her turn, "but we are quite as happy, I think, although it is not our golden wedding."

"Perhaps that will come some day, Diana."

"Fifty years, my dear; it's a long way off yet," said Mrs. Denzil dubiously.

"I am glad it is, for I shall have (D.V.,) fifty years of happiness with you to look forward to. Upon my word, Diana, I think you deserve happiness, after all the trouble you have had."

"With you I am sure to be happy, Lucian, but other people,

poor souls, are not so well off."

"What other people?"

"Jabez Clyne, for one."

"My dear," said Lucian, seriously, "I hope I am not a hard man, but I really cannot find it in my heart to pity Clyne. He was - and I dare say is - a scoundrel!"

"I don't deny that he acted badly," sighed Diana, "but it was for his daughter's sake, you know."

"There is a limit even to paternal affection, Diana. And putting aside the wickedness of the whole conspiracy, I cannot pardon a man who deliberately put a weapon in the way of a man almost insane with drink, in order that he might kill himself. The idea was diabolically wicked, my dear, and I think that Jabez Clyne, *alias* Wrent, quite deserves the long imprisonment he received."

"At all events, the Sirius Company got back their money, Lucian."

"So much as Lydia had not spent they got back, Diana; but when your father actually died they had to part with it very soon again, and some of it has gone into Lydia's pocket after all."

Diana blushed. "It was only right, dear," she said, apologetically. "When my father made his new will, leaving it all to me, I did not think that Lydia, however badly she treated him, should be left absolutely penniless. And you know, Lucian, you agreed that I should share the assurance money with her."

"I did," replied Denzil. "Of two evils I chose the least, for if Lydia had not got a portion of the money she would have been quite capable of trying to upset the second will on the ground that Mr. Vrain was insane."

"Papa was not insane," reproved Diana. "He was weak, I admit, but at the time he made that will he had all his senses. Besides, after all the scandal of the case, I don't think Lydia would have dared to go to law about it. Still, it was best to give her the money, and I hear from Miss Priscilla that Lydia is now in Italy, and proposes to marry an Italian prince."

"She has flown higher than a count, then. Poor Ferruci killed himself for her sake."

"For his own, rather," exclaimed Mrs. Denzil energetically. "He knew that if he lived he would be punished by imprisonment, so chose to kill himself rather than suffer such dishonour. I believe he truly loved Lydia, certainly, but as he wanted the assurance money, I fancy he sinned quite as much for his own sake as for Lydia's."

"No doubt; and I dare say Lydia loved him, after her own fashion; yet she seems to have forgotten him pretty soon, and - as you say - intends to marry a prince. I don't envy his highness."

"She has no heart, so I dare say she will be happy as such women ever are," said Diana contemptuously, "yet her happiness comes out of much evil. If she had not married my father, her own would not now be in prison, nor would Count Ferruci and Rhoda be dead."

"Ferruci, perhaps, might still be alive, and her husband," assented Lucian, "but I have my doubts about Rhoda. She was a wicked, precocious little imp, that girl, and sooner or later would have come to a bad end. The death of Clear was due to an accident, I admit; but Rhoda has still one person who laments over her, for, although Mrs. Bensusan knows the truth, she always thinks of that red-haired minx as a kind of martyr, who was led into wicked ways by Clyne, *alias* Wrent."

"I am sure Mrs. Clear doesn't think so."

"Mrs. Clear has got quite enough to think about in remembering how narrowly she escaped imprisonment for her share in that shameful conspiracy. If she had not turned Queen's evidence, she would have been punished as Clyne was; as it is, she just escaped by an accident. Still, if it had not been for her, we should never have discovered the truth. I would never have suspected Clyne, who was always so meek and mild. Even that visit he paid to me to lament over his daughter's probable marriage to Ferruci was a trick to find out how much I knew."

"Don't you think he hated Ferruci?"

"No; I am sure he did not. He acted a part to find out what I was doing. If Mrs. Clear had not betrayed him we should never have discovered the conspiracy."

"And if Rhoda had not spoken, the mystery of Clear's death would never have been solved," said Diana, "although she only confessed at the eleventh hour, and when she was dying."

"I think Link was pleased that the mystery was solved in so unexpected a way," said Lucian, laughing. "He never forgave my finding out so much without his aid. He ascribes the ending of the whole matter to chance, and I dare say he is right."

"H'm!" said Mrs. Denzil, who had no great love for the detective. "He certainly left everything to chance. Twice he gave up the case.".

"And twice I gave it up," said Denzil. "If it had not been for you, dear, I should never have gone on with what seemed to be a hopeless task. But when I first met you you induced me to continue the search for the culprit, and again when, by the evidence of the missing finger, you did not believe your father was dead."

"Well, you worked; I worked; Link worked," said Diana, philosophically, "and we all three did our best to discover the truth."

"Only to let chance discover it in the long run."

Diana laughed and nodded, but did not contradict her husband. "Well, my dear," she said, "I think we have discussed the subject pretty freely, but there is one thing I should like to know. What about the Silent House in Pimlico?"

"Oh, Miss Greeb told me the other day that Peacock is going to pull it down. You know, just before we were married I took leave of Miss Greeb, with whom I lodged for a long time. Well, she gave me a piece of news. She is going to be married, also, and to whom, do you think?"

"I don't know," said Diana, looking interested, as women always do in marriage news.

"To Peacock, who owns nearly all the property in and about Geneva Square. It will be a splendid match for her, and Mrs. Peacock, will be much richer than you or I, Diana."

"But not happier, my dear. I am glad she is to be married, as she seemed a nice woman, and made you very comfortable. But why is the Silent House to be pulled down?"

"Because no one will live in it."

"But it is not haunted now. You know it was discovered that Rhoda was the ghost, and the ghost, as Miss Greeb suggested, killed Clear."

"It is haunted now by the ghost of Clear," said Lucian gravely. "At all events, he was murdered there, and no one cares to live in the house. I confess I shouldn't care to live in it myself. So, Peacock, finding the house unprofitable, has determined to pull it down."

"So there is an end to the Silent House of Pimlico," said Diana, rising and taking her husband's arm. "Come inside, Lucian. It grows chilly."

"'Tho' winds be cold and nights be drear,
   Yet love makes warm our hearts, my dear,'"

quoted Lucian, as they went up to the house. "That is not very good poetry, but it is a beautiful truth, my love."

Diana laughed, and looked up proudly into the bright face of her husband.

So they went inside, and found that Miss Priscilla had made the tea, and all were very happy, and very thankful for their happiness. In this condition, which is sufficiently pleasant, I think we may leave them.

Choose from Thousands of 1stWorldLibrary Classics By

A. M. Barnard
Ada Leverson
Adolphus William Ward
Aesop
Agatha Christie
Alexander Aaronsohn
Alexander Kielland
Alexandre Dumas
Alfred Gatty
Alfred Ollivant
Alice Duer Miller
Alice Turner Curtis
Alice Dunbar
Allen Chapman
Ambrose Bierce
Amelia E. Barr
Amory H. Bradford
Andrew Lang
Andrew McFarland Davis
Andy Adams
Anna Alice Chapin
Anna Sewell
Annie Besant
Annie Hamilton Donnell
Annie Payson Call
Annie Roe Carr
Annonaymous
Anton Chekhov
Arnold Bennett
Arthur Conan Doyle
Arthur M. Winfield
Arthur Ransome
Arthur Schnitzler
Atticus
B.H. Baden-Powell
B. M. Bower
B. C. Chatterjee
Baroness Emmuska Orczy
Baroness Orczy
Basil King
Bayard Taylor
Ben Macomber
Bertha Muzzy Bower
Bjornstjerne Bjornson
Booth Tarkington
Boyd Cable
Bram Stoker
C. Collodi
C. E. Orr

C. M. Ingleby
Carolyn Wells
Catherine Parr Traill
Charles A. Eastman
Charles Amory Beach
Charles Dickens
Charles Dudley Warner
Charles Farrar Browne
Charles Ives
Charles Kingsley
Charles Klein
Charles Hanson Towne
Charles Lathrop Pack
Charles Romyn Dake
Charles Whibley
Charles Willing Beale
Charlotte M. Braeme
Charlotte M. Yonge
Charlotte Perkins Stetson
Clair W. Hayes
Clarence Day Jr.
Clarence E. Mulford
Clemence Housman
Confucius
Coningsby Dawson
Cornelis DeWitt Wilcox
Cyril Burleigh
D. H. Lawrence
Daniel Defoe
David Garnett
Dinah Craik
Don Carlos Janes
Donald Keyhoe
Dorothy Kilner
Dougan Clark
Douglas Fairbanks
E. Nesbit
E.P.Roe
E. Phillips Oppenheim
Earl Barnes
Edgar Rice Burroughs
Edith Van Dyne
Edith Wharton
Edward Everett Hale
Edward J. O'Biren
Edward S. Ellis
Edwin L. Arnold
Eleanor Atkins
Eliot Gregory

Elizabeth Gaskell
Elizabeth McCracken
Elizabeth Von Arnim
Ellem Key
Emerson Hough
Emilie F. Carlen
Emily Dickinson
Enid Bagnold
Enilor Macartney Lane
Erasmus W. Jones
Ernie Howard Pie
Ethel May Dell
Ethel Turner
Ethel Watts Mumford
Eugenie Foa
Eugene Wood
Eustace Hale Ball
Evelyn Everett-green
Everard Cotes
F. H. Cheley
F. J. Cross
F. Marion Crawford
Federick Austin Ogg
Ferdinand Ossendowski
Francis Bacon
Francis Darwin
Frances Hodgson Burnett
Frances Parkinson Keyes
Frank Gee Patchin
Frank Harris
Frank Jewett Mather
Frank L. Packard
Frank V. Webster
Frederic Stewart Isham
Frederick Trevor Hill
Frederick Winslow Taylor
Friedrich Kerst
Friedrich Nietzsche
Fyodor Dostoyevsky
G.A. Henty
G.K. Chesterton
Gabrielle E. Jackson
Garrett P. Serviss
Gaston Leroux
George A. Warren
George Ade
Geroge Bernard Shaw
George Durston
George Ebers

George Eliot
George Gissing
George MacDonald
George Meredith
George Orwell
George Sylvester Viereck
George Tucker
George W. Cable
George Wharton James
Gertrude Atherton
Gordon Casserly
Grace E. King
Grace Gallatin
Grace Greenwood
Grant Allen
Guillermo A. Sherwell
Gulielma Zollinger
Gustav Flaubert
H. A. Cody
H. B. Irving
H.C. Bailey
H. G. Wells
H. H. Munro
H. Irving Hancock
H. Rider Haggard
H. W. C. Davis
Haldeman Julius
Hall Caine
Hamilton Wright Mabie
Hans Christian Andersen
Harold Avery
Harold McGrath
Harriet Beecher Stowe
Harry Castlemon
Harry Coghill
Harry Houidini
Hayden Carruth
Helent Hunt Jackson
Helen Nicolay
Hendrik Conscience
Hendy David Thoreau
Henri Barbusse
Henrik Ibsen
Henry Adams
Henry Ford
Henry Frost
Henry James
Henry Jones Ford
Henry Seton Merriman
Henry W Longfellow
Herbert A. Giles

Herbert Carter
Herbert N. Casson
Herman Hesse
Hildegard G. Frey
Homer
Honore De Balzac
Horace B. Day
Horace Walpole
Horatio Alger Jr.
Howard Pyle
Howard R. Garis
Hugh Lofting
Hugh Walpole
Humphry Ward
Ian Maclaren
Inez Haynes Gillmore
Irving Bacheller
Isabel Hornibrook
Israel Abrahams
Ivan Turgenev
J.G.Austin
J. Henri Fabre
J. M. Barrie
J. Macdonald Oxley
J. S. Fletcher
J. S. Knowles
J. Storer Clouston
Jack London
Jacob Abbott
James Allen
James Andrews
James Baldwin
James Branch Cabell
James DeMille
James Joyce
James Lane Allen
James Lane Allen
James Oliver Curwood
James Oppenheim
James Otis
James R. Driscoll
Jane Austen
Jane L. Stewart
Janet Aldridge
Jens Peter Jacobsen
Jerome K. Jerome
John Burroughs
John Cournos
John F. Kennedy
John Gay
John Glasworthy

John Habberton
John Joy Bell
John Kendrick Bangs
John Milton
John Philip Sousa
Jonas Lauritz Idemil Lie
Jonathan Swift
Joseph A. Altsheler
Joseph Carey
Joseph Conrad
Joseph E. Badger Jr
Joseph Hergesheimer
Joseph Jacobs
Jules Vernes
Julian Hawthrone
Julie A Lippmann
Justin Huntly McCarthy
Kakuzo Okakura
Kenneth Grahame
Kenneth McGaffey
Kate Langley Bosher
Kate Langley Bosher
Katherine Cecil Thurston
Katherine Stokes
L. A. Abbot
L. T. Meade
L. Frank Baum
Latta Griswold
Laura Dent Crane
Laura Lee Hope
Laurence Housman
Lawrence Beasley
Leo Tolstoy
Leonid Andreyev
Lewis Carroll
Lewis Sperry Chafer
Lilian Bell
Lloyd Osbourne
Louis Hughes
Louis Tracy
Louisa May Alcott
Lucy Fitch Perkins
Lucy Maud Montgomery
Luther Benson
Lydia Miller Middleton
Lyndon Orr
M. Corvus
M. H. Adams
Margaret E. Sangster
Margret Howth
Margaret Vandercook

Margret Penrose
Maria Edgeworth
Maria Thompson Daviess
Mariano Azuela
Marion Polk Angellotti
Mark Overton
Mark Twain
Mary Austin
Mary Catherine Crowley
Mary Cole
Mary Hastings Bradley
Mary Roberts Rinehart
Mary Rowlandson
M. Wollstonecraft Shelley
Maud Lindsay
Max Beerbohm
Myra Kelly
Nathaniel Hawthrone
Nicolo Machiavelli
O. F. Walton
Oscar Wilde
Owen Johnson
P.G. Wodehouse
Paul and Mabel Thorne
Paul G. Tomlinson
Paul Severing
Percy Brebner
Peter B. Kyne
Plato
R. Derby Holmes
R. L. Stevenson
R. S. Ball
Rabindranath Tagore
Rahul Alvares
Ralph Bonehill
Ralph Henry Barbour
Ralph Victor
Ralph Waldo Emmerson
Rene Descartes
Rex Beach

Rex E. Beach
Richard Harding Davis
Richard Jefferies
Richard Le Gallienne
Robert Barr
Robert Frost
Robert Gordon Anderson
Robert L. Drake
Robert Lansing
Robert Lynd
Robert Michael Ballantyne
Robert W. Chambers
Rosa Nouchette Carey
Rudyard Kipling
Samuel B. Allison
Samuel Hopkins Adams
Sarah Bernhardt
Sarah C. Hallowell
Selma Lagerlof
Sherwood Anderson
Sigmund Freud
Standish O'Grady
Stanley Weyman
Stella Benson
Stella M. Francis
Stephen Crane
Stewart Edward White
Stijn Streuvels
Swami Abhedananda
Swami Parmananda
T. S. Ackland
T. S. Arthur
The Princess Der Ling
Thomas A. Janvier
Thomas A Kempis
Thomas Anderton
Thomas Bailey Aldrich
Thomas Bulfinch
Thomas De Quincey
Thomas Dixon

Thomas H. Huxley
Thomas Hardy
Thomas More
Thornton W. Burgess
U. S. Grant
Valentine Williams
Various Authors
Vaughan Kester
Victor Appleton
Victoria Cross
Virginia Woolf
Wadsworth Camp
Walter Camp
Walter Scott
Washington Irving
Wilbur Lawton
Wilkie Collins
Willa Cather
Willard F. Baker
William Dean Howells
William le Queux
W. Makepeace Thackeray
William W. Walter
William Shakespeare
Winston Churchill
Yei Theodora Ozaki
Yogi Ramacharaka
Young E. Allison
Zane Grey